Beyond 400

Beyond 400

Exploring Baptist Futures

EDITED BY
David J. Cohen
and Michael Parsons

☙PICKWICK *Publications* • Eugene, Oregon

BEYOND 400
Exploring Baptist Futures

Copyright © 2011 Wipf and Stock Publishers. All rights reserved. Except for brief quotations in critical publications or reviews, no part of this book may be reproduced in any manner without prior written permission from the publisher. Write: Permissions, Wipf and Stock Publishers, 199 W. 8th Ave., Suite 3, Eugene, OR 97401.

Pickwick Publications
An Imprint of Wipf and Stock Publishers
199 W. 8th Ave., Suite 3
Eugene, OR 97401

www.wipfandstock.com

ISBN 13: 978-1-60899-337-6

Cataloguing-in-Publication data:

Beyond 400 : exploring Baptist futures / edited by David J. Cohen and Michael Parsons

xvi + 270 p. ; 23 cm. Includes bibliographical references.

ISBN 13: 978-1-60899-337-6

1. Baptists. 2. Church. I. Title.

BX6231 B49 2011

Manufactured in the U.S.A.

Dedicated to the faculty, staff and students of
SPURGEON'S COLLEGE, LONDON, UK, and
VOSE SEMINARY, PERTH, WA

Guard the good deposit that was entrusted to you—
guard it with the help of the Holy Spirit who lives in us.

—2 Timothy 1:14

Contents

Foreword by Brian Winslade ix
Foreword by Jonathan Edwards xi
Preface xiii
List of Contributors xv
List of Abbreviations xvi

1. Baptist Christians: Repentant and Unrepentant – *Nigel G. Wright* 1
2. Humane Religion: Evangelical Faith, Baptist Identity, and Liberal Secularism – *Nigel G. Wright* 17
3. The Sound of Silence? Baptist Thought in Obama's World – *Martin Sutherland* 34
4. Meeting for Minutes? Baptist Congregational Life in the Age of Twitter – *Martin Sutherland* 46
5. Beyond Identity Crises? The Future of Baptist Theology – *Michael D. O'Neil* 56
6. Is a Denomination a Church? – *Peter Ralphs* 73
7. Emerging-Missional Ecclesiology and the Future of Denominational Leadership and Affiliation – *Graham J. G. Hill* 86
8. The Little Church That Could – *Steve McAlpine* 101
9. Cyprian and *The Pilgrim's Progress* – *Edwina Murphy* 116
10. Leadership Style and Church Culture – *Janice Howard Newham* 131
11. Baptists in Mission to and with the Poor: What Do We Need to Learn? – *Scott Higgins* 154
12. Baptist Witness to New Testament Baptism beyond 2009 – *Richard K. Moore* 171
13. An Immodest Proposal for the Practice of the Lord's Table – *Ian Packer* 187

Contents

14 Church as (Covenant) Community—Then and Now
– *Michael Parsons* 207

15 Worship and the Unity of Baptists Today – *Neville Callam* 222

16 The Emerging Portrait: A Response
– *Brian Harris and Nigel G. Wright* 236

*Appendix A: Explicit Baptismal Vocabulary
in the New Testament* 251

*Appendix B: The Nine Instances of Christian Baptism
Reported in Acts* 252

Bibliography 255

Foreword by Brian Winslade

The year 2009 was significant for the movement of Christians called *Baptists* as we commemorated the 400th anniversary of the founding of the first Baptist church. From a small group of English "dissenters" fleeing persecution to the more tolerant climes of Amsterdam, the Baptist movement today is the largest Protestant communion in the world. We've actually had quite a journey, and as the children of Israel would often ponder and give thanks for their forebears, we too have much for which we give thanks to God.

But we also need to keep our focus on what is up ahead of us as a movement of Christians and local churches. The twenty-first century is very different from the seventeenth century in which the first Baptist churches emerged. The issues they faced in terms of religious freedom, politics, and social reform were quite severe. Indeed, Leon McBeth describes the period in which the Baptists first emerged as a "cauldron bubbling with revolutionary changes in economics, politics, and religion."[1]

Baptist history and ecclesiology, as with the study of the Scriptures, requires careful exegesis in order to distill the context behind why our forebears wrote and organized themselves as they did. Baptist identity is not solely the domain of historians—there is also room for creative missiological disciplines that help us critique our past patterns for more effective application to the era in which we live. The Baptist way of being church is sound and theologically defensible; but it is not necessarily immutable.

I am unashamedly a Baptist in terms of my ecclesiological convictions. I am obviously a follower of Christ first and foremost, but I am not ashamed of my "tribal" affiliation. I am proud of our four hundred years of history which have shaped my faith and commitment to the

1. McBeth, *Baptist Heritage*, 22.

Foreword by Brian Winslade

local church. I am in awe of our early Baptist forebears for their courage and tenacity, and am inspired to emulate their radicalism. I am also confident of God's ability to help the current and future generations of Baptist church leaders to plot an appropriate course in the missional context in which they serve.

The chapters of this book contribute to the ongoing evolution of Baptist ecclesiology. They began as a series of papers presented at a commemorative conference at Vose Seminary in August 2009 entitled "Beyond 400." I think they strike a healthy balance between looking back and looking forward. You may not necessarily agree with every comment you read, but I commend them to you as further grist for the mill as we wrestle with what it means to be Baptist Christians in the twenty-first century.

Brian Winslade
National Director, Baptist Union of Australia

Foreword by Jonathan Edwards

As Baptists we need to live close to our historical roots. For some people history might seem like a harmless luxury for those with too much time on their hands, but we Baptists need to listen hard to those who have lived and died for Baptist convictions through the past four tumultuous centuries. The reason for this is that Baptists constitute a movement and not an institution, and if we are to stay healthy and true to our Lord then we need to listen to those who have worked out their Christian calling as Baptists in a myriad of historical, cultural, and geographical contexts.

Baptists cannot ignore the fact that we form merely one part of the church of Jesus Christ. Throughout the world we need to find ways of expressing generous partnership with people who love Jesus no less than we do but who express and practice their faith in a glorious variety of ways. There was a time when it looked as if such ecumenical cooperation was based upon a dilution of everyone's distinctive convictions. However, that is absolutely not the case, and the richest of ecumenical partnership depends upon everyone at the table recognizing the riches of one another's different faith journeys. Baptists have much to share, and this helpful book will assist us as we reflect on the diverse riches that God has graciously given to us through the centuries.

One of the other reasons why it is good to look back is that although the world changes vastly from century to century, most of the fundamentals remain exactly the same. As one reads of the early Baptists, the resonances are very strong with our own time. Our ability to communicate and travel across the world would have been unthinkable to early Baptists, but as we peer into their churches and church meetings we sense that we are meeting sisters and brothers with whom we could easily share a meal and join in worship. The superficial differences be-

Foreword by Jonathan Edwards

tween us are self-evidently immense, but the deep bonds of fellowship in the risen Christ span the centuries with consummate ease.

I am delighted that the "Beyond 400" conference at Vose Seminary proved to be such a stimulating occasion, and I pray that as you read the papers that were presented at that time you will be encouraged to further reflection and research into these crucial Baptist themes. The movement of Baptists has still got a lot of journeying to do.

Jonathan Edwards
General Secretary, Baptist Union of Great Britain

Preface

The year 2009 marked a celebration of 400 years of Baptist history and witness. As a part of the worldwide celebration, Vose Seminary hosted a conference entitled "Beyond 400: Exploring Baptist Futures." The idea for such a conference emanated from an appreciation of the examples we can observe from Baptist history and the lessons that can be learned. It also acknowledges the debt owed to those who have travelled the road before us and recognizes that stepping out into the future requires a consideration of and mindfulness concerning the past. The focus of the conference remained firmly on ecclesiology. Conference presenters and participants reflected on the history of Baptists both being and doing church. From this foundation they offered a variety of ecclesiological images for Baptists as we contemplate being and doing church in the present and future *as* Baptists.

This book represents a collection of the papers presented at the conference, with some valuable additions. A variety of perspectives on Baptist ecclesiology and Baptist futures are addressed from each presenter's reflection on their research and experience in many different contexts. Some have considered Baptist ecclesiology from a biblical standpoint, some have examined the issue theologically, and others have done so in the realm of praxis. Together we believe they present a valuable reflection on the past and a collection of challenges for Baptists in the present and into the future. We are thankful to each contributor for allowing us to use their material in this book.

We are grateful to Pickwick Publications for publishing this work. Our thanks also go to Brian Winslade and Jonathon Edwards for reading the entire text and offering thoughtful reflections in their respective forewords to this volume. We are thankful for the support and encouragement of Vose Seminary and both our families in our research and scholarly endeavors. Without their support the production of this book would have been impossible.

All conferences require both physical and financial support in order to run successfully. We are grateful to our three sponsors, the Australian College of Theology, Christian Super, and Baptist World Aid, for their generous assistance. We also acknowledge the tireless efforts from all the staff at Vose Seminary who contributed many hours in preparing for and running the conference.

Finally, a few thoughts regarding the dedication of this book: Though of course they are not unique in this, it seems to us that both Vose Seminary and Spurgeon's College exemplify what it means to aspire to excellence in training men and women for Christian ministry in its various forms. And, though these institutions sit at opposite sides of the world in different hemispheres, both similarly seek to apply biblical exegesis and theological reflection to current problems and contemporary culture in order that their graduates leave with a genuine sense of the church's mission to today's needy world. Part of our hope is that geographical distance will not lessen the fellowship and mutual calling we share in Christ.

David J. Cohen, Western Australia
Michael Parsons, United Kingdom
2010

Contributors

Neville Callam, General Secretary, Baptist World Alliance (Jamaica)

Brian Harris, Principal, Vose Seminary, Perth, Western Australia

Scott Higgins, Baptist World Aid, Australia

Graham J. G. Hill, Director of the Centre for Leadership, Morling College, Sydney

Steve McAlpine, Emerging Church leader, Western Australia

Richard K. Moore, Research Associate, Vose Seminary, Perth, Western Australia

Edwina Murphy, Lecturer in Church History, Morling College, Sydney

Janice Newham, research student at the Bible College of Victoria

Michael D. O'Neil, Director of Postgraduate Research, Vose Seminary, Perth, Western Australia

Ian Packer, Director of Public Theology, Australian Evangelical Alliance

Michael Parsons, Associate Research Fellow, Spurgeon's College, London

Peter Ralphs, Lecturer in Systematic Theology, Bible College of Queensland

Martin Sutherland, Vice Principal, Laidlaw College, New Zealand

Nigel G. Wright, Principal, Spurgeon's College, London

Abbreviations

ANF	*The Ante-Nicene Fathers*, edited by A. Roberts and J. Donaldson (1885–87; repr., Grand Rapids: Eerdmans, 1965)
BHH	*Baptist History and Heritage*
CBQ	*Catholic Biblical Quarterly*
CT	*Christianity Today*
Ch	*Churchman*
DLNTD	*Dictionary of the Later New Testament and Its Developments*, ed. R. P. Martin and P. H. Davies (Downers Grove, IL: InterVarsity, 1997)
Ep./Epp.	*Cyprian Epistles*
JSNT	*Journal for the Study of the New Testament*
JBL	*Journal of Biblical Literature*
JECS	*Journal of Early Christian Studies*
JPT	*Journal of Pentecostal Theology*
JRE	*Journal of Religious Ethics*
NPNF[1]	*Nicene and Post-Nicene Fathers*, ser. 1, ed. P. Schaff, 14 vols. (1886–89; repr. Peabody, MA: Hendrickson, 1994)
NTS	*New Testament Studies*
PJBR	*Pacific Journal of Baptist Research*
RevExp	*Review and Expositor*
SBL	*Society of Biblical Literature*

1

Baptist Christians: Repentant and Unrepentant

NIGEL G. WRIGHT

Introduction

There is a difference, so it is said, between having 40 years' worth of pastoral experience and having one year's experience 40 times over. The difference lies, one presumes, in the ability to learn from one's experience, to rethink one's past, and to accumulate wisdom, and in its turn this requires the discipline of honest theological reflection. This is what we are about in this conference. Baptist Christians now have not 40 but 400 years' worth of experience since John Smyth and Thomas Helwys founded the first Baptist congregation amongst the English exiles of Amsterdam in 1609. It seems appropriate then to begin a conference entitled "Beyond 400" with some kind of evaluation of what up to this point we may have learnt. After all, the Pauline injunction to "test everything; hold fast to what is good" (1 Thess 5:21) applies to us as well.

To set the scene rather than to inform us of things we do not already know, it is worth pointing out that Baptist identity is now commonly spoken of in some circles in two ways. The first is to describe it as "a way of being church."[1] I shall return to this phrase in due course, but for the moment simply notice its modest implications. A second is that the concept of identity has led in turn to the idea of a genetic

---

1. An early use if this phrase is in Haymes, *Question of Identity*, 1. This brief booklet sparked off an extensive and productive discussion.

code of beliefs, principles, and practices that might together constitute a particular identity. Several Baptist thinkers have therefore attempted their own genome project and have put forward several more or less similar definitions of what that code might be.[2] My own abbreviated version of this code is that, once the reality of church (what is sometimes called "ecclesiality") is present in the first place, the particular Baptist expression of church contains the practice of believer's baptism added to congregational church government and a commitment to religious liberty. Where these elements are present it is difficult to deny that there is a Baptist church.

Baptist Christians—Unrepentant

The title for this paper is not entirely my own idea. In 1958 the Baptist historian and denominational leader Dr. Ernest Payne delivered an address in the United Kingdom as moderator of the then Free Church Federal Council with the title "Free Churchmen, Repentant and Unrepentant." He began by referring to Jesus' parable of the Pharisee and the tax collector (Luke 18:9–14) in which the Pharisee is heard to pray, "God, I thank you that I am not as other people," while the tax collector simply cries out, "God, be merciful to me, a sinner!" Religious groupings sometimes give way to the temptation to give thanks that they are not like the rest, and this temptation is at its strongest, says Payne, "when we come together in gatherings such as this."[3] We should heed his warning. The theme chosen for this conference is one that helps us in this regard, for it has a future perspective and so provokes us not only to recollect the achievements of the past but to go beyond them into a better and wiser future. It is not defending the past that is our concern, but positioning ourselves for the future. This should be our concern today since the study of history has its perils. One of these is the danger that we might relive and perpetuate past enmities that have no future potential. This is where the theme of repentance is a helpful one, and this is a note I hope to strike along the way. Awareness of our history, its strengths and its

---

2. See for instance, Grenz, *Baptist Congregation*, 92; Beasley-Murray, *Radical Believers*, 6–7; Wright, *Free Church*, 42–43. On a slightly different tack see McClendon, *Ethics*, 28, 31.

3. Payne, *Free Churchmen*, 2.

weaknesses, can help guide us as we chart a course into the future that draws us on.

However, risking the pharisaical, let us begin here with unrepentance rather than repentance. Speaking in a more broadly Free Church context, E. A. Payne in the address I have referred to quickly identified four "most vital freedoms" contributed by the Free Church or "dissenting" traditions to the church's common good.[4] It should be clear that I regard Baptists as pre-eminently and classically free church. These freedoms are: (1) freedom from state connection and control, (2) freedom from essential dependence on a priestly succession, (3) freedom from fixed liturgical forms, and (4) freedom of conscience and inquiry.[5] The repetition of the word "freedom" here is striking, and it is a principle I identify at the core of Baptist identity. The tradition of English Dissent that gave rise to these freedoms, in Payne's view and that of many others, offered a more adequate interpretation of the religion of Christ than those of the churches of Christendom, and was not to be surrendered. It belongs to the non-negotiables. Indeed, in Payne's view this interpretation was gaining ground ecumenically and would become the medium for the church's life once the "national Churches of the Old World" collapsed.[6] I suggest that this is exactly what we see happening, and that it is taking place on two fronts simultaneously.

The first front concerns the growth of churches that have adopted the Free Church form and have proven themselves to be well adapted to the work of transmitting the faith. This is particularly true of charismatic and Pentecostal groups, which are at the forefront of church growth. Such churches combine passionate spirituality with flexibility of church leadership and structures in reaching communities that other forms of church life seem unable to touch. The second front is actually within the established, national, or institutional churches themselves, in which a process of steady "congregationalization" seems to be at work, despite the official ecclesiological stances of their hierarchies. Miroslav Volf, from whom I draw some of these ideas, even cites the concerns of Joseph Cardinal Ratzinger, now Pope Benedict XVI, about this trend:

---

4. I use the initial capitals when speaking of Free Church institutional forms and dispense with them when speaking of free church ideas or principles.

5. Payne, *Free Churchmen*, 3.

6. Ibid., 45.

> My impression is that the authentically Catholic meaning of the "Church" is tacitly disappearing, without being expressly rejected.... In other words, in many ways a conception of Church is spreading in Catholic thought, and even in Catholic theology, that cannot even be called Protestant in a "classic" sense. Many current ecclesiological ideas, rather, correspond more to the model of certain North American "Free Churches."[7]

We shall ignore the apparent assumption that Free Churches are an American phenomenon. Perhaps what the former Cardinal had in mind were the base communities of South America and their need to reinvent the church in the light of the lack of priests and other institutional support.[8] But what seemed to the Cardinal to be a bad thing might not seem so to us. Indeed, the process he identifies has otherwise been described by Martin Marty, perhaps more journalistically, as one of "baptistification"—the increasing tendency of congregations in many traditions to live and act like Baptist churches, and in Marty's own American context this would be not least because of the pressures of the American constitution towards non-established religious existence.[9] In favor of this insight I think we might call to witness in the established churches the growing focus upon the life of the local congregation, the increasing stress in many traditions on a realized rather than nominal faith, on the participation of the "laity," on the willingness to accept and value the religious plurality of society, and on the valuing of personal conscience as what John Henry Newman called "the aboriginal vicar of Christ."[10] "Baptistification" may lack elegance as a word, but the idea is not wholly unwelcome. The modality of the free church way has been steadfastly shaping the sodality of the inherited tradition, and to good effect.[11]

So far the language has been of the Free Church. This is deliberate since we need to be rescued from the idea that being Baptist is all about having a particular view of baptism. Rather, we should see that believer's baptism is an indicator of a certain way of being church the essence of which is freedom. The note of freedom is clearly picked up by Payne, as

---

7. Volf, *After Our Likeness*, 12.

8. Boff, *Ecclesiogenesis*. The conflict between Ratzinger and Boff is well known.

9. Marty, "Baptistification," 32–36.

10. Newman uses this term in a letter to the Duke of Norfolk, published in *Certain Difficulties*, 248.

11. Snyder, *Signs of the Spirit*, 52–53.

I have mentioned. It needs to be grasped that this is first and foremost a theological freedom. It is freedom for God in and through Christ. It is because Christ has set us free for this freedom that we are to refuse to submit again to a yoke of slavery (Gal 5:1). It is because in Christ there is a new creation, and we are liberated from our bondage to sin and from subservience to the religious and political powers of this world, that we are to refuse to go back to where we once were. Yet this theological freedom translates into a freedom within the Christian community to know God, and then into a personal freedom formed by this community to exercise our consciences and to know the mind of Christ (1 Cor 2:14–16). The first Baptists came into being in large part as a rejection of forms of church and state that would deprive them of this freedom. There were others before and alongside them who made similar shifts. I think we may claim that they reinvented the church and they did so in a way that genuinely recaptured the spirit of the New Testament community and released a revolutionary social impetus into human society.

At this point interesting themes emerge, themes in which I have taken a particular academic interest.[12] Many of the greatest discoveries, as we know, are made accidentally. In his insight into justification by faith and his insistence on fidelity to the Word of God, I doubt that Martin Luther was aware that he was unleashing a revolutionary principle into the Western world.[13] Likewise, I doubt that in feeling after a true New Testament church the first Baptists were doing other than following the immediate demands of their religious consciences. But the wider ramifications of their religious dissent have been immense. In advocating a particular ecclesiology, they were also implying a certain kind of sociology. As Ian Randall has said about the pioneering Thomas Helwys, "Helwys was not only seeking to establish a new model of church, but also a new model of society, one free from the oppression which he saw in a national, state church."[14] In pursuing a religious community free from ecclesiastical or episcopal control, they were also pioneering a political community that set a limit to the bounds of the temporal power and relegated the jurisdiction of that power to the maintenance of outward order rather than specifically religious observance. And it is here that we may locate the emergence not only of the Free Church but also

12. Wright, *Disavowing Constantine*.
13. Naphy, *Protestant Revolution*.
14. Randall, *Communities*, 23.

of the free state, built around the consensus of the people rather than the command of the ruler. We can trace behind this move two different kinds of religious logic.

Free Church dissenters are used to employing a *disjunctive* rather than a *conjunctive* logic. Conjunctive logic has at times in the history of church-state thinking been used to justify monarchy. It finds divine realities reflected in earthly ones: there is one God, and so there should correspondingly be one pope, and one emperor. Divine monarchy is used in this way to validate both political monarchy and the ecclesiastical monarchical episcopate as more "Godlike" than any other system of spiritual or temporal government. Divine lordship therefore legitimates the exercise of lordship in both church and state. Disjunctive logic proceeds in the opposite direction. If God holds absolute power then no power on earth can be absolute.[15] Because the Lord is King, there can be no other king. Divine kingship does not validate human kingship but undermines it and calls it radically into question since God has no rivals. Compared with God, all powers are relativized and put in their place. It is this disjunctive logic that we find Jesus employing in Matthew 23:8–12.

> But you are not to be called rabbi, for you have one teacher, and you are all students. And call no one your father on earth, for you have one Father—the one in heaven. Nor are you to be called instructors, for you have one instructor, the Messiah. The greatest among you will be your servant. All who exalt themselves will be humbled, and all who humble themselves will be exalted.

Here Jesus effectively subverts the system. He offers a very different way of seeing and thinking, and it is this that Baptists and others like them both noticed and made the signature of their approach to the social order. The temporal power is a relative power—useful, indeed essential, in its own way and for limited purposes, but by no means a rival for the kind of supreme loyalty to be given to God alone. A disjunctive approach is apt to set the church community at a critical distance from the organs of the state, a distance that although respectful will always retain the possibility of non-cooperation. The Free Church will insist on its freedom to be the church. In this way the reinventing of the church that took place through radical Free Church movements can be seen to

---

15. Chan, *Spiritual Theology*, 51.

have had a significant political implication. What has been achieved in this movement has not only helped to reshape the church but also to reshape the civil and political communities. We are the beneficiaries—as church members and as citizens—of both these areas of reform and renewal, and four hundred years on may give thanks not only for a new way of being church pioneered by our forbears, but also for new ways of being together in free societies that they helped to bring about.

After four hundred years there are things for Baptists to celebrate. We may celebrate the seriousness with which our tradition has taken the New Testament as the norm for its faith and conduct even when this has meant breaking with the overwhelming consensus of churchly practice, as in the rejection of infant baptism in favor of believer's baptism. We can give thanks for the evangelical conviction that we must be converted to God and experience the transformation of which believer's baptism by immersion is an effective sign. We can appreciate the instinctive conviction that for spiritual acts to be real they must be freely chosen, and that nominal rites and acts in which the heart is not invested are, at best, a debased and, at worst, an abusive form of religion. We can celebrate the vision not only of life in Christ for the individual believer, but for participating as members in an ordered community life in which we engage intentionally with how we are to live together, own and manage power communally, and exercise discernment together with the "mind of Christ." We can celebrate the kind of logic that has inspired Baptists to disengage from the use of coercive state power in matters of religion and conscience and seek not only religious freedom for themselves but also its corollary: the same kind of freedom for every other person whatever their religious choices may turn out to be. We can celebrate the theological instinct that has enabled Baptists to see that even though the civil powers are incapable in matters of religion, they still have a role in the providence of God to preserve and to protect. For this reason there is a duty owed by believers to seek the good of the civil order and to serve its honorable purposes at the same time as one may criticize it when it goes beyond its proper boundaries. We can be glad that our tradition is one that holds together a firm belief in the uniqueness of Christ and of the joy and duty of believers to offer him confidently to the world as the Redeemer whilst at the same time guarding people's freedom to decline the. We have combined a "theology which is both inclusive of others with an exclusive commitment to Jesus Christ as the revelation of God."[16] This is an honorable record of witness and achievement.

All of these facts of our history, and others we could no doubt go on to list, are things of which we do not need to repent. They belong to our patrimony, to that which has been passed on to us by those who were in Christ before us. Conversely, we have a calling to pass them on to faithful persons in our turn. Baptists are, in a theme to which I would like to return, radical Protestants. We thank God that we are not as other people. Or are we, perhaps?

Baptist Christians—Repentant

Reading Baptist history, and observing Baptist life generally, yields many rich insights and often a generosity of spirit that is impressive. It inevitably also confronts us with attitudes and assumptions with which we may rightly struggle. Not everything that belongs to the tradition, or to contemporary Baptist life, should be carried forward into our futures. There must be a case for Baptist revisionism, but one which is convergent rather than divergent, holding fast to and taking further the genius of the tradition rather than rejecting and departing from it. This ought not to sound exceptional since it must be true of every person and every communion to some degree. Rather than congratulate itself on its virtues, modern Baptist life might well be more aware than former generations of its own poverties and of the richness of other traditions, including those it has previously rejected. This more chastened approach is welcome. Here I wish to single out some past attitudes and to suggest they should play no part in our future.

Earlier on I referred to the tendency now to refer to "the Baptist way of being the church" and indicated that I welcome this expression for its modesty. This is to be contrasted with previous assumptions that Baptists had discovered *the New Testament way* of being the church and therefore could claim to be the "true church" over against any (or at least most) rival claims. In this regard the fact that Baptists emerged from the Separatist movement becomes significant.[17] Separatism rejected the Roman Church and its derivative, the Church of England, as false forms of the church. The fact that Baptists went so far as to reject the very

---

16. Haymes et al., *On Being the Church*, 186.
17. White, *English Separatist Tradition*.

baptism of these churches is a sign of the extent to which they wished to disassociate themselves from what had gone before. Baptist churches saw themselves as more than an option within the spectrum of church life; like restorationist groups since, they understood themselves as the authentic expression of church in contrast to corrupt and counterfeit versions—the recovery of the church of Christ of the New Testament. The fact that they were persecuted for their claims only served to push them more deeply into their conviction. In this regard John Smyth, who is one of our story's heroes, was also one of the worst offenders. Take his words in *The Character of the Beast* (a choice of title significant in its own right):

> The true constitution of the Church is of a new creature baptized into the Father, the Son and the Holy Ghost. The false constitution is of infants baptized. We profess therefore that all those churches that baptize infants are of the same false constitution, and all those churches that baptize the new creature, those that are made disciples by confessing their faith and their sins, are of one true constitution. And therefore the Church of the Separation being of the same constitution with England and Rome is a most unnatural daughter to her mother England and her mother Rome.[18]

This is a sample of an enduring theme in Smyth's brief career, himself a one-time clergyman in the Church of England, and it is notable that even the "churches of the Separation" with which he had so much in common were to be rejected on this reading as false. It is not surprising then that even the congregation which he founded was unable to resist further schism for very long.

As another sample of the "true church" mentality, witness the somewhat later words of the admirable Benjamin Keach (1640–1704), pastor of the Horselydown church in Southwark, when speaking words of commendation to his own congregation:

> You have not made Men, General Councils, nor Synods your Rule, but God's Holy Word: your Constitution, Faith and Discipline, is directly according to the Primitive Pattern; God hath made you (in a most eminent manner) to be Builders of the old Wastes, and Raisers up of the former Desolations, and Repairers of the Waste Cities, the Desolations of many Generations, Isa 61:4. . . .

18. From John Smyth, "The Character of the Beast," in Freeman et al., *Baptist Roots*, 77.

> You have laboured to sever the Gold from the Dross, and to build with proper and fit Gospel-Materials, viz., Spiritual and Living Stones, well hewed and squared by the Hammer of God's Word and Spirit, and will not take one Stone of Babylon for a Corner.[19]

It is not the clear restorationist theme here that we might find problematic but the assumption that everything else is of Babylon, that beyond the circle of the enlightened the rest is apostasy and defection.

It is no doubt true that for a movement like the Baptists to get underway there had to be a stark and somewhat apocalyptic analysis of the prevailing state of affairs. It is also no surprise to see following generations drawing back from this to a considerable degree once their own identity and survival had become secure. But even the remnants of this mentality should not, I suggest, be perpetuated. Baptists have a way of being church that has integrity, has a firm New Testament foundation, and which is worth defending over against other models of the church. It is right to engage in dialogue, critique, and even polemic. We may even believe that this way of being the church can claim to be the most faithful imitation of New Testament Christianity. But this is no reason for unchurching others and denying their own ecclesial identity. To be sure it is not only Baptists who have sung this song—it has been a common claim of both church-type and sect-type movements in the history of the church.[20] The Church of Rome has insisted historically that it is the one, holy, catholic, and apostolic church to the exclusion of all others. In this way it has shown itself to be as negatively sectarian as any so-called sect. With all its willingness to open up since Vatican II, it continues to insist that although other movements may contain "ecclesial elements" and "many elements of sanctification and truth," the fullness of church is to be found within its own bounds and the whole church "subsists" only within it.[21]

The dispute as to who can claim to be the "true church" is frankly a fruitless one that leads to excommunicating one another. Yet the desire as churches to be "true" is clearly fruitful and entirely right. At this point I make the modest proposal that Baptists repent of portraying themselves, in so far as they still do, as "true church." And with this should go

---

19. From Benjamin Keach, *The Breach Repair'd in God's Worship*, in McBeth, *Sourcebook*, 67.

20. Troeltsch, *Social Teaching*, 335–37.

21. *Catechism of the Catholic Church*, paragraphs 816–18.

an awareness of that apparently endless capacity of Baptist and baptistic churches, and indeed Protestant churches in general, to divide and fragment. If there is one longstanding criticism of Protestantism made by those true to the Roman Catholic faith, it is that once people take the Bible in their hands for themselves and insist, as Luther did, upon the right and duty of personal interpretation without some form of *magisterium* to arbitrate between interpretations, the capacity to divide and go on dividing is virtually unstoppable. Erich Geldbach put this regrettable mentality nicely: "When in doubt let's split."[22] If Baptist DNA contains some good genes, we must also confess that it has some defective ones, division being one of them. This enthusiasm for schism is, I suggest, an unsolved problem within the Free Church tradition, and it should trouble our consciences more than it apparently seems to do.

In place of the rhetoric of "true church" we might adopt an eschatological perspective. Seen in the light of the end and goal of our existence, the "true church" is something that has yet to be but towards which we, along with all faithful communities of Christ, are moving. The vision in Revelation 7 of "a great multitude that no one could count, from every nation, from all tribes and peoples and languages, standing before the throne and before the Lamb" is of a reality still to come, yet which may be seen proleptically and fragmentarily in the churches of the present. It is the future church that is the truly gathered church and which unambiguously displays the marks of being one, holy, catholic, and apostolic. No currently existing Christian communion can credibly claim to embody these qualities. An eschatological perspective avoids any claim to be as such the "true church," but sees that we are on our way to what we shall be and that there are higher and lower degrees of faithfulness both to the visions of church given in the New Testament and to the eschatological hope. Our own way of being church is relativized over against the eschatological vision so that we see the extent to which we fall short of what we shall be. Other ways of being church can be seen as also on their way to this shared future. None of us is the true church. To some degree we are all defective. Yet we face the challenge to realize in the present as much as we can of what we shall be.

We return at this point to the traditional four marks of the church, and suggest that in place of seeing them as qualities that churches can claim to possess (who after all can credibly claim to be "one, holy, catho-

---

22. Geldbach, "Petrine Ministry," 158, 162, 164.

lic, and apostolic"?) we understand them as a missionary agenda as we move towards their eschatological realization. In this sense then, the church is to be understood as a proclaiming, reconciling, sanctifying, and unifying community. These activities are the work of Jesus Christ in the world and of the church as Christ's instrument.[23] They are the qualities of a living community and in this way represent the task, or the agenda, of every Christian community.[24] The challenge is to *realize* this agenda and to avoid sinning against it. A potential cause for self-congratulation or exclusion of others is thus transformed into a humbling challenge truly to become the church. The challenge is to repent and to rethink what we mean by "the true church."

Closely allied to this discussion lies another one to do with the place of Baptist Christians within the catholic tradition of the church. As restorationists, Baptists have understood themselves as returning to the Bible to begin the work of building the church from the bottom up. Such a perspective obscures the degree to which they are also the product of the universal church which pre-existed them and gave rise to them. Insofar as Baptists see themselves as set apart from the Great Tradition of Christian faith and life, they may become prone to a mentality that sets them to mutual disadvantage on the edge of the whole church's existence. As in many parts of the world Baptists are a minority community within a wider community that owes some kind of allegiance to religious nationalism, it may be seen how such a mentality is reinforced. The accent therefore falls on the ways in which Baptists might differ from others, and not on what is shared. Read retrospectively, traditional Baptist hostility towards Roman Catholicism can look to modern eyes like bigotry and prejudice. I would resist that interpretation in favor of understanding it as profound resistance to the papacy's one-time claims to universal jurisdiction both religiously and politically—a resistance that was at the time entirely justified.[25] Yet this history has confused the entirely valid distinction between "catholic" and "Roman Catholic" and hindered Baptists from seeing how much they owe to the catholic tradition and how much, in journeying towards the future true church, they need to draw from its resources. Baptists are part of that project that we call the catholic Christian church and cannot disengage themselves from it. Yet

---

23. Here I am following closely Grenz, *Renewing the Center*, 319–21.
24. Ibid., 313.
25. Geldbach, "Petrine Ministry," 161–62.

they belong within that project as those who are radically Protestant, and it is precisely this duality that constitutes our future identity and our future contribution to the whole church. If there is a thesis in this lecture, therefore, it exists in the combination of the truly catholic and the radically Protestant as equally basic aspects of our future identity.

Dr. Rowan Williams, Archbishop of Canterbury, has remarked that at the time of the Protestant Reformation the question "Is the pope a Catholic?" was not a joke. It was the whole point of the Reformation—to what extent was the pope truly a representative of catholic, normative, faithful Christianity? Could it be that the putative representative of the catholic tradition had in fact become an "antichrist," a claim that was, of course, frequently made and passionately believed by the Reformers? It should also be noted that despite the often-made claim that Baptists are not a creedal movement, that they have "no creed but the Bible," some of them did not hesitate in their early confessions to specify allegiance to the ecumenical creeds, clearly indicating their sense of place within the traditions and taking a reference point from those early statements.[26] There is every reason, therefore, for contemporary Baptists to see themselves as deeply rooted in the catholic traditions of the Christian church and should define themselves as faithful catholics. In some circles this is a process well under way, and we are seeing a new "catholic consciousness" among certain parts of the Baptist community.[27] In large measure the emergence of the "catholic Baptist" represents a new awareness of the place of tradition within the formation of particular theologies.

This calls into question whether it is ever possible to have a theology formed by Scripture alone. The notion that we are or can be wholly and solely subject to the teaching of Scripture without mediation is another of those illusions, like the idea of the true church, of which our tradition should repent. "The reality is that no Christian community lives with the Bible alone."[28] The doctrine of *sola Scriptura* needs to be replaced, therefore, by a doctrine of *suprema Scriptura*, recognizing Scripture's primary and normative role in a complex process of interpretation that includes

---

26. The Orthodox Creed of 1679 specifies in article 38 that the Apostles' Creed, the Nicene Creed, and the Athanasian Creed ought "thoroughly to be received, and believed." See Lumpkin, *Baptist Confessions*, 326.

27. As examples, see Holmes, *Listening to the Past*; Harmon, *Towards Baptist Catholicity*; Colwell, *Promise and Presence*. See also Haymes et al., *On Being the Church*.

28. Haymes et al., *On Being the Church*, 49.

reason, experience, tradition, and context.[29] The effect of such a repentance should not lead us to the wooliness of a twilight in which all cats are grey, but to existence as a community of witness and conviction with an appropriate and modest sense of its own frailty and its dependence upon those interpreters who have gone before or who stand alongside us in the present.

The dependence of Baptists upon the tradition is after all illustrated by the very Bible to which they make appeal and by the doctrine of the Trinity, which they would vigorously wish to affirm. Neither has dropped from heaven in some unmediated form but are the gifts of the tradition to those who have followed after. The hard work of preserving, receiving, recognizing, and then canonizing the New Testament writings was a lengthy process, involving discussions through time and across space before it was complete. Yet the canon of New Testament scriptures was accepted by Baptists as a given that needed not to be re-evaluated. Likewise, the outcomes of the debates and controversies about a truly Christian doctrine of God that occupied the churches in the patristic age were accepted by most Baptists as givens to be defended against the encroachments of Unitarianism. Honesty compels Baptists to acknowledge that the very Bible to which they appeal as the supreme earthly authority is itself the product of the catholic tradition of the church of whose work they are the beneficiaries. And, if this be the case, in these two central areas there are no coherent reasons why the tradition of the catholic church might not be received, if not uncritically then at least gratefully, at many other points.

Yet a caveat should be added at this point: the distinction between what is catholic and what is Roman Catholic needs to be maintained. Here I return to my characterization of Baptists as radical Protestants. And this is where the future must lie, in the combination of catholic consciousness allied to radical Protestant commitment. Embracing the catholic tradition of the whole church does not mean ceasing the critique of those distortions of it that we find in Roman Catholicism. Against the trend in some quarters to minimize the need for the Reformation, it is encouraging to see a recent resurgence of interest in what it means to be faithfully Protestant.[30] More of this is needed since the ability to find greater agreement on the doctrine of justification than was once

---

29. Harmon, *Towards Baptist Catholicity*, 32.
30. McGrath, *Christianity's Dangerous Idea*.

thought possible was not, and is not, the only point at issue.[31] Baptists have rightly understood that the nature of the church, its composition and its order, have been crucially at stake, and, as we have seen, how we view the social order and contribute to it is likely to follow on from what we have determined about the place of the church. However much Roman Catholicism can honestly claim to have Christ at its centre, the issue is whether the heavy weight of Roman Catholic tradition as currently received can ever do anything other than obscure the Jesus in whom it believes. This is the mystery of it all: how Jesus of Nazareth, the humble carpenter and rabbi who is also God's Son and our Savior, can be called in to validate a religious system that seems to resemble him so distantly and sometimes not at all.

To repeat: Baptists are at the radical end of the Protestant spectrum and represent a markedly different way of being the church of Jesus Christ. They have broken with the idea that the church was ever called to be an imperial institution exercising sacred power over its members and with the power to command. They came to see it as a free community of the redeemed, of those committed to voluntary and wholehearted commitment to the way of Christ pursued in solidarity and mutual affirmation. To assert their participation in the catholic faith is not to lessen the critique of distorted versions of that faith which is both radical and Protestant, but it is to affirm the need for Baptists to be aware of their connectedness in Christ with all who have confessed the faith before them and with all who do so today. Their vision is that the church might become the church, faithfully honoring and embodying the way of the living Christ. Their radical Protestantism is part of what they offer for the sake of the whole church.[32]

Baptist Christians: repentant and unrepentant. I hope I have said enough by way of affirmation and denial to make the point. None today can escape the chastening effect of self-criticism. Baptist tradition is not an unambiguous good, and it needs to be tested. But when it is tested there is that to which we do well to hold fast. One of the supreme

---

31. See the summaries of these discussions in Lane, *Justification*.

32. Stephen Harmon makes an eloquent and, to me, convincing plea for greater Baptist catholicity in his book *Towards Baptist Catholicity*. But surprisingly, he has little to say about believers' baptism, and his reason for "not becoming a Catholic" has to do with not wanting to add to the church's disunity by jumping ship rather than the belief that radical Protestants have still much to offer on the nature of the church. See my review in *Ecclesiology* 5 (2009).

strengths of the tradition embedded within its core is a critical and corrective principle. Its essence was captured by that early Separatist congregation in Gainsborough, Lincolnshire, founded in the 1600s and out of which the first Baptists were to emerge. The covenant they made together, echoed by many others since, was "as the Lord's free people . . . to walk in all His ways, made known to them or to be made known unto them, according to their best endeavours, whatsoever it might cost them, the Lord assisting them." The tradition itself is one that has a dynamic built into it: to continue listening to the free Word of God that arises from the Scriptures and that causes us to see things in new ways whilst maintaining faithful continuity with what has gone before. The openness to change that is part of the further-light principle is written into our DNA. It is our tradition that we can change our tradition. This is the way of open-ended pilgrimage which sets us free to embark upon and explore our futures.

2

Humane Religion:
Evangelical Faith, Baptist Identity, and Liberal Secularism

NIGEL G. WRIGHT

Introduction

John Smyth (c. 1665–1612), the founder of the first Baptist church in 1609 and the first Baptist theologian, included the following article of faith in his publication *Propositions and Conclusions*:

> That the magistrate is not by virtue of his office to meddle with religion, or matters of conscience, to force or compel men to this or that form of religion, or doctrine: but to leave Christian religion free, to every man's conscience, and to handle only civil transgressions (Rom 13), injuries and wrongs of man against man, in murder, adultery, theft, etc., for Christ only is the king, and lawgiver of the church and conscience (James 4:12).[1]

Leon McBeth comments on this article that although the words "separation of church and state" are not present here, the concept certainly is.[2] If so, we discover what I have previously argued: that the first Baptists were not only reinventing the church, they were pioneering a new way of conceiving the temporal power. The ruler, the magistrate, and the state

---

1. John Smyth, "Propositions and Conclusions concerning the True Christian Religion, containing a Confession of Faith of certain English people, living at Amsterdam" (1612) in Lumpkin, *Baptist Confessions*, 140.
2. McBeth, *Sourcebook*, 70.

do not, theologically conceived, have complete authority over every aspect of social and personal life. They have a role that is limited to the maintenance of good order, to the punishment of offenders, and to the protection of the virtuous. But it is not for the civil power to command or to coerce in matters of religious conscience. As Thomas Helwys famously expressed in his publication of the same year,

> For our lord the King is but an earthly King, and if the Kings people be obedient and true subjects, obeying all humane laws made by our King, our lord the King can require no more. For mens religion to God, is betwixt God and themselves; the King shall not answer for it, neither may the King be judg betwene God and man. Let them be heretikes, Turks, Jewes, or whatsoever, it apperteynes not to the earthly power to punish them in the least measure.[3]

Seminal statements as these were over time to win the day and, no doubt along with other social and philosophical forces, lead to the theological and political doctrine of the separation of church and state. From the theological perspective this doctrine intends to set a limit to the invasion or coercion of religious conscience by the secular power. From the political perspective the reverse is the case: it intends to limit the ability of religious and clerical authorities to impose upon the citizen religious requirements or limitations that they do not embrace for themselves. However, the separation of church and state remains a contested doctrine for some who insist that the gospel of Christ lays claim to the whole of life and that therefore to separate the realm of the spirit from that of the body is to offend against Christian holism. It is helpful therefore to set out what the separation of church and state is not before explaining what it is.[4]

Separation of Church and State

First, it does not imply *the separation of church from society*. Churches and other faith communities and the multiple institutions they generate are an integral part of community life and society at large. The state, or government, is not society itself, but the hard edge of society, given

---

3. Ibid., 72.

4. In what follows I am adapting material from my chapter "Government as an Ambiguous Power" in Spencer and Chaplin, *God and Government*, 16–39.

in order that society might be maintained. Separation of church and state does not therefore imply a strategy of withdrawal on the part of the church whereby it retreats from society into the private and mystical realm and takes no part in the public realm.

Second, it cannot imply *the independence of the church from the state* as though what takes place in one can have no effect upon the other. To the contrary, institutions shape each other. State legislation, policing, taxation policy, financial security, legal provisions for charities, and the general well-being or otherwise of state institutions will make their impact upon faith communities. Traffic will also flow the other way as church initiatives, especially in the area of education and social care, contribute to, supplement, and sometimes replace government activity.

Third, it does not mean *the separation of the church from politics*. This is especially the case when "politics" is understood more broadly than the central organs of national or local government alone. All of life is political in that it involves processes of negotiating, agreeing, and managing our common life. "Politicalness" is intrinsic to corporate life, whether this is in schools, trades unions, local councils, charities, or congregations.[5] Moreover, in all of these realms there is a continual discussion about what constitutes the goods that we have in common and how on the basis of shared or sometimes contested values we are to find the ground that will make life most fulfilling for all. This inevitably touches on the moral and existential beliefs we bring to the discussion, whether as people of religious or secular faith.[6]

Fourth, separation of church and state ought not to mean *the systematic exclusion of religion from public life*. This is what some have taken it to mean with a strong but negative emphasis, especially in the US, on Thomas Jefferson's "wall of separation" between the church and the state.[7] The complete exclusion of religion from the public realm is pre-

---

5. The word "politicalness" comes from Wolin, *Presence of the Past*.

6. I put it like this because it is impossible to divide, as some people do, between voices that speak only out of "reason" or only out of "faith." All secularists hold beliefs they cannot prove (the sanctity of human life, for instance) and all people of faith have their characteristic ways of reasoning.

7. Jefferson, who was in his own idiosyncratic way a religious man, used this celebrated phrase in his 1802 reply to a letter from the Danbury Baptist Association, but it was first used by the Baptist theologian and founder of the Rhode Island colony Roger Williams in "Mr. Cotton's Letter Lately Printed, Examined and Answered" (1644), in his *Complete Writings*, 1.108.

sumably based on the idea that religion is potentially a poison.[8] This is clearly the goal of a certain kind of secularist. But it would simply signify the introduction of a different kind of established religion, the secularist version, with its own forms of priesthood and control. Secularism of this kind has already demonstrated throughout the twentieth century that it is capable of greater atrocities than religion has ever managed to achieve.

How then is the separation of church and state to be understood? It represents a clear desire to distinguish between the order of preservation served by government and the order of redemption served by the church.[9] Both are necessary, but since the order of preservation requires the use of coercion and force, there needs at this point to be a clear separation between the way governments fulfill their mandate and the way the church (and, indeed, any religious movement) pursues its mission. Coercion, force, and violence do not serve the coming of the kingdom of a God who is supremely revealed in a Messiah who gave himself up to death on a cross and taught his disciples to love their enemies and do good to those who persecute them (Matt 5:43-48). This is because the highest goods of which human beings are capable are essentially internal rather than external and, therefore, require the free exercise of the will for them to be realized. The external preservation of human societies is an essential work but it cannot achieve human redemption. What it can do is provide the framework of peace and security within which the gospel of Christ can be proclaimed, and that gospel is the power of God for salvation (Rom 1:16-17).

To separate church and state allows the church to be itself and frees it for its prophetic task of witness. All Christians are called to be exemplary citizens and to seek the welfare of whatever society to which they belong (Jer 29:7; Rom 13:7; 1 Pet 2:13-17). Since they are no longer subservient to the agenda of governments and the powerful, however, free churches are not under any obligation to give religious legitimation to the powers. This increases their value to society since communities of constructive dissent have the capacity to incubate new ways of living together and stimulate social change. Reciprocally, freeing the state from religious control (if not religious influence) means that it can take its place as a modest instrument of the common good and can do so

---

8. It might be noted that the American version of Christopher Hitchens's atheistic bestseller, *God Is Not Great*, carries the subtitle *How Religion Poisons Everything*.

9. Yoder, *Christian Witness*, 12-13.

impartially and fairly. It need penalize none for their beliefs, but can grant the space in which people can negotiate their own freely chosen religious decisions rather than acting out of fear of coercion should they fail to conform. In this way "a free church in a free state" works both for the benefit of true religion and for a free, non-persecutory society.[10]

To separate religion and state in the way indicated suggests that churches should not have any form of "established" status in the sense that they are bound in partnership with the temporal power,[11] nor should they seek any privileges for themselves that are not equally to be shared by other faiths and ideologies. This is required by the theological distinction between church and state, but it also represents a form of love for neighbor since it seeks the same kinds of advantage for others that it does for itself. Christian churches and religious bodies maintain a critical distance from power in order to fulfill their mandate faithfully. But individual members of the church should be free and encouraged to participate freely in all dimensions of government activity as conscience allows them. When they do so it is as citizens who happen to be Christians rather than as Christians enjoying some kind of established privilege that others might be entitled to resent. If Jesus' metaphor of being salt and light is to be followed, Christians have the capacity by their presence and quality of life both to work against any corruption that they find and to encourage and stimulate the good that they will also find (Matt 5:13).[12]

Here I wish to insert a claim that may begin to make sense of the title of this lecture. The sustained Baptist attempt to uncouple church and state was an attempt to return the Christian religion to being a humane influence rather than a punitive and persecutory one. It was a denial of the implication of religion in state violence, which had been a longstanding and abhorrent aspect of established religion. It was an evangelical impulse in that it represented a return to the peaceful proclamation of the gospel of peace on behalf of a Messiah who endured violence rather

---

10. The slogan "a free church in a free society" is a useful one. It appears to have been coined by Camillo Cavour (1810–61), united Italy's first prime minister. See Wright, *Free Church*, 206–7.

11. It is inevitable, of course, that it will assume some kind of legal status, but this is not what is intended by the word "established." On the various possibilities for "established" models of church see my article "National Churches" in Briggs, *Dictionary of Baptist Life*, 345–46.

12. Apparently salt was used both to preserve and to fertilize.

than inflict it. It was also politically liberal in that it aimed at increasing the element of freedom within the social order. By contrast with both the established churches of Christendom and some of the Protestant movements that emerged in the Reformation, Baptists saw that church discipline might rightly be exercised among those who had embraced the covenant of church membership, but not outside these voluntary boundaries. Whereas the Puritans were prepared to follow the pattern of Calvin's Geneva and actively enforce, with the help of the civil power, external obedience to what was deemed to be the will of God,[13] Baptists saw the Christian community as the appropriate means by which the life of discipleship was to be instilled among the church's members, but not among outsiders. This is not to say that Baptists were not themselves enthusiastically willing from time to time to take up the sword for certain causes, as their sometimes belligerent role in the English Civil Wars clearly revealed. But if this stance needs a defense it is along the lines that they were struggling for a non-dictatorial social order in which the religious conscience would be free. Since it is manifestly and lamentably the case that in the contemporary world religion is frequently associated with physical, psychological, and rhetorical violence and at times is rightly to be feared, the early Baptist impulse that true Christian religion is intrinsically humane and non-coercive needs to be re-emphasized. Humane religion should still be high on our agenda. The ability to articulate and embody an appropriately gracious, merciful, and compassionate public theology appears to me to be highly necessary.

Of all the fundamental principles that belong to our patrimony, the one it is easiest for contemporary Western Baptists to overlook, or so it seems to me, is that to do with religious freedom. Perhaps this is because in the West religious liberty has become an accepted given of our political culture and because all the Western churches, even those that once denied this right, now endorse it, at least in principle. We therefore take it for granted. Yet it remains the case that the struggle for full religious freedom is still a major concern in many places, many more than we might imagine, especially in countries that enact anti-conversion laws. My suspicion, however, is that alongside this, although often as irritants rather than as violations of human rights, issues of religious freedom continue in liberal democracies in mutated form, and Baptist futures will require thinking carefully about the relation between firm evangeli-

---

13. Haymes et al., *On Being the Church*, 111.

cal conviction and the constraints of secular liberalism. To help negotiate this quite complex territory I have sought to develop a contemporary typology.

A Contemporary Typology

The use of typology in understanding the relation of the church to society is an established one. Ernst Troeltsch, after surveying the history of Christian social thinking, concluded that there were to be found within it three broad types, which he distinguished as the church-type, the sect-type, and mysticism.[14] The church-type, the majority, is characterized by *universality*, the desire to comprehend and dominate the whole of society; and the contrasting sect-type by *intensity*, the desire to be faithful to Christ even though this might mean accepting a minority role and somewhat alienated place in the social order. Mysticism is characterized by *inwardness*. In this typology Baptists are firmly of the sect-type. Troeltsch's work has achieved classical status. Something similar might be said about H. Richard Niebuhr's seminal work *Christ and Culture*. Here again Niebuhr worked with ideal types, five in number, of the ways in which Christ has been deemed to relate to created but fallen human culture throughout Christian history. The *Christ against culture* type, which Niebuhr saw illustrated by the various Anabaptist movements and particularly by the Amish of North America, sets fidelity to Christ over against accommodation to culture. The *Christ of culture* type accommodates to culture to the point where no conflict between the two is experienced, and so could be exemplified by Liberal Protestantism. The *Christ above culture* type represents the centre ground occupied historically by the church according to which Christ makes sense not only of the church's story but of the whole of creation, which finds its true nature in the Logos from whom all things derive their rationality. *Christ and culture in paradox*, illustrated chiefly by Lutheranism, detects a kind of dualism between Christ and culture so that any relation between them is more likely to be derived dialectically rather than in smooth cohesion. Finally, Niebuhr works towards his preferred type, *Christ the transformer of culture*, illustrated by names in Christian history such as Augustine, Calvin, and F. D. Maurice. Christ redeems and transforms the public culture.

14. Troeltsch, *Social Teaching*, 2.993.

It is arguable of course that the church's relationship to culture will conform to all of these types at some point depending on the context or the issues at stake. Typologies can be illuminating, but also misleading in that they invite people to pigeonhole movements and groups according to a set of preconceived identities. It is particularly unhelpful therefore when baptistic groups are stigmatized as both of a "sect-type" and "against culture." The word "sect" is usually interpreted negatively, and the idea of being "against" culture is surely flawed in that even sect-type groups have their own culture. My own typology has attempted to avoid this by offering a different set of categories. I summarize these briefly as I have written about them elsewhere.[15]

Participating and Possessing

In these perspectives, the Christian church lays claim not only to participating in the public realm but also to possessing it. It lays down the truths that determine that realm. This may take the form of *theocracy*, in which any distinction between sacred and secular is abolished, or of *Constantinian Christendom*, where the distinction between the two is maintained and the two act in each other's interest, employing coercion to do so. Or it may be in the much-overlooked form of *non-Constantinian Christendom*, which advocates the separation of church and state to distinguish more clearly between the coercive powers of the magistrate and the persuasive power of the gospel and its advocates, but is still within a vision of Christendom in which Christian truth is determinative for the public realm. The difference between this and the other modes is that in it the decisive example of Jesus and the voluntary nature of Christian faith is held to lead to a social order that allows for religious freedom and excludes religious coercion, all for specifically Christian reasons. This brings us then to the position antithetical to that we have just examined.

Not Participating and Not Possessing

The real focus in this section concerns what I identify as *hard secularism*. Hard secularism is more than a political theory. It is a metaphysics and takes its lead from scientism, which is more than a method of gaining knowledge and understanding; it is a materialistic, atheistic worldview

15. Wright, *Participating without Possessing*; idem, *Free Church*, 270–79.

hostile to religion, which it sees as a force for superstition and conflict and which it is only prepared to tolerate insofar as it does not have significant social or political effects upon public existence . Privatization of religion is, according to this account, a containment strategy. Faith is neither allowed to possess the public realm nor to participate in it except on terms laid down for it by secularism itself. Twentieth-century Communist regimes clearly fall into this category, but the rhetoric of hard secularism based upon disregard for religion is not hard to find even in liberal democracies.

Participating without Possessing

In this category Christians participate in the social and political order but are aware that they do not possess it. Rather it is shaped by a different religious tradition, or by an alternative political philosophy, or perhaps by a variety of forces and influences in tension with each other. However, not being disqualified from participating, they do so as a minority presence, even though they may be aware that at specific points they need to accommodate to conditions they would not themselves as Christians have chosen. We may imagine that this is the condition under which Christians live in many parts of the world where the overwhelming majority adhere to a different religion, whether Hinduism, Buddhism, or Islam, or where, as in many Western countries, secular liberalism dominates.Crucially at this point I identify the philosophy of *soft secularism*. Just as it is a mistake to regard all forms of Christianity as the same, so it is a mistake to regard all forms of secularism as the same. As science and scientism are not the same so it is with secularism. Scientism is an ideology, whereas science is a methodology. It is possible, therefore, to distinguish between *ideological secularism* and *civic secularism*; or between *programmatic secularism* and *procedural secularism*.[16] Whereas ideological or programmatic secularism is hostile to religion, civic and procedural secularism has more the character of a practical political philosophy designed to enable people of differing convictions and postures to share equally in the public benefits of society without discrimination. When it comes to public goods and the public square, people should neither be favored nor disqualified from sharing in them on the basis

16. This is a distinction developed by Rowan Williams, Archbishop of Canterbury, in a lecture entitled "Secularism, Faith and Freedom."

of their religious beliefs or conformity. A parallel distinction might be made here between a *hostile secularism*, which wishes to exclude religion from the public realm, and a *hospitable secularism*, which sees the public realm as exactly the kind of place where people of differing religious persuasions and identities can meet without fear of being disadvantaged or disqualified and, therefore, are enabled to meet authentically. What complicates the issue is that it is not always clear what form of secularism is operative, and the suspicion can sometimes be that hard secularism is concealing itself in the more generous form of soft secularism. The failure to distinguish between the different secularisms is at the heart of some current misunderstandings in the Western world. I suspect it is not only Christians who are party to such misunderstandings. The potential for rhetorical miscommunication is considerable. When we are told that religion should be a private affair, for instance, Christians are apt to think that we are being excluded from the realm of public discourse on the grounds of religion. This feels like being told to conceal or even abandon our identity in the public sphere. When Christians counter with the claim that their truth is a public truth, secularists are apt to hear that Christians wish to impose upon others a religious position with which they do not agree. This is the ground of resentment about the role of religion in the public sphere, and as religious judgments often come into play in relation to beginning- and end-of-life issues—such as abortion, assisted suicide, and euthanasia—it is not surprising that these issues sometimes become the scene for conflicts. The concern around religious freedom and state constraints, therefore, has mutated to take new forms and raise new questions in advanced democracies. Just as former generations had to wrestle with the issue for some time before it dawned upon them that religious nonconformists could still be valuable and loyal citizens, so perhaps we have now to wrestle with questions about the relation between our evangelical convictions and our secular liberal context. This is where our Baptist identity can guide us.

Non-Constantinian Christendom

Let me backtrack to the category of non-Constantinian Christendom I previously identified. It has now become widely accepted that Christendom has been superseded and that this is a good thing.[17]

17. See Murray, *Post-Christendom*; idem, *Church after Christendom*; Bartley, *Faith and Politics*.

Christendom itself is widely regarded as a mistake. But the judgment about whether it is a good or a bad thing depends on whether we can talk about *Christendom* or *Christendoms*. If Christendom is essentially a coerced reality in which the Christian faith is imposed by the powerful then its passing is not to be lamented. The confusing of the orders of preservation and of redemption can only lead to the distortion of both. If, however, it is a way of speaking about a society that has been shaped by the predominant, willingly-embraced faith of its population then this is a different case.

I contend that the historical free church vision has been of this latter order and so has been in its own distinctive way still a Christendom vision. It has not contended for a paganized society or for the abandonment of the desirability of a social order shaped by Christian faith. Where it has differed from Constantinian Christendom has been in its belief that the outcome of such a society would be a firm commitment on the part of the temporal power to disengage religious belief from compulsion, to protect the rights to religious freedom, and to dissent and to foster principled pluralism rather than religious conformity. This is a Christendom vision in that the social order is understood and undergirded by reference to Christian beliefs, but to the free church version of those beliefs, not the established or state church version. Baptist Christians have had no problem with the idea that the gospel can and should shape social reality, nor even with the idea that the state might possibly be a confessional state.[18] They have differed about the corollaries of such a possibility and insisted that a truly Christianized state would look very different from nearly all the versions of the religious state that have been on offer.

So far the analysis goes. It is unlikely however that in the kind of societies in which most of us at this conference are living twe can anticipate living within any kind of Christendom, Constantinian or otherwise. In other parts of the world where Christianity is on the rise or still dominant it might be possible to think otherwise—but not here. Christendoms depend upon people maintaining an active and dominant allegiance to the Christian faith, and these days seem to have passed for most liberal democracies. We may once have been in the category of

---

18. In fact even those who place themselves in the anti-Christendom camp seem to have theologically informed views about what states should or should not do. Is this still a ghost of a Christendom vision?

participating and possessing, but now more accurately should think of ourselves as participating without possessing. If anything, the predominant consensus, shared across a broad spectrum of political parties, is most accurately understood as liberal secularism. The challenge in the realm of religious freedom is to ensure as best we can that this is the hospitable, civic, procedural secularism to which I have referred and that it is not allowed to become the ideological, programmatic, hostile secularism that could use the former as a cloak for its own agenda. I do not believe this to be an easy task.

As it happens, non-Constantinian Christendom and liberal secularism seem to me to have much in common and to be perspectives on the social order that can do business with each other. I would go so far as to say that liberal secularism has grown out of soil well fertilized by free church principles. Both represent responses to the kind of religious politics that devastated Europe in the post-Reformation period and led to the conviction that both politics and religion are better served when specific religious interests are kept at a distance from temporal power. If there is any virtue in the dictum that politics and religion should not be mixed, it is at this point it is to be found, however untrue it may be at other points. They share a common commitment to maximizing freedom for persons to determine their own destinies and to maintaining the impartiality and fairness of the public realm. Each seeks to be non-persecutory and to avoid disadvantaging people through discrimination. Both operate according to declared agendas to which they may be held accountable. Both value equality and human rights, although how exactly these concepts are understood may differ. It is all the more surprising, therefore, that at times they appear to come into conflict with each other.

After achieving fundamental rights, it need not be surprising that a further stage in the area of religious liberty concerns the balancing of appropriate rights. It remains to be seen whether such tensions are a temporary stage in an otherwise productive relationship or whether there are deeper issues at stake. A fundamental difference, for instance, is that for all its emphasis on human dignity and freedom, the non-Constantinian perspective locates human flourishing in obedience to a divine Other rather than in strict autonomy. It has a clearer vision of the virtuous life. It might also be observed that a public culture founded on rights and anti-discrimination legislation can become oppressively dogmatic and lacking in sensitivity to anything that falls outside its immediate parameters.

To illustrate some of these tensions, and take them from the abstract into the practical, it might be observed that Christian Web sites in the UK currently abound with what are claimed to be discriminatory actions taken against Christians in the name of diversity and equal opportunities. Examples include:

- a Christian registrar in Islington being dismissed from her post because of her refusal to register same-sex partnerships on grounds of conscience;
- a second registrar in the same London borough being demoted for the same kind of refusal;
- the owners of a Christian boarding house being reported by a homosexual lobby group for indicating on their Web site that gay couples would not be accommodated, contrary to new legislation about non-discrimination in the provision of goods and services;
- a Baptist nurse being reported by a colleague and temporarily suspended for offering to pray for a patient in her care;
- a British Airways worker at Heathrow being threatened with dismissal on health and safety grounds for refusing to remove a cross she was wearing;
- a Christian worker being dismissed for expressing negative views about homosexuality in a conversation with a colleague while at work;
- Catholic adoption agencies being forced to cease their long-standing adoption work because of their unwillingness, following church teaching, to consider same-sex couples as prospective parents.

There are many other examples like the above contributing to a general sense that Christians are at the bottom of the pile when it comes to the protection of their rights. The impression is that well-meaning equality legislation generates conflicts of rights and is being used oppressively with the suspicion that, whatever the outer rhetoric behind diversity and rights legislation, the inner reality is a hostility to strong religious conviction. Is this, therefore, a case of hard secularism masquerading as soft secularism in order to pursue an anti-Christian and anti-religious agenda? Or is it a form of Christian paranoia that adopts the posture of victim for its own advantage? Or is it that there is a deeper level of productive dialogue and debate about the appropriate balancing of rights that we have yet to discover? It should be clear enough that debates about religious freedom have not been resolved but have simply mutated.

Of course, to quote the Roman Catholic Archbishop of Cardiff in a recent article,

> It would be a strange world where there were no tension between Church and State: either the Church would have become the compliant tool of a totalitarian regime, or Christ's kingdom would have arrived on earth without our noticing it.[19]

Some degree of tension is surely to be expected. Yet the reported cases I have just referred to may not be altogether what they seem to be. Are Christians apt out of over-sensitivity to interpret genuine concerns for health and safety as attacks upon their faith? This may have been the case with the British Airways employee, and BA revised their position in the light of the ensuing outcry. Could it be that in some situations Christians are genuinely offensive in the way they put their point of view? Ought they perhaps to take the point that in a commercial transaction it is none of their business what people are up to in a room they may have legitimately rented? Or could it be that we have examples here not of oppressive legislation but simply of poor implementation and management? Or might it even be that Christians should just get over it and treat others not as categories but as human beings who in a fair and just society should be allowed to get on with their lives, and that the law is entirely right to insist that this should happen? Or may it be that there is a whole complexity of issues here that need to be disentangled before we can see what issues are matters of religious freedom and what are not? I am inclined to this latter view and believe that we are in a new process of learning.

In his foreword to a recent publication, Michael Scott Joynt, Bishop of Winchester, makes the following point:

> A society that makes room only for a few thin, minimal, rootless, generic values, like "fairness" and "tolerance" in the public square, whilst effectively requiring people to hide the things they value most in some private realm, will be a weak society

---

19. Smith, "Voice That Must Be Heard."

because its public and political life will be drained of the values that truly animate people and that mobilise self-sacrifice. Such a project might like to make much of its "liberal" credentials, but in truth it only really manages to cater for diversity by pushing it into the private sphere, rather than making room for its proper celebration. In an age where there is growing concern about our weakened social capital and civic apathy, it is imperative that we pursue a model of liberal democracy that makes good room for people and their values in the public square.[20]

The issue is not whether or not we believe in freedom and plurality. We most certainly do. But we also believe in freedom of religious expression, and not only in freedom of worship. The issue is that a dogmatic public culture might end up seeking to control what people say and think in the same way as the established religions once sought to do, punishing those who were regarded as deviants and nonconformists. Part of our future challenge is to contend for new understandings of what it means to be free.

Late last year I attended a lecture given by Sir Jonathan Sacks, Chief Rabbi of the United Kingdom and the Commonwealth, who is highly respected among Christians not least because of his unique ability to articulate the kind of "participating without possessing" position I have tried to outline. The Jewish community in the UK is a model of a distinctive community living responsibly and fruitfully in a society it does not control. In describing his role Dr. Sacks explained that the terms of his office expressly forbade him from excommunicating anybody and he explained why this was the case. Many Jewish citizens of the UK have had their origins in the *shtetls* within the Pale of Settlement across Poland and Russia, where they would live in relatively isolated and homogeneous communities. If a Jew fell foul of the religious authorities and was excommunicated from the religious community they would have nowhere to go, and so their very existence would be under threat. Because the communities were inherently religious and lacked "secular" space, the loss of religious status would lead to the loss of any kind of status. This helped me see how important it is in the present age that there should be secular space and that religious faiths need there to be such space. Secular space is necessary not just to protect people from abusive religion but to ensure that when people do heed the call of discipleship

---

20. Foreword to Boucher, *Abolition of Slavery*, 6.

they do so for genuinely spiritual reasons and not just for the sake of conformity.

Paradoxically, therefore, the authenticity of the church in this age is dependent upon there being that sphere which is not church. If people then choose to belong to the church they do so freely and not for fear of being disadvantaged. Historically Christians have called this sphere "the world" and have been clear that the church is not the world. There is, therefore, a kind of duality that belongs to authentic Christian existence that comes to expression in varying forms. The "now" is not the same as the "not yet." We are called to be in the world but not of the world. In the words of the well-known parable, the wheat and the weeds must grow together until the end of the age (Matt 13; 24:30, 36–43). The duality is not a dualism that insists we can divide ultimately between redemption and creation or between spirit and matter. But neither is it a monism that insists that here and now we can abolish the distinction and collapse church and world into one. It is a provisional duality with which we need to learn how to live, rendering to God what is God's and to Caesar what is Caesar's until the day of final resolution when God will be all in all.

For these reasons I wish to take a more positive view of the context of liberal secularism than some others may wish to do. It has its own moral force in insisting upon the value of freedom and a public space, which need not be understood as morally neutral or empty but as imbued with the positive values of fairness and impartiality. This is a moral force with which we can identify and which in our way we wish to embody. The challenge is to ensure that liberal secularism lives up to its own self-definition and its own claims and does not fall prey to harder forms of secularism that are potentially as destructive and cruel as has been any established religion through time.

This is not to say that liberal secularism is enough, but only that it is the best of the options that are currently realizable. No Christian, it seems to me, is going to consider any version of the social order sufficient which does not knowingly have Christ as its centre and sphere. But that vision is an eschatological one and awaits the time when "the kingdoms of this world will become the kingdom of our Lord and of his Messiah" (Rev 11:15). Liberal secularism has arisen partly out of the soil of free church principles, but partly also as an entirely understandable reaction against domineering, violent, bigoted religion. It came out of grasping that no one religious tradition could be trusted to hold open the ring of human flourishing but would come to place its own interests above the humane concerns of a truly compassionate community. Baptists of the future should be committed to the patient work of building up such a community, of offering it a critique where required, of resisting it when it exceeds its proper bounds, and of working as learners ourselves towards its increased maturity.

3

The Sound of Silence? Baptist Thought in Obama's World

MARTIN SUTHERLAND

Introduction

The election of Barak Obama as President of the United States was a truly extraordinary event, more perhaps for its symbolism than even for its specifics, remarkable as they were. That an African American should stand on the steps of the Capitol Building to give his inauguration address is significant enough, but Obama represents more than ethnicity or race—he is a symbol of a new world.

It is, of course, an interconnected world. It is telling that one of Obama's early personal demands was that he be able to retain his Blackberry mobile device. This presented potential security problems. Terrorists might be able to trace his movements. But Obama insisted that he wanted to maintain his own network of contacts, free from the intrusion of his minders. The solution was to assign him his own security frequency. (In a demonstration of how things had changed in sixteen years, ex-president Clinton pointed out that the equivalent problem when he came to the White House was addressed by giving him his own postal code!)

To such problems of "the age of Twitter™" I shall return in the next paper. "Obama's World" is bigger than technology, but the inescapable fact of the explosion of interconnectivity (or "globalization"—call it what you will) in the last two decades or so makes for a host of opportunities, a range of new threats, and some intriguing challenges for Christian thinkers and leaders.

Obama is, of course, at pains to point this out. In his inaugural address he spoke of foreign relations in confident but conciliatory terms.

> We can meet those new threats that demand even greater effort—even greater cooperation and understanding between nations. For we know that our patchwork heritage is a strength, not a weakness. We are a nation of Christians and Muslims, Jews and Hindus—and non-believers. We are shaped by every language and culture, drawn from every end of this Earth; and because we have tasted the bitter swill of civil war and segregation, and emerged from that dark chapter stronger and more united, we cannot help but believe that the old hatreds shall someday pass; that the lines of tribe shall soon dissolve; that as the world grows smaller, our common humanity shall reveal itself; and that America must play its role in ushering in a new era of peace.[1]

Addressing directly the Muslim world, Obama then spoke of seeking "a new way forward, based on mutual interest and mutual respect."

This is the nub of Obama's world. It is no longer possible merely to dismiss the foreign as exotic and other, alternative religions as "heathen" or "infidel," unfriendly nations as "the axis of evil." We are truly and increasingly each other's neighbors. Via satellite or over the fence we look directly, even intimately, into each other's lives. Our affairs are no longer separated, and in many cases they no longer merely collide; inexorably they are enmeshed. We cannot get on without one another and must find a way to get on *with* one another.

Christians are troubled by this. If it is true "that the lines of tribe shall soon dissolve" and that "as the world grows smaller, our common humanity shall reveal itself," is there any more a place for religious identities? Obama himself is a Christian (*not* a closet Muslim as some have mischievously suggested!) so commitment itself is not a problem. Yet it is notable that his own account of his conversion in his autobiographical *The Audacity of Hope* has less to do with truth than with security.

> I came to realize that without a vessel for my beliefs, without an unequivocal commitment to a particular community of faith,

---

1. Obama, inaugural address, online: http://www.gpoaccess.gov/crecord/09crpgs.html.

> I would be consigned at some level to always remain apart . . . ultimately alone.[2]

As Baptists we may resonate with some of that, but is church a club for the like-minded or is there something to declare? In particular, do *Baptist* distinctives matter any more? Do they even survive? What might Baptist thought look like in such a climate? Have the perspectives forged 400 years ago run their course? Asked less defensively, do Baptists have anything to contribute in Obama's world?

It is first worth noting that the local and specific has not dropped out under the pressure of globalization. Whatever our complaints about McDonald's golden arches being found all over the world, Levi's on everyone's hips, and Hollywood's pervasive reach, a counter-momentum is also observable. In geopolitics we now have more governments and states than ever. Indigenous cultures all over the globe claim a new voice. In Australia and certainly in Aotearoa-New Zealand this is very evident. It is the old paradox seen between Enlightenment and Romanticism—the stronger the forces of interconnection, the greater the energy for unique expressions—the "one" never consumes the "many." This is a crucial factor, as it is in this desire for the local, that, I suggest, Baptist thought finds a natural role.

The Sound of Silence: The Mishearing of Baptist Voices

Anabaptist/Baptist theology has struggled to maintain meaningful conversation in the theological mainstream. This is in part due to the perception (often meekly shared by Baptists) that this line of radical Protestantism has produced few significant theologians to talk to. I want to explore aspects of Baptist method that have set it apart from the Great Tradition. What emerges is an approach that eschews a linear progression of ideas, driven by philosophical imperatives. At the heart of this *tikanga* is the dynamic presence of Christ in the gathered community. Doctrines are defined in terms of their relation to that centre. Among the results are a heightened emphasis on practical ecclesiology and an active interest in personal narrative.

Baptists are found in all countries where there is a significant Christian population. They are numerically one of the largest Protestant

---

2. Obama, *Audacity of Hope*, 206.

groups in the world. They have achieved a certain profile, not to say notoriety, of which they are not always proud. They have entered the folklore of hypocrisy, of puritanical attitudes, and demanding moral codes. More positively, they have often exemplified an impressive activism. Who can describe the modern missionary movement without reference to William Carey? Or ignore Charles Spurgeon, who sits like a huge spider in the center of a web of Victorian developments that influence the church today—popular preaching, evangelicalism, revivalism. No study of public religion in the United States can disregard the Southern Baptist Convention—effectively the established church of the South.

Yet this vibrant, energetic communion *is* virtually ignored in the history of theology. Curiously Baptists themselves have rarely demurred. Keith Jones, although an enthusiast for the recovery of Anabaptist insights, happily concedes:

> We have no great patterns or guides, nor many examples of baptistic groupings working at these issues in a systematic theological way. Unlike other parts of the Christian world family we appear not to have been good at systematic theology.[3]

Even such a significant thinker as James McClendon (to whom I will return) opens his three-volume *Systematic Theology* with an analysis entitled "Why baptists have produced so little theology."[4]

So is Baptist theology truly the "sound of silence" or is there a Baptist noise we have failed to hear? Understood in conventional ways, the silence motif seems to reflect an undeniable reality. The popular piety of Baptists has been and remains frequently anti-intellectual, suspicious of learning. If one was asked to rank the top one hundred Protestant theologians since the Reformation, it is very likely that not a single Baptist would make the list.

Why would this be? There are some obvious historical reasons—oppression, exclusion from universities in Britain, etc. Yet to understand Baptist theology only in such terms is merely to repeat the dismissive attitudes of the past. "Poor souls, they have done their best under trying circumstances, we must have patience with them."

Yet there is something inherent to the Baptist *tikanga*—the Baptist "way"—that adds another level of explanation to the apparent primi-

---

3. Jones, *Believing Church*, 51.
4. McClendon, *Systematic Theology*, 1:20–27.

tiveness of Baptist theology. Indeed, I suggest that, rather than Baptist theology failing to reach the highest levels of Christian thought, it is actually a distinct *way* of doing theology. When it is true to its own lights, the Baptist *tikanga* results in an articulation of the faith that admittedly doesn't always adhere to the "rules." But, then, they are other people's rules.

A Baptist Dynamic

McClendon, who made more effort than most to address the nature of Baptist method, put the problem this way:

> The truth, I believe, is this; the baptists in all their variety and disunity failed to see in their own heritage, their own way of using Scripture, their own communal practices and patterns, *their own guiding vision*, a resource for theology unlike the prevailing scholasticism round about them. Some were attracted to current fashions and tried theologizing in those fashions. The results were seldom good, and the consequence was further distrust of theology in baptist ranks.[5]

What McClendon in his generalization refers to as "scholasticism"—and what I, in equally sweeping terms, name the "Great Tradition"—is a dominant model of theological method that set up a series of expectations. This tradition, representing the mainstream of "orthodoxy" for centuries, found a natural conversation partner in philosophy. Thus, metaphysical problems, epistemology, the divine attributes, and such are expected foundational elements in the theological discourse. Now, it has often been just those questions that Baptist theologians have ignored or treated lightly—not always, I contend, because they couldn't cope with them, but principally because these are *not* key questions in a Baptist *tikanga*.

There are exceptions. I would want to be more generous than McClendon. The results have not always been bad. Augustus Strong at the turn of the twentieth century and Stanley Grenz at the turn of the twenty-first were Baptists who produced significant systematic theologies. But they are exceptions that tend to prove the rule. They maintain standard Baptist views on government and baptism, etc., however, their method is not distinctly Baptist at all.

5. Ibid., 1:26.

This is particularly evident in Grenz's approach. Although he spent the better part of his career at Baptist institutions, Grenz primarily addressed the questions of evangelical theology rather than Baptist thought. Although it is certainly arguable that Grenz had an understanding of and vision for evangelicalism that reflected his Baptist assumptions, his principal methodological interest was the search for ways in which evangelical theology might be "re-visioned" in a postmodern age.[6]

What then might we look for in Baptist thought? There have been numerous attempts to define what it means to be Baptist in terms of content—to suggest that there are a number of Baptist distinctives that uniquely combine to build the Baptist vision. There are four main candidates:

1. Baptism of believers only
2. Congregational autonomy
3. Separation of church and state
4. Freedom of conscience (or "soul competency" in American Baptist parlance)

This last is problematical. It is derivative of the other three, with the addition of Enlightenment ideas of the autonomy of the individual. For reasons that will become clear later in this paper, I suggest that it is an unfortunate distortion of the Baptist way. As to the first three, each is actually an ecclesiological position: determining, first, membership of the body; next, relationships to other parts of the body; and thirdly, the relationship of the body to civil authorities. It is my contention that the preoccupations of Baptist polemics are significant, but for what they *signal* rather than what they contain.

Rather than the paradoxes of metaphysics, the beating heart of Baptist theology is ecclesiology. Not, it must be stressed, a general attention to the nature of the church, but a particular, "baptistic" understanding of the dynamics of the community of Christ. McClendon identifies a core sense of immediacy—the sense that the church now *is* the primitive church, being created anew in every moment, and that each generation stands with the apostles at the brink of the new day. It is a vision

---

6. This is most acutely demonstrated in Grenz's essay "Conversing in Christian Style." In it he makes virtually no comment on "Baptist . . . method," being really interested in the "postmodern context."

"neither developmental nor successionist, but mystical and immediate . . . better understood by the artist and poet than by the metaphysician and dogmatist."[7] Underlying traditional Baptist distinctives, then, is an understanding of the dynamics of being church or, better, the dynamics of *becoming* church.

A "Gathered" Theology

But if this describes the vision that drives Baptist life, we can be a bit more specific as to the essence of Baptist theological method. Here we must turn to the biblical passage that Miroslav Volf correctly notes has "shaped the entire free church tradition"—Matthew 18.[8]

Now what Volf and generations before refer to are the words in Matthew 18:20, "where two or three are gathered in my name, I am there among them." Theologians from all traditions have acknowledged this as a powerful statement of how and where the church is constituted, but none have placed more importance on it than Baptists. There are two crucial consequences of this concentration.

The first is sacramental. I have explored this elsewhere.[9] There is no passage of Scripture of greater sacramental import than Matthew 18:20. Indeed, in the baptistic tradition there is, I suggest, only one true sacrament: the sacrament of gathering. Baptists are happy to agree with Karl Barth on baptism and Zizioulas on Eucharist that these practices are not in themselves sacramental but that they attain iconic significance as eschatological events in the gathered community. So, Zizioulas:

> The eucharist, as distinct from other expressions of ecclesial life, is unthinkable without the gathering of the whole Church in one place . . . consequently, it manifests the Church not simply as something instituted, that is, historically *given*, but also something, *con-stituted*, that is, realized as an event of free communion, prefiguring the divine life and the Kingdom to come. . . . In this way the eucharist is not a "sacrament," something parallel to the divine word: it is the eschatologization of the historical word, the voice of the historical Christ, the voice of the Holy Scripture

---

7. McClendon, *Systematic Theology*, 1:33.
8. Volf, *After Our Likeness*, 135.
9. Sutherland, "Gathering, Sacrament."

which comes to us, no longer simply as "doctrine" through history, but as life and being through the *eschata*.[10]

In Baptist application, then, there is no such thing as private baptism, and the elements of communion have no significance in themselves, but only in the context of the gathering. Taken most radically, *all* eating together by the Christ community is understood as sacramental. This recovers the New Testament picture of Eucharist as a real meal that prefigures the eschatological feast. It also sharpens the ongoing significance of grace before meals, a practice in constant danger of degenerating into "form without substance."

Much can obviously be said of this sacramental aspect of Matthew 18. But we need to note a second aspect—the question of authority. Matthew 18:20 is far too often shorn of its textual context, that is, a case of discipline exercised by the community. I am happy to concede the historical/critical issues surrounding this passage in Matthew. For this discussion it is immaterial whether Jesus himself spoke these words or if they reveal an early self-understanding of the church. Whatever the history of the passage, Baptists have always cited it as a model of community life in action. The development of ideas in the passage is crucial. In verses 15–18 a relational problem is progressively taken to the wider community. This process depends on the audacious statement on authority in verse 19: "If two of you agree on earth about anything you ask, it will be done for you by my Father in heaven." Now, crucially this is not the end of the *pericope*. The promise of divine response to agreed requests is not an indication of any power inherently possessed by the gathered community. Rather, it turns on what follows in verse 20. Community discipline may be exercised "because"—"for"—"where two or more are gathered in my name, *I* am there among them." The authority is Christ's authority, discerned and made visible in the gathered church.

All these aspects of Matthew 18, Eucharist, discipline, community decision, are of crucial significance to Baptists. Indeed, as Paul Fiddes notes, they have often come together at the centre of Baptist church life.

> In [the church] meeting members of the church gather together to find the mind of Christ. They vote on issues, not to impose a majority view but to find the purpose of the risen Lord for

---

10. Zizioulas, *Being as Communion*, 21–22.

their life and mission. Because Christ is embodied among them through the meeting of their bodies, they expect to be able to discern his mind for them. In the seventeenth century it was common practice for members to hold the church meeting either immediately before or after the Lord's supper. So the church book, that recorded the names of the members, the church covenant and all the decisions taken in the church meeting, was kept in a drawer in the bench behind the Lord's table, or in the "table pew."[11]

The gathered church is thus both the *site* of Christ's presence and the *means* of discerning his will. The implications of this understanding are huge. Most importantly, it identifies the life of the congregation as the visible center of the faith.

Thus all theological questions are ecclesiological questions. Baptists have little incentive to establish linear progression of ideas or to begin their efforts to understand their faith with other people's issues. Everything derives from the dynamic experience of Christ in the community. Doctrines are of significance only for what they add to or draw from an understanding of that event. Baptist theology is "systematic" only in the sense of being a "centred set" of concepts. Doctrines emerge not by philosophical logic but as interrelated ideas driven centrifugally from, and drawn centripetally to, the centre.

And always at stake are the implications for community life. That is why when one goes searching for the early theology of Baptists mostly one comes up with ecclesiology or ethics. In colonial New Zealand this was certainly the case. The principal question, debated endlessly through the pages of the *NZ Baptist*, was "How do we organize ourselves? How are we to become church?" There were the occasional derived debates over questions current in Britain, but even here the interest lay in the effects on evangelism and conversion—securing the future gathering.

So Baptist theology will look different. How life is lived in the Christian community is of great interest. So, McClendon pioneered the notion of biography as theology. The first installment of his *Systematic Theology* is a volume on narrative ethics. Doctrine is second, and foundational theory is in the third volume. Compare Stanley Grenz (a fine theologian, but one I suggest is a Baptist doing non-baptist theology) and Paul Fiddes. Grenz works in a classical style; his project before

---

11. Fiddes, *Participating in God*, 283.

he died was building a "matrix" of theology from the doctrine of the Trinity. Fiddes, too, has a volume on the Trinity, but it is intentionally a *"Pastoral* Doctrine of the Trinity." Fiddes, doing something closer to baptistic theology, asserts

> this is no new venture, for the doctrine of the Trinity has been a pastoral theology from its formulation. The Christian idea of a personal God begins historically in pastoral experience, that is, in the experience of the Christian congregation.

Do, then, Baptist distinctives have a future? If defined as certain distinguishing doctrines, possibly not. Much of what came to be the Baptist noise was defensive—justifying separation or even survival. In Obama's world such defensiveness can retreat into the silence. We do, on the other hand, have something to contribute, something to celebrate, something tribal that adds to the whole. In Australasia I suggest there are particular opportunities here.

First, there is the latent energy of our congregations. Two "Church Life Surveys" of recent years have revealed a troubling uncertainty among Baptists over their denominational identity. Yet, when positive statements of what attracts Baptists to their communities are examined, a consistent interest in the events of worship and in small groups appears. For all our frustrating ways, we are still a people committed to the encounter with Christ in the gathering.

Second, there is a contextual opportunity. The drive to globalize and reconcile is matched by a compulsion to establish roots and relational anchors. In Australasia we may find ourselves ever more bound to the world, but at the same moment we need to embrace unique local expressions.

I would speak only in ignorance of Australian specifics, but let me illustrate from my own context in Aotearoa-New Zealand. There is much talk in New Zealand of bicultural theology. Baptists have not walked far down this path—yet. (Again, perhaps because the agenda is dominated by other theological *tikanga*.) The structural response of the Anglicans will not be our way. Moreover, historically committed to the separation of religion from the state and with a vision of immediate contact with the gospel story, Baptists are unlikely to find bicultural ground around the treaty of Waitangi. The treaty may quite properly find its place in law, and historical injustices must be righted. But Baptists will find the treaty an inadequate basis for theology.

Far richer potential lies in the developing theory of *Kaupapa Maori*. This approach to research and knowledge emphasizes the importance of "a local approach to critical theory." This rings bells. Of particular interest to Baptists is one of the key concepts—that of *whanau*. In terms of research methodology, Linda Smith summarizes the approach in this way:

> All Maori initiatives have attempted to organize the basic decision making and participation within and around the concept of *whanau*. . . . It is. . . argued that the *whanau* remains a persistent way of living and organizing the social world. . . . *Whanau* is one of several aspects of Maori philosophy, values and practices which are brought to the centre in Kaupapa Maori research. . . . We have a different epistemological tradition which frames the way we see the world, the way we organize ourselves in it, the questions we ask and the solutions we seek.[12]

Now this has clear resonances with *Tikanga Papita*—the "Baptist way." There is much that Baptists do not understand. But we do understand the local, and here I believe a meaningful conversation can take place.

Conclusion

To risk a troubling shift from Paul Simon to Neil Diamond, Baptist thought can shake off the imposed cloak of the "Sound of Silence" and celebrate its own "Beautiful Noise." Noise is a useful metaphor. Baptist thought can be cacophonous, chaotic even, more like jazz than baroque, more Dizzy Gillespie than Mozart. The joyous celebration of the presence of Christ in the moment of our gatherings cannot be simply codified.

There will remain a crippling dissonance, a gulf between academic theological debate and the common life of Baptist communities, until the dynamics of Baptist way, the *Tikanga Papita*, are recognized and celebrated. The principal responsibility for this lies with Baptist themselves. It is our job to explore the rich potential of our method. To others this will at times appear strange, and its outcomes difficult to measure. Multivolume systematic theologies will likely continue to be rare. The most authentic outcomes will be in the evolving lives of the communi-

---

12. Smith, *Decolonizing Methodologies*, 187–88.

ties themselves. The best indicators of Baptist theology will be in our worship, in our sermons, in the pages of our denominational magazines, rather than in the writings of Baptist academics. As always we will encounter rules of debate that have been set by others. These we must respectfully resist, perhaps with the suggestion (and the risk!) that our theology be not just heard or read, but seen.

Our challenge will be to find ways of communicating these understandings on wider canvasses. Importantly, the very demands of global interconnectedness give us an unexpected freedom. We can move away from defensiveness to embrace new ways to bear witness to the presence of Christ. As we move beyond 400 years we need not be intimidated by the problems, but enlivened by the possibilities, of Obama's world.

4

Meeting for Minutes? Baptist Congregational Life in the Age of Twitter

MARTIN SUTHERLAND

Introduction

Baptists supposedly place a great premium on community. Expressed historically in terms of the covenanted congregation of believers, the gathered community lies at the heart of Baptist ecclesiology. In the preceding chapter I attempted to bind into this expression a dynamic of Christology, sacrament, and theological method. Thus, not surprisingly, I am committed to congregational life as a fundamental part of the Baptist future.

Yet this very aspect of Baptist polity is under enormous pressure. It must be admitted of course that congregational life, at least as manifested in business meetings, has been slowly committing suicide. We all have horror stories. Many can, I suggest, be put down (at least in part) to inadequate chairing or preparation. Nevertheless, the impression can emerge that we have been "meeting for the sake of the minutes," an exercise in form without substance in which there appears to be more interest in process for its own sake than in gathering to discern the voice of the Spirit.

In New Zealand congregational meetings have been progressively stripped of decision-making powers. The corporate leadership model is increasingly portrayed as the way forward, with members reduced to a role as in a company annual meeting—tasked only with electing a board and receiving reports. On top of this, Baptists have shared in a general Western "crisis of belonging" that has made the notion of covenanted, committed membership a very hard sell. All of this in an age when technology supposedly makes community easier.

Let me illustrate from my own recent experience. Earlier this year I was surprised to be contacted by a woman whom I had employed when I worked at the Law Courts some twenty years ago. She was also, with her parents, a member of the small church I was in at the time. That was in Invercargill in the South of New Zealand. She has since married and moved to Sydney, while I have been in Auckland for most of that time. Our lives had taken different paths; we had had no contact. My friend got in touch after finding my page on the social networking Web site Facebook. I had actually forgotten that I had even signed up to it. I had experimented with it a few months earlier to test if it was a suitable vehicle for faculty to use for personal academic Web pages. Concluding that it was not, I had forgotten about it only to be reminded one summer morning with Diane's message.

Immediately a most transfixing process began. Once I responded to Diane the mechanisms and conventions of Facebook took over. Contacts, and contacts of contacts, were notified of my response and presence. Within days I had 40 friends, within a couple of weeks I had over 100. And, of course, that is nothing. My adult children each have over 200 friends and many of their acquaintances have over 400—some over a 1000. All of which is more than a little bemusing. One hundred friends! I don't have that many friends. I am pretty sure that I don't even *like* 100 people, and I am confident that there are not 100 who truly like me! Yet Facebook tells me that I do, and there are.

I am at best ambivalent about the whole experience. There is a sense, often commented on by the pundits, that it all highlights the shallowness of these social sites—people with whom I have only nodding or functional acquaintance counted as friends and sharing with me the most trivial details of their lives.

Some examples of recent postings:

- "X has had a flippin' awesome chat, now has ideas sparking everywhere, watch out!"
- "Y is trying to get his desk into some sort of order."
- "Z is contemplating the merits of fruit toast bread."

Yet my experience also demonstrates something of the glory of the medium. Diane had been in my church. We had known her well. Yet there was no hint (and, I suggest, no likelihood) of us making contact via church connections. That form of community I instinctively rate the most profound could not do it; the form I count as banal made it happen.

Facebook is of course merely one example of the phenomenon of "Web 2.0" or the "participatory Web," which transcends the offering of fixed information as prodominated in the earlier age of the Internet. The first triumphs of the Worldwide Web enabled the posting of monumental amounts of information. If this "Web 1.0" was like a digital encyclopedia, "Web 2.0" enables a workshop in which all may participate. The former majors on knowledge transference; the latter creates conversations.

The current popular flagship is Twitter. If the core of Facebook is a profile of your life, Twitter is less interested in your life than in your opinions. It is a "micro-blogging" site on which you can create or participate in a string of discussion—as long as each entry is less than 140 characters. (That is less than the last two sentences!) Blogging in general and Twitter in particular have been criticized. Jewish commentator Lief Leibovitz suggests they "reduce the mysteries of life into minutiae."[1] Recently the Catholic Archbishop of Westminster, Vincent Nichols, cautioned that social Web sites substitute transient relationships for real relationships, potentially contributing to societal breakdown and even youth suicide rates.[2]

Is this fair? A recent study of Twitter traffic has found that over 40 percent of the postings are "pointless babble."[3] But let's face it, most conversations with, say, casual acquaintances at parties, would fit such description. Trivial connection is not a digital invention.

Yet are these technological developments, ostensibly great ways of keeping in touch, actually Trojan horses of alienation and distancing? More importantly for our purposes, do they promote or undermine the possibility of community life, which lies at the heart of the Baptist vision?

Sociologist Zygmunt Bauman has a singular take on these questions. Bauman is most recently famous for his term "Liquid Modernity," denoting what he sees as the pernicious state of a contemporary modernity in which all is transient and there is neither time nor capacity to

---

1. Leibovitz, "Communication Breakdown."
2. Wynne-Jones, "Facebook and MySpace."
3. R. Kelly, "Twitter Study."

establish and maintain deep or "solid" relationships and commitments.[4] Inhabitants of such a world, Bauman argues, risk losing even the desire for solidity, with real "relationships" having come to be perceived as restrictive, enclosing, oppressive. "Instead of talking about partners" Bauman suggests, "they prefer to speak of 'networks.'" Crucially,

> In a network, connecting and disconnecting are equally legitimate choices, enjoy the same status and carry the same importance. . . . "Network" suggests moments of "being in touch" interspersed with periods of free roaming. In a network, connections are entered on demand, and can be broken at will. An "undesirable, yet unbreakable" relationship is the very possibility that makes "relating" [a feature of "solid" life] as treacherous as it feels. An "undesirable connection," however, is an oxymoron: connections may be, and are, broken well before they start being detested.[5]

In specific relation to the digital world Bauman suggests such mechanisms allow us to substitute quantity for quality.[6]

Are we thus being lured towards a world in which relationships are made remote events, with technology interposed, removing the dirtiness of dissent, in which confrontation can be avoided merely by pushing "delete?" Will we be reduced to "moments of 'being in touch' interspersed with periods of free roaming"? Instead of meeting for the sake of the minutes will we be literally just "meeting for minutes?"

There has been quite a level of discussion on these issues in church circles. Alan Jamieson from New Zealand, for instance, has explored the phenomenon of "believing without belonging."[7] Some have directly picked up Bauman's language. The most notable is Pete Ward in his 2002 book *Liquid Church*. Interestingly, Ward makes positive the very liquidity that Bauman sees as pernicious. For Ward the church must move away from defining human "need" towards responding to human "desire." The "solid" church characteristics of weekly meeting and membership must give way to occasional "festival" and networking.[8]

---

4. Among Bauman's key works are *Liquid Modernity*; *Community*; *Individualized Society*; *Liquid Love*; *Liquid Life*; *Liquid Fear*; *Liquid Times*; *Consuming Life*; *Art of Life*.

5. Bauman, *Liquid Love*, xi–xii.

6. Ibid., 58.

7. Jamieson, *Churchless Faith*.

8. Ward, *Liquid Church*.

Paul Fiddes has recently put forward the case that a form of virtual communion may properly be posited in the context of sites such as Second Life, in which one constructs a representative persona around which is built a "second," virtual life and interacts with the personas or "avatars" of other participants.

> An avatar can receive the bread and wine of the Eucharist *within the logic of the virtual world* and it will still be a means of grace, since God is present in a virtual world in a way that is suitable for its inhabitants. We may expect that the grace received by the avatar will be shared in some way by the person behind the avatar, because the person in our everyday world has a complex relationship with his or her *persona*.[9]

So where, then, for Baptist congregationalism? The very notion of covenant that has historically lain at the centre of the congregational model seems an inescapably "solid" concept. Can it thrive in a "liquid" world? We will not progress this issue if we confuse it with the forms that congregationalism takes. The Westminster system of governance, for instance, need not be crucial to the future of Baptist life. What we must do is delve deeply into the theology of what church is—how being church reflects the *missio Dei*.

There is an old chestnut that goes, "Jesus came preaching the Kingdom; what he got was the church"—the implication being that Jesus didn't get what he expected and had to settle for second best. It is a lie. The truth is more startling. To the church is uniquely revealed what once was hidden. The "secret" is no secret anymore. Essential to that secret is the discovery that believers have been chosen before the world began (Eph 1:4) for "adoption." More specifically, those who believe, those who have the Spirit, those who have received Christ, are "children of God." More pointedly still, they are "heirs of the Father," "joint heirs with the Son." But this change of status, immense as it is, does not, of itself, focus our enquiry. There is more—a central, active role for the church in the movement of God's cosmic plan. We find it outlined most fully in Romans 8 and Ephesians 3.

---

9. Fiddes, "Sacraments in a Virtual World," reproduced with permission in M. Brown, "Virtual Sacraments?" See also the fascinating blog discussion that follows. I am grateful for this reference to my colleague Andrew Picard at Laidlaw College.

Romans 8:14-25

Nowhere is it more clearly stated that Christians are "children of God," "heirs of God," "joint heirs with Christ" than in this passage. Crucially, we also suffer with Christ, so that, in Paul's phrase, we may be "glorified with him" (Rom 8:17). This phrase is interesting. What can it mean? What is it for Christians to be "glorified with him"? Having in a number of places laid out the cosmic role of Christ, Paul goes on to explore the cosmic significance of the church. This is outlined in verse 19. Creation waits for the revealing of the children of God, because God intends creation to attain the same freedom already gained by those children of God.

Here is something truly significant. To be "children of God" is important not just for humanity, but for the universe. As "children," Christians have been fully reconciled to God—once we were estranged, we are now family—"joint heirs." But this is not the end. Rather it is just a further installment of the unfolding plan of God. In the next phase the children of God declare, in the very fact of their new status, the coming redemption of the universe. The church is thus the test case, the example, the "first fruit" of what is to come. To be sure, in our time, as Paul acknowledges, we wait and groan to see the new thing. But it is already an eternal reality—in Christ it has been achieved. This unseen reality is the basis of our hope and a fundamental element of a missional ecclesiology.

Ephesians 3:1-21

Here Paul makes this cosmic vision more personal. This is a startling passage in many ways, rewarding serious contemplation. What is Paul saying? The mystery of Christ (that is, that Gentiles are fellow heirs) is now revealed to apostles and prophets. Paul is a servant of this gospel, so that through him all people may see the plan and then, in turn, that through the church the wisdom of God may be made known to the universe. Here again is the cosmic mission of the church.

In verse 21 we find a fascinating gloria: "to God be glory *in the church* and in Christ Jesus to all generations." Again we are presented with an unexpected, indeed staggering, role for the church. Paul declares here that God may be glorified in the church in a way that parallels the way Christ himself glorifies God. This "glorification" is a key concept tio which we will return.

These foundational New Testament passages on the mission of God and the role of his children are part of a bigger picture still. They connect directly to the distinctive Christian understanding of the nature of God, the coming of Christ, and the end of time. Crucially, they underpin the Baptist understanding of congregational life. When we explore the links between the Trinity, the incarnation, eschatology, the church, and mission in the context of passages such as we have noted, a dynamic picture emerges of the saving love of God.

At the centre of the Christian understanding of God is the life of the Trinity. God exists not as some remote lonely figure but as a community of love—Father, Son, Spirit. Three, whose connection to one another is so perfect, so complete, that they are properly called "one." This relationship is so perfect that it does not require anything else. But the love of God is a giving love, *agape* love, not selfish in any sense. With such a love perfectly in operation, creation is neither surprising nor inexplicable. Put in simple form: this was a love too good not to share. So God created the universe—not merely as an object "out there," nor as a plaything, but as a further focus of divine love. The plan of God, the end in mind, was a universe wholly in harmony with himself. Though disrupted by the fall, this plan has not altered. This is the vision of "all things coming under Christ" (Eph 1:20), of God "reconciling to himself all things, whether on earth or in heaven" (Col 1:20).

The aim, then, the eternal plan, the mission of God, is for a created order in harmony with himself. This is natural, in the sense that it reflects exactly the life of the Trinity, the very nature of God. As the three persons subsist together in perfect harmony, so it is planned that the created order too will ultimately exist in such harmony with God. Now, of course, at least when viewed from our perspective, this harmony is not yet achieved. The world seems fractured, out of kilter with God. We have located the cause for this in humanity's rebellion from God, which we call "sin." Its product is separation from God, "death."

Sin and death—these together constitute the "problem" to be overcome. So, with that ultimate goal of perfect harmony always clear, God sets about solving the problem. Crucially, everything about that solution is natural. It reflects the nature of God, the nature of the problem, and the nature of the ultimate goal. Of God's saving plan we may say the following:

a) God's action is a Trinitarian movement. (John 3:16, *God so loved... that he sent his Son.*) The Son, through whom creation came to be, is the one sent to be with creation. This is the incarnation. The Son becomes a man—fully divine, fully human.

b) In Christ the mission is fulfilled. The very act of incarnation is a triumphant demonstration of the ultimate goal. God's plan for the universe is that it will be in perfect harmony with himself. In Christ that plan is seen fulfilled—in miniature, perhaps, but the perfect demonstration of what God intends. Divine and human, in one person. This is the plan for the *end* of time enacted *in* time. As the New Testament, and especially the writer to the Hebrews, makes clear, this process of becoming one of us includes suffering. The cross is a true pivot in history. There is so much built into that event—penal substitution, ransom, example, victory—but a part at least is this: that the incarnation of the Son was completed in that moment. The Son was "perfected" in suffering (Heb 2:10). On Calvary he shared even our ultimate limitation—death itself. Christ is the initiative of God, solving the problem—or, better, beginning the unfolding of a new reality. Jesus came declaring the reign of God, the fulfillment of God's mission. And the mission includes us.

c) The church is a part of the plan. When we recall what Paul says about continuing the suffering of Christ, about Christians being children of God and joint heirs with the Son, about how the church is the body and "fullness" of Christ, and about how the creation looks for the revealing of the children of God, we see the true enormity of what God has done in Christ and is doing through the church.

In Christ, by the power of the Spirit, Christians have been reconciled to God. Thus, in us too the plan for the end of time is now mysteriously fulfilled. The church plays an integral part in the unfolding plan of God. We are imperfect to be sure. We may still groan and wait for adoption to become evident in our midst, but, for all that, we are the body of Christ, declaring God's new order to the universe. This is what is signaled in Ephesians 3:21. Amazingly, God may be glorified in the *church* as well as Christ. The concept of "glorifying" God here is a rich one. The Greek *doxa*, when applied to God in the New Testament, transcends the simple notion of praising God. It is determined by the very divine nature. Christians do not merely offer praise; they participate in God's glory as they participate in Christ. Conversely, in manifesting the fulfillment of the *missio Dei*, the church glorifies God, displaying to the universe who God is and what God has done, demonstrating by its very existence the divine nature.

Now, this notion that the church tells forth the glory of God is a little troubling for those of us who know the church! We think of our own congregations and wonder just what exactly this poor specimen of the children of God is unveiling to the universe. But this is only problematic if we have an over-realized eschatology that imagines we become some perfect community in this time. We *are* fallen, often inadequate, frequently quarrelling, "a fractious and divided people." That being so, what can a congregation hope to show of the mission of God? It shows the mission in action. It shows the reconciling power of the Spirit being worked out *in real time*.

This is our role in the mission of God. This is the cosmic dynamic that we call non-believers to join. As an incarnation of the *missio Dei*, church does not merely *do* mission, it embodies it. Crucially, the mission is demonstrated not in our perfect *being* but in the development of our *becoming*. In this openness to the transforming power of the Spirit we incarnate the *missio Dei*.

I use "incarnate" deliberately, not to diminish the unique role of Christ of course but to emphasis it. If we are to "glorify" God we will do so incarnationally. Here congregational life becomes crucial. We may joke that "we love the church but it is Christians we can't stand," but that jibe does identify a key issue. Jesus came to his own in flesh and blood. The Baptist vision forbids us to pretend we can be church in general without being congregations in particular. It is a conceit to imagine that we love the people of God otherwise than in loving *these* people of God.

Thus, I suggest the face-to-face–ness of the congregation simply cannot be escaped. It does not glorify God to press "delete" on difficult relationships, or on those who don't look, smell, or sound like us. Facebook and Twitter attract the easily connected; the gospel brings together the irreconcilable.

Communion (as in the Eucharist) will surely only be authentic if it exemplifies incarnation rather than denying it. I thus find myself disagreeing with Paul Fiddes. I do not see that communion in Second Life is at all analogous to a meal shared in the name of Christ between flesh-and-blood people. Second Life, you see, is not a digital reality and therefore a site for the grace of God. It is not a reality at all. It is fiction, no more "real" in that sense than a novel.

With its insistence on face-to-face covenant solidity, the Baptist view of church is the one most overtly challenged by the age of Twitter. Other ecclesiologies, especially those that emphasis the universal over the particular, might seem most fitted to soak up "liquid modernity," but I suggest this is a delusion. The very particularity of the gathered congregation demands recognition of what Christ has done in becoming one of us (indeed, making himself present in that very moment of gathering). Our forms can (and undoubtedly must) change, but Facebook will not be a substitute. If we are to fulfill our part in the mission of God it will not be in "meeting for minutes" but truly in meeting for life.

5

Beyond Identity Crises? The Future of Baptist Theology

MICHAEL D. O'NEIL

Introduction

The 400th anniversary of the founding of the first Baptist church provides a welcome occasion to reflect on the history, faith, and theology of those churches claiming the name "Baptist." Harried out of England during the reign of James I, John Smyth fled from Gainsborough, in northern England, to Amsterdam in 1607. Convinced through his own study of the New Testament that infant baptism was not a scriptural practice, and that both the Christian life and the Christian church were established upon the confession of faith, in 1609 Smyth baptized himself and forty adult members of his congregation.[1] Over time Smyth's central convictions have become indelibly written in Baptist heritage, including his belief in regenerate church membership upheld through believer's baptism, the self-government of the church, and religious freedom.[2] Other beliefs also characterize Baptist thought and life, including the sufficiency and authority of the Bible, the autonomy of the local church not only in relation to other ecclesiastical bodies but also to the state, the notions of "soul competency" and the priesthood of all believers, and a congregational form of church government in which each believer has

---

1. Shelley, *Church History*, 296.
2. Buschart, *Exploring Protestant Traditions*, 147.

a voice in the life of the church.³ Taken together, these characteristics form a critical aspect of Baptist identity, and function in service of the primitive Baptist vision, which sought a true and pure church living in free and faithful obedience to the lordship of Jesus Christ mediated to his people via the Scriptures illumined by the Holy Spirit.

In recent years, however, some have expressed concern over the loss of these particular distinctives, and the corollary loss of Baptist identity. For example, R. Stanton Norman considers these distinctives as constitutive of "the Baptist Way," and he insists that adherence to and propagation of these distinctives is an expression of our loyalty and obedience to Christ.⁴ Similarly, David Coffey laments that Baptists have "been robbed of our distinctive identity," and calls for a new generation to

> restore this identity with the conviction that we are not building a Baptist empire for the twenty-first century but rather are dealing with Gospel, Church and Kingdom issues in ways which justify our description as *Radical Believers*'⁵

These distinctives are not the only aspect of Baptist identity, however. "Baptist history is replete with self-doubt and identity crises," says William H. Brackney,⁶ and these identity crises have much to do with broader issues of theological method and content, as well as practical matters of polity and style. Theological controversy along liberal-conservative or Calvinist-Arminian lines may stir the question, "Who are the *real* Baptists?" So, too, can matters of heritage, church government, women's ministry, or myriad other issues. Baptist identity may also suffer dilution under the pressure of pragmatic concerns in local church ministry, or as a result of congregational indifference to such matters in a post-denominational or ecumenical era. And for some the question is simply, "Does distinctive Baptist identity actually matter?"

According to Timothy George, distinctive Baptist identity *is* important, and he celebrates the significant contributions Baptists have made to the Christian church generally. Nevertheless, there is also a crisis in contemporary Baptist life, which he diagnoses as a "crisis of identity rooted in a fundamental theological failure of nerve."⁷ The way forward

3. Ibid., 162–63.
4. Stanton, *Baptist Way*, 187–88.
5. Coffey, "Foreword," 4; emphasis original.
6. Cited in Mohler, "Call for Baptist Evangelicals," 227. See further the whole essay.
7. George, "Renewal of Baptist Theology," 13.

in the midst of this crisis is the way of recovery—mining and reappropriating the Baptist confessional heritage, which in turn is deeply rooted in the theological themes and priorities of the Reformation.[8] So too, R. Albert Mohler would subsume Baptist distinctives within an overarching theological framework, though "without abandoning that which is distinctive to the Baptist heritage."[9]

While it is a right and salutary practice to inculcate the distinctives in the minds and lives of Baptist Christians and so nurture Baptist identity, it is surely the case that Baptists are *Christians* first and *Baptists* second, with the result that Baptist identity is a subordinate category. Further, the kinds of tensions and divisions that have at times divided the Baptist communities generally concern broader theological issues. As such, the approach suggested by George and Mohler is sound, providing substantial theological underpinning for the specific contributions of the Baptist ecclesiological vision.

The question that arises, however, concerns the form, structure, and content of the overarching theological framework. Is it possible to develop a distinctively Baptist form of theology? That is, is Baptist theology *Baptist*, or merely Evangelical or Reformed? To borrow a turn of phrase from a Pentecostal scholar, can Baptist theology bring the main dish or can it provide only the sauce?[10] The purpose of this paper is to ask whether a peculiarly Baptist approach to theology is possible, and what shape the formal and material principles of that theology might take. The paper begins with a brief survey of several systematic theologies produced by contemporary Baptist theologians before evaluating a particular proposal by Martin Sutherland. It concludes by offering pertinent suggestions for ongoing dialogue regarding this important topic.

Exploring Baptist Theological Method

The Baptist Vision

One major problem confronting the possibility of a distinctive Baptist form of theology is the fact that no single person or doctrinal expression exercised a definitive theological influence on Baptist origins, with the

---

8. George, "Reformation Roots," 9–11.
9. Mohler, "Call for Baptist Evangelicals," 239.
10. See Cross, "Rich Feast."

result that contemporary Baptists experience an undeniable plurality of belief. Baptists as such are not committed primarily to a particular theological persuasion but to a particular way of being *church*. What Stanley Grenz has asserted of Evangelical believers generally may be ascribed also to Baptists particularly: that the initial statement to be made about Baptists cannot focus on doctrinal formulations, for being a Baptist refers first of all to a specific *vision* of what it means to be a Christian.[11]

What is the content of this Baptist vision? In his *Radical Believers: The Baptist Way of Being the Church* (1992), Paul Beasley-Murray writes,

> In ideal terms the Baptist way of being the church is God's way for his people to live their life together. . . . Our study of God's Word leads us to believe that this is God's way for living our life together."[12]

More recently, Nigel Wright titled his work *Free Church, Free State: The Positive Baptist Vision* (2005). Both these works clearly indicate that the essence of the Baptist vision concerns ecclesiology—indeed, *practical* ecclesiology, a claim further substantiated by the nature of each of the classic Baptist distinctives already noted.

The origins of this vision can perhaps be found in the origins of the Baptist movement itself. While it may be the case that there was no single person or doctrinal expression that led to the founding of the Baptist churches, it may be argued that there was a definitive context: the existence of small communities of sincere believers recently empowered to read Scripture for themselves, in the context of either an imperial-style Roman Catholic Church or state-sponsored national churches, each of which had grown corrupt, authoritarian, and spiritually lax. These small communities soon found a glaring disparity between the church ideal portrayed in the New Testament and the national churches of their age. When efforts towards reform were frustrated, separatist movements developed which then drew the ire of the established churches, often accompanied by violent suppression. In this context the Baptist vision of

---

11. See Grenz, *Revisioning Evanglical Theology*, 30–31. It is worth noting that this is true primarily of those who are Baptist by conviction. In the contemporary Western church there are many who attend Baptist churches for reasons of convenience rather than conviction, and thus for whom the particular *vision* of being a *Baptist* church is somewhat irrelevant. So too, for them, is the task of developing an identifiably Baptist theology.

12. Beasley-Murray, *Radical Believers*, 6.

a believers' church began to emerge with the concomitant development of the particular distinctives and practices that facilitated the existence and ministry of the new church style. The Baptist vision was, again, of a true and pure church living in free and faithful obedience to the lordship of Jesus Christ mediated to his people via the Scriptures illumined by the Holy Spirit.

The suggestion that the Baptist vision and associated distinctives arose in a particular context raises the question of whether this vision and these distinctives were normative. That is, did the cultural and political context in which the Baptist movement arose exercise undue influence on Baptist ecclesiology, and if so, is this ecclesiology still applicable in very different contexts? Or was it the case that a variety of cultural factors converged to create a new context in which legitimate though novel interpretations of Scripture issued in a new, transhistorical ecclesiastical polity? Any attempt to construct a distinctively Baptist theology must of necessity probe and address itself to this question.

Contemporary Baptist Theology

When we turn to examine contemporary systematic theologies written by Baptists, we find little to assure us that there is, in fact, a distinctive form of Baptist theology. The theologies written by Grudem, Grenz, and Erickson seem more self-consciously "evangelical" than Baptist.[13] Grudem is explicit, "I write as an evangelical and for evangelicals."[14] His systematic theology falls squarely into the Reformed tradition, and with regard to Baptist distinctives, Grudem is equivocal. For example, he concludes that the "form of government adopted by a church is not a major point of doctrine," and, while arguing for believers' baptism he

---

13. It is beyond the bounds of this paper to analyze and discuss the distinction between evangelicalism and Baptists. Certainly there is much common ground between the two groups, and it is possible to view Baptists as a subset of the broader category evangelicalism. Other, shorter and more popular theologies written by Baptists are not considered here. For example, Hart, *Truth Aflame*, writes an edifying and homiletic form of systematic theology as a charismatic Southern Baptist. Milne, *Know the Truth*, follows a more Reformed trajectory than Hart, and is more equivocal with respect to Baptist distinctives in matters of church government and the sacraments.

14. Grudem, *Systematic Theology*, 17. See also p. 1168, where Grudem acknowledges the very close relation between his own work and the Westminster Confession.

will also allow conscientious paedobaptists to become members of the local church.[15]

Grenz confesses that his systematic theology is "avowedly evangelical and unabashedly Baptist,"[16] and his Baptist convictions are certainly prominent in his treatment of ecclesiology, where he views the church as a voluntarist covenant community, upholds believers' baptism, and argues for congregational government and a symbolic understanding of the sacraments. Further, deeper resonances with Baptist thought might be discerned in his choice of "community" as the integrating motif of his theology, his emphasis on ethics and religious experience over against "rationalism," and his insistence that humanity is basically "open" to God. But whether these resonances actually arise from the Baptist vision cannot be demonstrated, and one suspects that they arise, rather, out of Grenz's confrontation with postmodernism.[17]

Perhaps the dean of contemporary Baptist systematic theologians is Millard Erickson. Certainly David Dockery suggests so: "While a Baptist and evangelical theology can probably be done better than Erickson has done it, it must be said that to-date, no one has done so."[18] Yet even so appreciative an interpreter as Dockery can also say that "it cannot be said that Erickson's theology is necessarily consciously and distinctively Baptist," and that Erickson himself aimed for a larger audience.[19] Even in his ecclesiology Erickson is only moderately Baptist, cautiously favoring congregational government while giving his assessment that the New

---

15. Ibid., 936, 982–83. Note, however, that in the 2007 edition of his volume, Grudem revises his position regarding church membership on pragmatic grounds to argue that church membership should be restricted to those baptized as believers.

16. Grenz, *Theology for the Community*, xxxi.

17. Grenz's attempt to do theology in the light of postmodernism exposes his project to serious criticism in terms of method and content. See, for example, Erickson et al., *Reclaiming the Center*. My own assessment of Grenz's theology is that his attempt to develop a postfoundationalist form of theology is compromised by the question of the truthfulness of theological construction. Without some degree of a correspondence theory of truth, our theological assertions risk becoming nothing other than assertions, and thus an imposition of power. In terms of material content, Grenz develops a personal and relational ontology in place of the more traditional substantialist ontology. This raises issues for his theology in several places, but no more so than in his Christology, where his non-substantial ontology threatens to divide the person of Christ and tends towards adoptionism. See, for example, Grenz, *Theology*, 308–14.

18. Dockery, "Millard J. Erickson," 654.

19. Ibid., 644.

Testament evidence for it is "inconclusive," and demonstrating openness to modes of baptism other than immersion, although insisting on believers' baptism.[20]

A quite different approach to Baptist theology is adopted by James McClendon. McClendon broadens his focus from specifically Baptist groups to those which may be considered baptistic, including virtually any group from the Free or Believers' Church tradition, or that has some root in the Radical Reformation. Thus, McClendon's proposal would embrace many groups not typically considered Baptist in a stricter sense, including Adventists, Assemblies of God and other Pentecostals, Brethren, Churches of Christ, Disciples of Christ, Mennonites, Quakers, and so on. Further, he elucidates the "baptist vision" in terms of five distinctive marks: biblicism, liberty, discipleship, community, and mission.[21] Noting the breadth of these churches and the corresponding paucity of their constructive theology, McClendon suggests that the primary reason for this paucity is that

> baptists in all their variety and disunity *failed to see in their own heritage, their own way of using Scripture, their own communal practices, their own guiding vision*, a resource for theology unlike the prevailing tendencies round about them.[22]

He proposes as an organizing principle for an authentic baptist theology the idea of *"shared awareness of the present Christian community as the primitive community and the eschatological community."*[23] Further,

> This is not merely a reading strategy by which the church can *understand* Scripture; it is a way—for us, it is *the way*—of Christian existence itself. For my thesis here in brief is that just such a reading of the Bible and especially of the New Testament, read as

---

20. Erickson, *Christian Theology*, 1084, 1104–5.

21. McClendon, *Systematic Theology*, 1:27–28, 33–34. Note that McClendon's use of the small "b" in *baptist* intends to identify the broader ecclesial "type" rather than denominationalist Baptists particularly. In this essay I will use the small "b" as appropriate to accurately represent the stance of a particular theologian or theological view, and will retain use of the capital "B" when referring to those groups who self-consciously adopt the tag to indicate either their belonging to a Baptist denomination specifically, or to the Baptist tradition generally.

22. Ibid., 1:26; emphasis original.

23. Ibid., 1:30; emphasis original. The "as" in this sentence is all-important, serving as the underlying hermeneutical criterion which gives McClendon's theological vision its central focus and power.

> interpreting the present situation, is characteristic of the baptist vision wherever we find it. . . . I claim, in sum, *that the vision so understood is a necessary and sufficient organizing principle for a (baptist) theology.*[24]

McClendon's proposal has undoubted merit as well as penetrating insight, and is as such a valid and viable proposal for systematic theology, as his own project has demonstrated. Nevertheless, his method sharpens and forces the question of identity which is the focus of this paper. That is, McClendon's "baptist ecumenism,"[25] in broadening the term "baptist" to include many groups with quite distinct identities, and in flattening the typical Baptist distinctives by incorporating them into generalized categories more suited to the broad ecclesial grouping he envisages, seems ultimately to require the dilution of a distinctively *Baptist* identity.

Further, McClendon's method also raises an additional question, that is, whether Baptist identity is correctly identified as a genetic development of the Anabaptist tradition, or whether the early English Baptists developed independently of the Anabaptists. Conyers, for example (and contra McClendon), argues that the early Baptists arose independently of the Anabaptists and self-consciously adopted a Reformed expression of theology, which they proceeded to adapt in accordance with their own distinctive convictions regarding human rationality, agency, and faith, together with the ecclesiological implications of these convictions.[26] The question remains contentious, with thorough-going implications for the nature and future of Baptist theology.

A "Dramatic" Proposal for Baptist Theology

More recently, New Zealand Baptist Martin Sutherland has taken McClendon's lead to suggest a uniquely baptist mode of theological method.[27] Sutherland's proposal unfolds over a number of stages. He

---

24. Ibid., 1:33; emphasis original.
25. McClendon, *Systematic Theology*, 2:371.
26. Conyers, "Changing Face," 22–28. For a brief statement of McClendon's view, see his *Systematic Theology*, 1:19–20, and the references there. Also, note the articles by Timothy George referenced above for a view similar to that of Conyers.
27. Sutherland, "Gathering." Like McClendon, Sutherland adopts the small "b" to denote baptist movements in general rather than Baptists in particular.

begins with an assertion that baptists have a "distinct *way* of doing theology" that does not conform to the dominant method of doing theology because of the latter's predilection with philosophy as a conversation partner and the place of metaphysical problems as a primary element of theological discourse.[28] Rather than "the paradoxes of metaphysics, the beating heart of baptist theology is heard in our views of church and sacrament."[29]

Sutherland then argues that underlying traditional baptist distinctives is a fundamental notion of what it means to *become* the church. Adopting Matthew 18:20 and its context as his central biblical passage, Sutherland contends that the "dynamics signaled in this key ecclesiological passage both explain and sustain an authentically baptist way of doing theology."[30] He suggests that the passage portrays the church as a disciplined community of discernment and authority constituted by the "mystical presence" of Christ in the event of its gathering.[31] So important is the concept of "gathering" that it must be viewed in sacramental terms as both the occasion of Christ's presence and the means of discerning his will. In Sutherland's proposal, the life of the congregation is "the visible centre of the faith."[32]

> It is the inevitably local, gathered community which is the focus of the promise Christ makes in Matthew 18:20. The language there attached to gathering is far stronger than any attached in the New Testament to baptism. It is more direct, I would argue, even than the "this is my body/blood" declarations at the last supper. If "real presence" is sought then surely it is here, where two or three gather in his name. . . . This I propose is a "trace" of an authentically baptist sacramentality. The most truly sacramental moment is the gathering itself. . . . All other rites gain their sense and validity from their exercise in that context, rather than the community gaining its visibility and form from the rites. . . . Indeed, the gathering *is* the sacrament, the moment of Christ's presence, the *telos* at once for the church and for the world.[33]

---

28. Ibid., 43–44; emphasis original.
29. Ibid., 44.
30. Ibid., 45.
31. Ibid., 45–46.
32. Ibid., 46–47.
33. Ibid., 51–52, 52–53; emphasis original.

Sutherland concludes his exploration of a sacramental mode of baptist theological method by drawing out two primary implications from his proposal. First, since the life of the gathered community constitutes the visible centre of the faith, all theological questions are necessarily ecclesiological questions, for it is "the mystical presence of Christ in the gathered community [which] generates the church's theologising."[34] Consequently, baptist theology is necessarily practical, concerned with the life of the community as it encounters the mystical presence of Christ in its midst. "Baptist theology," says Sutherland, "is 'systematic' only in the sense of being a 'centred set' of concepts. Doctrines proceed not by philosophical logic but as radiating spokes from the centre."[35]

Second, Sutherland considers the question of the veracity of theology. In what sense can theology or theological propositions be considered "true"? In addressing this question he opts for a narrative account of theology in which the local gathered community seeks to align its story with the normative Christ story as revealed in Scripture. The reason the Christ story is normative is grounded in the conviction that the local community is only constituted as church as they gather "in his name." Hence, theology is necessarily local and contextual, and also more or less true in accordance with the degree of alignment of its story with the normative Christ story.[36] This way of construing the truthfulness of theology inevitably exposes Sutherland to the possibility of postmodern relativism. He is not unaware of this possibility, however, and states his position with some clarity:

> The truth of theology therefore is not primarily that of correspondence, which arrogantly claims an unmediated grasp of reality. Neither is it merely one of self-referential coherence. *Both understandings remain necessary and useful*, but closer to the heart of a baptist approach to theology is an understanding of theological truth better described as "consonance." In this concept, drawn from music, theology's task is to establish and enable the harmony of the local story with that of Christ, so that the church truly gathers "in his name."[37]

---

34. Ibid., 53, 46.
35. Ibid., 53.
36. Ibid., 54.
37. Ibid., 54–55; emphasis added.

Sutherland's construal of truthfulness in terms of consonance need not make the truthfulness of theology relative, but it does acknowledge the fact that every theological formulation is inherently contingent. In this view Scripture functions truly as canon—as measure—guiding the theology and life of the community into closer approximation of the normative Christ story. Thus Sutherland utilizes the dramatic metaphor proposed by Kevin Vanhoozer to suggest that the role of Scripture in the life of the community is to cultivate good theological judgment, such that the community is equipped to take their place "fittingly" in the ongoing drama of redemption on the stage of history.[38] The role of tradition is less formal in Sutherland's proposal. Previous generations of Christians provide a sense of continuity, experience, and discovery by which baptist theology might be enriched, but rarely directed. The focus of a truly baptist theology will ever be "the vision of Christ himself, forever renewed in his presence among us."[39]

Assessing Sutherland's Proposal

Martin Sutherland's proposal for baptist theological method has provided a creative and useful starting point for thinking about the way of Baptist theology into the future. His selection of Matthew 18:20 as the foundational text is apposite and in accordance with historical Free Church ecclesiology.[40] He considers matters of theological sources and authority, broaches the question of the truthfulness of theology in this mode, and reflects on the goal and purpose of theology in relation to the ongoing life of the Christian community. His central material proposal in which he posits the sacramentality of the gathered community itself is creative and somewhat daring, and yet has within its overall scope the possibility of encompassing the major themes of the gospel if he will go on to explicate the theme of the mystical presence of Christ in terms of Trinitarian theology and identity. Finally, his vision of Christian ex-

---

38. Ibid., 56. See Vanhoozer, "Voice," 100–104. Note, also, the similarity of this dramatic understanding of the role of theology and Scripture to Nigel Wright's understanding of the authority of Scripture, and of the Christian life in terms of *improvisation*, in Wright, *Scripture*, 89–93.

39. Sutherland, "Gathering," 56.

40. Volf, "Community Formation," 216. Also, Kärkkäinen, *Introduction to Ecclesiology*, 134–50.

istence in terms of participation in the redemptive narrative, and his view of doctrine as comprising a "centred set," is not only theologically satisfying, but missionally relevant—the more so if he is able to translate his doctrinal "centred set" into inclusive ecclesial practice. Thus, my aim in posing the following questions to Sutherland is not by way of polemics, but dialogue and examination, for the question at stake in this paper remains: will Sutherland's proposal enable the development of a distinctively *Baptist*—capital B!—theology?

The first question I raise concerns Sutherland's central material principle: the sacramentality of the gathered community. He writes, "In the event of gathering in his name, Christ is present. There is surely no greater promise of grace than that. And of this grace the gathering itself is the visible sign."[41] Later he provides more definition for what this gathering involves.

> It is more than coincidental presence together in one place. It is a gathering as a covenanted community in the name of Christ with all that that entails. It is a gathering of disciples who walk the road of suffering. It is an enactment of the Gospel and, in the committed, covenanted relationships of real, named, flesh and blood persons, it is a glimpse of the reconciliation God is bringing about for the universe. . . . This I propose is a "trace" of an authentically baptist sacramentality. The most truly sacramental moment is the gathering itself. . . . Indeed, the gathering *is* the sacrament, the moment of Christ's presence, the *telos* at once for the church and for the world.[42]

If by "sacramentality" Sutherland means that the gathered community is a sign and instrument of the kingdom, his point will likely be welcomed by most Baptists. However, the language of "sacrament," especially when applied to the church, is not without problems, for it can engender the idea that the gathered community is itself the locus and mediator of the grace it signifies. Such a view tends to posit too close an identification between Christ and his church, blurring the distinction between the two. By insisting that the gathering itself *is* the sacrament, *is* the moment of Christ's presence, *is* the telos—the perception and knowledge of Christ as the source, goal, and meaning of all existence—Sutherland comes close to this position. If the language of

---

41. Sutherland, "Gathering," 46.
42. Ibid., "Gathering," 52–53; emphasis original.

"sacrament" is to be used at all, it is better applied to Christ alone, who is the *Ursakrament,* "both the *sacramentum* and the *res sacramenti,* both the sign and the reality signified."[43]

The second question I would put to Sutherland concerns his portrayal of the truthfulness of theology. I have already cited his care in noting that both a correspondence and a coherence theory of truth "remain necessary and useful." Nevertheless, he is critical of these theories as arrogant and self-referential, and prefers to opt for narrative "consonance." In so doing it seems to me that he evades the question of the truthfulness of theology, for narrative consonance in and of itself is insufficient as a measure of truth. Why privilege *this* narrative?

Further, it may be that Sutherland has a fully developed doctrine of Scripture, but if so, it is not expounded here. Rather, Scripture is simply acknowledged as the normative document of Christian faith, being the source of the Christ story and the canon by which the community's faithfulness is measured and enabled to be "true."[44] Although he does not explicitly state his approach along these lines, it seems that Sutherland has developed a narrative account of theology with a non-foundationalist epistemology, perhaps following McClendon and/or Grenz. The problem here is that unless Sutherland can ground his narrative consonance with some form of theological realism—which in turn requires some form of correspondence theory of truth—his narrative consonance will collapse back into the self-referential coherence model of truth he wishes to avoid. Ian Markham argues cogently that we have only two options when it comes to developing a theological worldview. We either adopt a worldview that is both realist and theist, and which therefore provides coherence and rationality, or we adopt an explicitly anti-realist worldview. According to Markham, to dismiss questions of ontology and truthfulness and "simply articulate your narrative" is to give up "on intelligible explanations for the world, and therefore God."[45]

I have argued elsewhere the formal possibility of establishing the church as a faithful gospel community embodying the incarnational narrative in its particular context without capitulating before the question of truth.[46] The form of correspondence theory required is not

43. George, "Sacramentality of the Church," 32.
44. Sutherland, "Gathering," 56.
45. Markham, *Plurality and Christian Ethics,* 152–53.
46. O'Neil, "Ethics and Epistemology," 21–40.

thorough-going as though it were "windows all the way down," but is a form of critical realism predicated on the historical truthfulness of the resurrection of Christ. The truth claim of Christian theology is that "the events that transpired around the person of Jesus of Nazareth represent a divine disclosure of ontic reality, a disclosure given in particular historical context but which is nonetheless freighted with the weight of universal normativity."[47] Within such an ontology, space is prepared for the community of faith to become

> a witness within a pluralist culture to the truth that lies at the core of all reality, a witness which simultaneously confronts the deficiencies of alternate ontologies and invites consideration of the ontology held forth in the church.[48]

As such, the people of God exist in apologetic and dialogical relation to the surrounding culture, bearing witness to ultimate reality as a prophetic counterculture enlivened by the Spirit in a dispirited world.

In terms of the central concern of this paper, the final question I pose to Sutherland is the most significant. Sutherland's theological method, following Paul Fiddes, distinguishes between "tracks and traces" in respect to the development of a distinctively baptist theology.

> "Tracks" are those well-formed, discernable lines tramped down through agreed use and delineating the journeys of the past. Of these traditions there are relatively few in Baptist theology. More important are the vaguer, less certain "traces" which "evoke the picture of a shadowy after-image, or a scarcely worked-out trajectory; [hinting] at uncertainty, at ambiguity in both knowledge and direction."[49]

Sutherland agrees with the contention that baptists "have no great patterns or guides, nor many examples of baptistic groupings working at these issues in a systematic theological way,"[50] and so seeks to discover those "more important" traces. Thus, Sutherland regards his construal of the gathering of the community as a "'trace' of an authentically baptist sacramentality."[51] Similarly, as he considers the role of tradition in theo-

---

47. Ibid., 37.
48. Ibid., 38.
49. Sutherland, "Gathering," 41. Sutherland is citing Fiddes, *Tracks and Traces*, 1.
50. Ibid., 42, citing Jones, *Believing Church*, 51.
51. Ibid., 52–53.

logical method, Sutherland, despite his protest to the contrary, consigns the entire Baptist tradition to the status of traces that may enrich us, but which will rarely direct us.[52] His rationale for this decision is the immediate vision of Christ's mystical presence ever-renewed in the community, and the baptist responsibility to refer primarily and directly to Christ rather than the tradition.

By his own definitions, however, it appears that Sutherland's method is unwarranted at this point. If, as noted above, tracks refer to "those well-formed, discernable lines tramped down through agreed use and delineating the journeys of the past," and traces are characterized by "vague" and "shadowy uncertainty" and "ambiguity," or by "scarcely worked-out" trajectories, then Baptist tradition has certainly bequeathed tracks and not traces to succeeding generations to guide and direct their paths. These tracks are nothing less than the numerous Baptist confessions developed over time as an expression of the faith of a particular group. According to Lumpkin,

> These confessions represent the sincere desire of many Baptist communities to set forth their interpretations of the Scriptures regarding Christian belief and practice. No single confession has yet appeared which would be acceptable to all Baptists. On the other hand, all Baptist confessions demonstrate enough of essential agreement to procure for their proponents an acknowledgement of membership in the Baptist family. In every instance, they bespeak the theological and biblical awareness, the freedom, and the sense of responsibility of the movement through succeeding generations.[53]

While acknowledging the provisional nature of all confessions in the Baptist tradition, Timothy George nonetheless identifies five features common to the major confessions which he terms "identity markers."[54] The five features are as follows:

- orthodox convictions in which Baptists have typically stood in continuity with the dogmatic consensus of the early church;

---

52. Ibid., 56.
53. Lumpkin, *Baptist Confessions*, 422.
54. George, "Future of Southern Baptist Theology."

- evangelical heritage, by which George means that Baptists affirm the formal and material principles of the Reformation, specifically, Scripture alone and justification by faith;
- a Reformed perspective whereby "despite a persistent Arminian strain within Baptist life, for much of our history most Baptists adhered faithfully to the doctrines of grace as set forth in Pauline-Augustinian-Reformed theology"[55];
- Baptist ecclesiological distinctives, which most closely approximate the Anabaptist ideal of the church as an intentional community of baptized believers bound to the Lord and to one another;
- confessional character in which Baptists confess their faith as a witness to the faith they hold in sacred trust and catechize the rising generation by passing on their faith intact.

Historically, at least, there seems to be a quite definite *Baptist* way of doing theology, but perhaps we have missed the forest for the trees. The presence and character of these confessions indicate a definite trajectory of Baptist theology and identity, and Sutherland's almost peremptory dismissal of this confessional heritage appears overly hasty and unwarranted. The renewal of Baptist theology in accordance with this heritage does not, of course, entail a slavish adherence to this tradition. At every point, both the tradition and modern proposals remain subject to the authority of Jesus Christ as witnessed in Holy Scripture read in the community of faith. This community, of course, transcends temporal bounds, and in this light the confessional tradition, while not binding on the conscience of believers, is nonetheless a school in which contemporary believers learn to read Scripture faithfully while still retaining an openness to the contemporaneous voice of the risen Christ present in the midst when two or three gather in his name.

Conclusion: The Way Forward

The primary concern of this paper has been to investigate whether Baptist theology is distinctively *Baptist* or merely a more general form of Evangelical or Reformed—or baptistic or postmodern—theology. Other questions have arisen along the way. Does a distinctive Baptist identity

55. Ibid., 32.

actually matter, or might Baptists be absorbed into an amorphous baptistic ecclesiastical type as in McClendon's "baptist ecumenism"? Or, put differently, do Baptists have a unique and valuable contribution to make to the ongoing life of the Christian community? Were the classic Baptist distinctives a contextual development relevant only to a specific time, place, and context, or are they enduring biblical imperatives for the church in succeeding generations? What role do the Baptist confessions and tradition play in the formulation of contemporary Baptist theology? Is there a way forward for Baptist theology?

I suggest that the future of Baptist theology and the renewal of Baptist identity lies not in submerging Baptist distinctives into a generic baptistic Free Church type, but in reclaiming the ecclesiological, confessional, and missional heritage of the Baptist tradition. The early Baptist vision of a pure and free church living in free and faithful obedience to the lordship of Jesus Christ mediated to his people via the Scriptures illumined by the Holy Spirit remains compelling. Thus, the McClendon/Sutherland proposal to employ the gathered community as the formal organizing principle of a genuinely Baptist theology remains viable so long as it is carried out with a primary focus on the truthfulness of the biblical gospel as its central material content.

Utilizing a form of epistemic method as suggested in this paper will secure the development of a theology that witnesses truly to ontic reality, and fosters a vision of a gathered community that embodies the incarnational narrative in its particular context. The purity of the community will not be that of a narrow, defensive, exclusive, or sectarian people distinguishing strictly between insiders and outsiders. Rather, as a generous and welcoming community centred around Jesus Christ and oriented toward the coming kingdom of God, it will be faithful and responsive to the call of Christ, as it participates in his redemptive mission. Recovering the confessional heritage of the Baptist tradition supports and guides the theological and catechetical work of the churches, nourishing believers with a sense of identity grounded in the historical community of Christ as it moves towards the kingdom of his Father.

6

Is a Denomination a Church?[1]

PETER RALPHS

Introduction

I was once asked to give input from an evangelical's viewpoint at a forum where the UCA Assembly's Resolution 84 would be discussed from various perspectives. The person who invited me (a theologically conservative Christian) was very keen to check that I was not one of those evangelicals who were suggesting people might leave the UCA over the issue. As it turned out, I eventually declined the invitation, but I was struck by his mindset that the most terrible thing that could happen was for anyone to leave the UCA! I surmise that he thought this would be tantamount to leaving the church itself and suspect that his mindset

---

1. This paper is an adaption of one originally written in the context of the Uniting Church in Australia (UCA) as a theological and pastoral response to a situation where a number of UCA members were wondering whether to remain with the UCA or to seek fellowship with a church of a different denomination. The concern was to assist ordinary church members wanting to think through issues that revolved around the UCA's long debate over sexuality and its eventual apparent rejection of the long-held Christian position that God's will for people is faithfulness in marriage and celibacy in singleness. The UCA's position was summed up in Resolution 84 of the its 10th Assembly, held in 2003. (The UCA Assembly is the national regulating authority of the UCA with responsibility for determining doctrinal matters and the UCA's position on contemporary issues, though it is required to consult with other UCA councils and congregations on key matters.) For many evangelicals the issue has been not so much about sexuality per se but rather what they perceive as unfaithfulness to the clear teaching of Scripture on sexuality and so tantamount to a definitive rejection of biblical authority.

was shared by many people, especially those in leadership in the UCA bureaucracy. This mindset may well also be shared by leaders of other denominations in regard to their own denomination!

The catch cry of those trying to hold the UCA together, despite the irreconcilable positions held by its members on biblical authority and interpretation, has been "unity," suggesting that what is under threat is the unity of the church. Certainly, the unity of the church must be a matter of serious concern for biblical Christians, for Jesus taught and prayed for the church to be one and Paul strongly echoes this teaching (for example, the theme of unity in the local church permeates 1 Corinthians, and that of the universal church as well is to the fore in Ephesians). Cyprian argued likewise in his treatise *On the Unity of the Church* (251 CE) and it has rightly been acknowledged as an essential aspect of the church throughout its history, highlighted with the ecumenical movement of the twentieth century.

However, all this raises an important issue: is a denomination, including the UCA, a church? I would argue that biblically the answer is no. The New Testament in its teaching about the church knows nothing of anything that is comparable to a denomination. While it is not easy to define "denomination" precisely, I see it as referring to a common branding of churches that are associated with one another with some sort of overarching structure that helps support a shared tradition and values. Roxburgh sees denominations as performing a legitimizing function for their members in supporting a shared narrative and values; however, this legitimization is contingent upon the denomination having its members' trust and confidence.[2] A denomination may be as low-key as a voluntary association of like-minded congregational churches with minimal organization for mutual convenience (for example, ministerial accreditation, negotiation with civil government) or as highly hierarchically structured as the Roman Catholic and Anglican denominations. Of course, some denominations may see themselves as more than merely one of a number of denominations but rather as "the true church" with which all churches ought to be associated. Roman Catholicism is a clear example of this, though it is not uncommon for some evangelical denominations to regard themselves as holding to the gospel in its most pure form and so as more representative of "the true church" than other denominations.

2. Roxburgh, "Reframing Denominations," 79–82.

In the New Testament, the church, both by way of terminology (for example, *ekklēsia*[3]) and concept, is presented in two ways. From one angle it is a community of Christians in a particular geographical locality—for example, the church in Jerusalem, Ephesus, Philippi, Rome, etc. (see Acts 14:23; Phil 1:1; 1 Thess 1:1). Often a church's theological reality is stated (for example, "the church of God" or "of Jesus Christ"; see Rom 16:16; 1 Cor 1:2) along with its physical location (e.g., "in Rome"). In some places, the church would consist of a single "house church," in other places perhaps of a number of "house churches" (see Rom 16:5, which suggests there were churches in Rome that met at other people's houses as well as that of Priscilla and Aquila, perhaps including those mentioned later in vv. 10–11, 14–15). Just how a plurality of house churches in one city/town related to one another is difficult to say, but they must have related sufficiently for Paul to write a single letter to be read by them all (such as the Letter to the Romans), either by having a common meeting where it was read out or by passing it around. A variation on this theme is the reference to "churches" (plural) in a wider locality (for example, in Judea, Asia; see 1 Cor 16:1, 19; 2 Cor 8:1; Gal 1:22). No label comparable to our denominational labels today is ever used.

Given that *ekklēsia* is used in its normal secular sense in Acts 19:39, 41 for the assembly of a city's citizens, it could be argued that in like manner the church is only such when its members are gathered together.[4] Certainly Paul uses *en ekklēsia* in 1 Corinthians 14:19, 28 and *oun sunelthē hē ekklēsia* in 1 Corinthians 14:23 to refer to the actual Christian meeting at Corinth. However, this is too narrow a perspective to satisfy the New Testament's use of the term and concept, and we may rightly speak of the church gathered (where its members experience fellowship, praise God, and receive encouragement and instruction) and the church scattered (where its members live and witness as Christians in the world).

From another angle, the church is a trans-geographical, trans-cultural (and, some would add, trans-temporal[5]) reality, consisting of

---

3. Giles has an excellent discussion of *ekklēsia* in *What on Earth Is the Church?*, 230–43.

4. Winter, in "The Problem with 'Church,'" discusses the problem the early church faced in using *ekklēsia* given its secular political implications and the risk of importing aspects of the secular *ekklēsia* into the life of the church.

5. The church triumphant (consisting of departed saints) and the church of the age to come are real concepts but of little relevance for the discussion of denominations in

all people in communities of faith who acknowledge Jesus as Lord and Savior (see 1 Cor 1:2; Matt 16:18; 2 Cor 8:18; 11:28). This is probably the primary approach to the church found in Ephesians and Colossians (see Eph 1:22–23; Col 1:18). In this case, the church is not so much made up by adding together all the various local churches so that they are part of the universal church—rather it is probably better to see the local church as the *embodiment* in one location of the wider church of God.[6] From the totality of New Testament data concerning the church and its life, I would define the church as a community of believers who give their allegiance to Jesus, the crucified and risen Lord and Messiah, a community indwelt and empowered by the Holy Spirit; which proclaims the gospel and incorporates people into its life through baptism, models Christlike, self-giving love, and whose members share together in the Lord's Supper, as they live in anticipation of the fullness of God's kingdom at the Parousia.[7]

The church in the New Testament is both continuous with and discontinuous from the Old Testament people of God. The church flows out of its Jewish heritage. Jesus was a Jew and came to fulfill God's promises to the Israelites. The first Christians were Jews. Yet it is clear that Jesus intended to build a new people of God, a community centred on himself as Messiah (see Matt 16:18; "I will build my church"). And both in ministry (for example, the occasional healing of Gentiles) and in command (see Matt 28:18–20) he made it clear this movement was larger than could be contained within Judaism—new wine skins would be needed. Indeed, one of the big issues the early church faced (as reflected in the New Testament documents) was to define its identity over against Judaism, particularly in light of the fact that it was mainly Gentiles rather than Jews who were accepting Jesus as Lord and Savior (see Gal 3:7; 6:16; Eph 2:19).

We do not get the impression from the New Testament that any particular local church called the tune for all other churches. This hierarchical approach was certainly a later development in church history

---

the present era, except in so far as to point out that presumably Christians will have laid aside their denominational labels in the final eschatological reality of the church!

6. Ladd, *Theology of the New Testament*, 586. Grenz refers to the local church as "the church in miniature" (Grenz, *Theology for the Community*, 609).

7. As is often recognized, the communal nature of the church reflects the communal being of God as Trinity and is consistent with human creation in the divine image as communal beings (Gen 1:26–27).

(the church of Rome, leading to the Roman Catholic Church) but it is not a New Testament phenomenon. Certainly, all churches were expected to adopt common apostolic teaching and practices, but this was a general expectation derived from the gospel itself, not from a hierarchical structure imposing such standards (see 1 Cor 4:17; 7:17; 11:16). Paul appeals to churches he founded to fall into line with such orthodoxy and orthopraxy, but he never imposes it as coming from some authoritative body over all the churches. We are left wondering how the individual churches related to one another. Amongst the Pauline churches Paul himself probably provided the glue, and relationships were further cemented as Christians travelled from place to place and fellowshiped together. But this was an informal networking, not a formal structure.

The closest the New Testament might come to an authoritative assembly type approach (typical of some denominations) is with the "Council of Jerusalem" in Acts 15. This was an "assembly" of the early church that met in response to criticisms of Paul's ministry to the Gentiles, to determine the crucial issue of whether Gentile converts needed to adopt Jewish practices to be members of the church or whether salvation and membership in the church were based on faith in Jesus alone. This was a unique event in that it was made up of key original apostles through whom Christ was founding his church (and some other leaders), and Paul saw it as important that his gospel of salvation by grace through faith be endorsed by this foundational leadership, which it was. The enquiry was not initiated by the Jerusalem church but the pro-Gentile church in Antioch, which wanted clarification (it was not top-down!). The only stipulation the council gave was that Gentiles might follow a few practices that would make it easier for Gentile and Jewish Christians to have "table fellowship" together for the sake of the unity of the church. This matter having been decided, we read of no further such "assemblies/councils" in the New Testament. We certainly have no inkling of an overarching structure over local congregations nor of a structure where representatives of various churches come together to decide matters that will be determinative for all those churches.[8] This is unlike many contemporary denominations that have a conciliar structure where matters are discussed and decided by representatives of a denomination's various member churches, though how binding these deliberations are on member churches varies considerably.

8. Banks concurs with this observation in regard to Paul's writings (Banks, "Denominational Structures," 280).

Even the Jew-Gentile aspect of the early church is not comparable with denominations. Certainly the churches in Judea were predominately Jewish and those outside of Judea were predominately Gentile (see Rom 16:4), and Paul was concerned to cement their relationship especially through an offering by the Gentile churches to the Judean Christians in their economic need (see 2 Cor 8–9). But we never have the suggestion that these formed discrete groups like denominations. Paul was always concerned that Jew and Gentile relate to one another within a single community of faith (see Romans).

Now none of the above is meant to suggest that denominations are wrong per se. Indeed, as Kevin Giles points out, a denomination potentially has a number of positive aspects: it unites Christians with common concerns on a basis wider than the congregation, sometimes regionally, nationally, and internationally; it encourages interaction with those within this wider fellowship with whom we may differ on certain matters; it enables cooperation and centralization of resources for theological education, mission, and social action; it provides oversight of congregations and leaders for pastoral care and discipline.[9] The point is that denominations are a comparatively late development in the history of the church, really a phenomenon that came after the Reformation in the sixteenth century though anticipated in the split between the Roman Catholic Church and the Eastern Orthodox Church in the eleventh century.[10] To have coexisting mainstream denominations is largely due to European colonization.[11] In the colonial situation, in what was to become the USA no one denomination could claim ascendency or state endorsement, and denominations had no choice but to accept a plurality of expressions of being church. By way of contrast, in Europe churches in a given locality (such as a region or nation) largely were of the same "brand" (Roman Catholic, Anglican, Lutheran, etc.); dissent-

---

9. Giles, *What on Earth?*, 208–9.

10. The Reformers such as Luther had no intention (at least, at first) of setting up an alternate church but wanted the Roman Catholic Church to undergo reform; eventually they justified their split from Roman Catholicism on the grounds that it was no longer "the true church" on account of its departure from the biblical gospel. Unfortunately since then the same rationale has sometimes been used to justify schism and a multiplicity of denominations.

11. As Giles points out in *What on Earth?*, 199–200. Likewise, Gelder dates denominations from the mid to late 1700s (Gelder, *Missional Church*, 9, 21–22). Guder also discusses the distinctive shaping denominations have undergone over time in the American scene (Guder, *Missional Church*, 49–50, 62–66).

ing groups existed but were seen as aberrations that needed to conform rather than as legitimate, coexisting churches.[12] Thus, in the Old World non-conformist groups (for example, Baptist, Methodist) had to struggle to achieve legitimacy in the eyes of the religious establishment,[13] but in time did come to be seen as denominations against the backdrop of the established church.[14]

One commentator has estimated there are over twenty thousand denominations in the world today![15] It would probably be reasonable to also include independent megachurches, which may well perform functions traditionally performed by denominational structures on behalf of member churches (for example, leadership training, sending cross-cultural missionaries, church planting) and which can tend to self-replicate either through deliberate church planting or imitation by others. It can certainly be argued that denominational groupings of Christians were a historical necessity at particular moments for the sake of the church and its mission; that their birth was justified politically, pastorally, and missionally. We have to allow for the Holy Spirit to guide the church creatively through the centuries as it has adopted and continues to adopt structures appropriate to its sociological contexts.[16] But denominations are not biblical as such (that is, there is no real biblical precedent for them)[17] and they are in principle neutral phenomena that have to be assessed by wider biblical teachings, such as the extent to which they facilitate churches to live as the church.[18]

Since the church is either a church on mission or it denies its reason for being, at their best denominations assist the local congregations to

---

12. This is similar to the situation in Russia today where the Russian Orthodox Church is asserting itself as "the true church," endorsed by the state, over against other Christian groups, including evangelical churches, which it regards as heretical and needing to be brought into line.

13. A similar mindset can still persist on the part of some of the long-established mainline denominations towards newer Pentecostal/Charismatic churches/denominations today.

14. Ibid., Gelder, 17.

15. White, *Church*, 67.

16. A point well made by Giles in *What on Earth?*, 206–8.

17. As admitted by Gelder in *Missional Church*, 67.

18. See ibid., 67–69, for various ways in which denominations have historically attempted to explain their legitimacy.

engage in meaningful mission in their contexts and beyond.[19] Conversely, churches ought to rightly support the denomination to which they belong where it is fulfilling its proper role of facilitating churches in their mission and where the priority of the local church is recognized. At their worst, like other human institutions, denominations can become instruments in the hands of "spiritual powers" that seek to oppose God and his kingdom and oppress his people. Indeed the ultimate test of a denomination is whether it facilitates the church's mission through local congregations or hinders it. It goes without saying that denominations (including megachurches) should never see themselves as standing over against or in competition with other denominations or churches as this would suggest an independent spirit from the rest of the body of Christ and call into question its unity. It is worth reflecting on the rebuke of Jesus to his disciples when they thought they had a monopoly on the kingdom of God (Mark 9:38–41). Kevin Giles's comment is apposite: only those who think they have all the truth and have nothing to learn from other Christians can dare to stand apart.[20] I would add that an independent spirit also betrays a lack of preparedness to offer humbly to the wider church those gifts and insights with which God has blessed a denomination or a church.

From what has been said above, I believe it would be going beyond New Testament teaching to say that a denomination is a church. Rather a denomination is a grouping of churches along particular lines for various reasons, a way some churches relate to one another within a particular structure that may be more or less hierarchical. My view contrasts with that of Kevin Giles who argues that a denomination does have at least provisional theological endorsement as "church," though he admits that the local congregation does have a certain priority in God's purposes.[21] I find rather weak his argument that Paul's phrase "the churches of the Gentiles" (which Giles admits is plural in form) can allow for "church" to be used for Christians sharing a common heritage and confession.[22] Likewise, I find it somewhat anachronistic to extrapolate from supra-congregational aspects of the church in the New Testament

---

19. An important text in regard to the missional nature of churches and denominations is Gelder, *Missional Church*.

20. Giles, *What on Earth?*, 204.

21. Ibid., 196–211, 210.

22. Ibid., 206.

to the denominationalism of a much later era.[23] Giles rightly points to theological development in history[24] but fails to recognize that the classical developments (for example, the doctrine of the Trinity, person of Christ) were usually attempts to reflect on and reconcile *biblical data* and Christian experience, whereas, as I have argued, there is no biblical data in support of the concept of denominations. I am not arguing for the abolition of denominations, for they are a historical reality and at their best can serve a useful purpose; but I am questioning their status as "church" and so their claim to an allegiance that properly belongs only to the church as biblically defined.

Accordingly, the unity of a denomination is not equivalent to the unity of the church, for a denomination as such is not a church. It is a human organization that should facilitate the mission of God and the fellowship of his people. Accordingly, for a church or individual Christian to leave a denomination does not equate to leaving the church. Nor is it to threaten the unity of the church, which depends on the Holy Spirit and the practice of love and not on the maintenance of a particular denomination. It may well threaten the unity of a denomination as a human structure, but not that of the church. What will threaten the unity of the church is unfaithfulness to the revelation of God in Jesus Christ as we have it in the God-given record of the Scriptures and failure to engage in meaningful mission and to practice Christ-like love. Indeed, it would be quite arrogant for a denomination to suggest that to leave it is to leave the church[25] and that its unity is the church's unity; such a suggestion falls into the trap of elevating human conventions alongside or over the word of God.[26]

However, any Christian leaving a denomination should link with a community of Christians, and any church leaving a denomination should see to it that it somehow develops and maintains links with the wider church. Just as the New Testament knows nothing of denominations, it knows nothing of insulated churches or Christians. Even independent megachurches should seek suitable links with other churches lest they think and act as if the kingdom of God is summed up in their

---

23. Ibid.

24. Ibid, 206–7.

25. In recognizing the negative aspects of denominations Giles points out the constant danger of a denomination seeing itself as the only "true church" (ibid., 209).

26. As the Pharisees are said to have done in Mark 7:8.

existence and mission! Links might be sought, for example, through being part of a network of like-minded churches for mutual benefit and accountability, pastors joining a local pastors' fellowship, and engaging in appropriate ecumenical activities.[27] Robert Banks emphasizes the role networks can play in helping churches grow spiritually and engage in mission.[28]

Some Christians appeal to the biblical (mainly Old Testament) idea of a " remnant" to argue for remaining within a denomination that no longer facilitates the church's mission but effectively opposes it. The hope is that God will use this remnant by their witness either to turn the denomination around or at least act as a voice for truth in its midst. Of course, in regard to the Old Testament people of God, while God preserved and worked through a faithful remnant at times, it was rare for that actually to turn the whole people to God and his ways. God normally ended up judging and punishing his people as a whole but preserving the remnant so that his mission in the world would continue. However, I would challenge the application of "remnant theology" to the contemporary denominational scene on the grounds that we are not dealing with a comparable situation. The nation of Israel in the Old Testament was a unique entity brought into being by God to achieve his purposes, ultimately to bring his Son Jesus into the world as a first-century Jew, the Messiah. Israel was a theocracy created by God for a specific missional purpose. The modern counterpart to this is the universal church of God, which now serves his post-Calvary, post-resurrection, post-Pentecost missional purpose, fleshed out in local Christian communities that are at the forefront of mission (or ought to be!; see Gal 6:16; 1 Pet 2:9–10). The same cannot be said of a denomination. It is not the church or people of God *per se* but a human grouping of churches, and its legitimacy stands or falls with whether it facilitates mission or not. If it does, that is all well and good. If it does not, and it cannot be turned around without a massive investment of time, energy, and effort (that can distract from involvement in meaningful mission), then it is understandable if its members see it as no longer worthy of their allegiance and support.

---

27. Interestingly, the ecumenical movement no longer aims at the church's unity being outworked through a unified structure, but rather though mutual recognition and cooperation by the various denominations—unity with diversity.

28. Banks, "Denominational Structures," 297.

It may continue as a religious entity but will be largely irrelevant to the kingdom of God.

Another idea used to argue for staying within a denomination that is departing from biblical truth is that the church is to be a mixed bag until Christ returns. There is some truth in this. Indeed the New Testament presents the church warts and all (see Rev 2–3) and it would be a mistake to have a "docetic" view of the church, denying its true humanness, including its sinfulness in the "already and not yet" era of the kingdom of God. Augustine argued this way against the Donatists, who wanted a pure church cleansed of those who had denied the faith under pressure. Unfortunately, Augustine misapplied the parable of the wheat and tares (Matt 13:24–30) to the church whereas, according to Matthew, Jesus in his explanation of the parable clearly says the field is the world, not the church (Matt 13:36–43)—it is a parable about the presence of both good and evil in the world until the end when judgment occurs, not a parable about good and evil in the church. It is doubtful it can be used to justify ongoing involvement in a denomination when it has shown itself over a long period of time to steadfastly resist any real change in the direction of obedience to the gospel. The New Testament expects that a church will deal with false teaching and inappropriate conduct in its midst (e.g. 1 Cor 5:1–5; 1 Tim 1:19–20) in a spirit of humility (see Gal 6:1). In fact in Acts *ekklēsia* is first used in the context of disciplinary action (Acts 5:11)! If a denomination is such as to constantly hinder this from happening and there seems little evidence of prospect for change, it may be time to consider whether God's use for that denomination has come to an end. It may even be that the departure of churches from denominations that seem incapable of serving those churches as they seek to carry out God's mission leads to a situation where churches are being set free from bureaucratic structures that have departed from the biblical pattern of servant leadership and impede mission and to form new links with other churches that help facilitate mission.

What does all this have to say to Christians and congregations affiliated with denominations that seem to have lost their way in regard to the gospel and so who are struggling with the dilemma of whether to stay and continue to fight or leave?[29] It says that the issue is not about leaving *the church* or *its* unity, and that if one chooses to leave there should

---

29. See Guder, *Missional Church*, 61–62, for a good case study of a couple facing such a dilemma and some of the factors involved.

be no guilt in that regard. When this is accepted the matter is more a pragmatic missiological one than an ecclesiological one and needs to be assessed on that level: Which course of action better facilitates God's mission for his people? Does association with this denomination help or hinder fulfillment of that mission? While it is understandable that a church or Christian might want to stay and fight for the salvation of a denomination that they have valued and that has done many good things for the kingdom, God's revealed agenda is not the salvation of denominations but the salvation of the world through his church's mission. We need also to carefully consider whether God's judgment may not rest from time to time on a denomination as an organization and whether the very collapse of its unity and loss of congregations and members is part of that judgment.

To hang on to a denomination for the sake of reformation, property, security, or emotional attachment is very understandable and may well be the appropriate course of action for some. It is hard to leave the denomination in which one's spiritual heritage is found. For professional ministers, especially, there are major practical considerations of employment and financial security. For congregations, issues of property may loom large. While we must not make a god of property, it is an issue of stewardship. People have worked hard and given sacrificially so that certain buildings and resources can be used to worship God and witness to the community. It is no small matter to leave them and perhaps hand them over to a minority of people who may use them to promote a different, non-biblical gospel. And if evangelicals leave, would they be deserting good people who love the Lord but who lack the theological astuteness to see clearly the issues or who are too spiritually or emotionally insecure to make a move away from a denomination?

If we may liken a denomination to a ship, what do you do when it seems that those with their hands on the helm for the moment are steering the ship towards some rocks? Do you desert the ship to save your own life and join a ship sailing in safer waters? Do you try to wrest the helm away? Do you stay on board for as long as you can for the sake of the passengers, many of whom may be unable to appreciate that disaster is looming or may be fearful of leaving the supposed security of the ship? Which of these actions requires greater commitment and bravery?

In pondering all the factors, Christians need to keep in mind our call to the adventure of faith, knowing that God is our all-providing, all-comforting, all-judging God who has invited us to walk together with him as his church, whether that means moving out from under the shelter (or away from the storm of) a particular denomination with which we have been involved for a long time or staying with the ship through the storm and possibly its ultimate foundering. Christians who choose to stay with their denomination need to be sure that their attachment to it, which may be for a whole host of understandable reasons, is not seen by them to be the same as attachment to the church of Jesus Christ. They have freedom about being part of that denomination, which is only a human institution with no particular standing with God, just as others have freedom about not being part of it. However, no Christian has freedom about not being part of the church that is the body of Christ. It is important not to equate the two!

At the same time, to retain the allegiance and support of congregations and members, a denomination would do well to focus on serving the churches and facilitating them as they engage in God's mission rather than acting as a bureaucracy whose primary concern is to protect and promote its own self-interest, even if that self-interest is denominational survival (disguised as concern for the kingdom of God).[30] This is especially so in a post-denominational context where many of the traditional denominations are declining, where the shape of many churches is morphing into a similarity, and where denominational distinctives are no longer to the fore in people's minds translating into denominational loyalty. A healthy approach might be for denominations to see themselves as parachurch organizations standing alongside and serving their congregations for the sake of the gospel.[31]

---

30. As Migliore points out, it is the nature of bureaucracies to be marked by anonymity, fixed rules, hierarchical authority, and mimicry of secular models of management (Migliore, *Faith Seeking Understanding*, 187). Giles expresses similar concerns about such negative possibilities in regard to denominational structures (Giles, *What on Earth?*, 209–10). There is a good discussion of the corporate, bureaucratic model of denominations that predominated in the twentieth century in Roxburgh, "Reframing Denominations," 87–90. Roxburgh points to the "crisis of legitimacy" that denominations face today because of the general shift in culture away from the corporate model of the last century (90–92).

31. Banks' excellent article "Denominational Structures" argues for denominational structures being viewed by themselves as parachurch organizations. White adopts a similar view (White, *The Church and the Parachurch*, 64).

7

Emerging-Missional Ecclesiology and the Future of Denominational Leadership and Affiliation

GRAHAM J. G. HILL

Introduction

This chapter explores some of the implications of emerging-missional ecclesiology for the role of denominational leadership and affiliation in the postmodern and so-called post-denominational context. While denominations remain with us (and I suggest in this chapter that they have an important role to play in their relationship with local churches, especially if their structures and ministries are characterized by vitality, mission, and servant leadership), many Christians in Western cultures seem to feel at liberty to overlook or tolerate a variety of denominational labels in their quest to find a church that suits their needs and particular tastes. Nigel Wright observes, "It is this new freedom, or it could be an indifference, regarding specifically denominational values, that can be described as post-denominationalism."[1] This chapter examines what emerging-missional ecclesiology and perspectives have to say on denominational leadership and affiliation in this environment.

The phenomenon of the *emerging-missional church movement* can be traced back to the "Gospel and Our Culture Network" in the US and the UK through to such theologians as the British and South African

---

1. Wright, "Post-Denominationalism," 1.

missiologists Lesslie Newbigin and David Bosch. The perspectives of Newbigin and Bosch captivated the imaginations of a group of missional ecclesiologists such as Hunsberger, Guder, and Roxburgh, who in turn inspired an emerging generation of missional thinkers and practitioners such as McLaren, Kimball, Frost, McManus, and other emerging-missional authors and practitioners. All of these authors have become an influential part of the emerging-missional conversation or movement, whether they self-identify with it or not. Although it is a movement of *thought*, rather than an organized movement, its missiological nature, ecclesiological concerns, and most influential authors and writings are identifiable and examinable.

It is worth providing a brief definition of the core characteristics of this movement here. The emerging-missional church movement emphasizes emerging, contextualized, and culturally appropriate forms of community and worship. It is dedicated to refocusing churches on mission, sees Western society as a mission field, and finds mission sourced in the *mission Dei*. Its ecclesiology combines a notion of the church as a contrast society, the development of ecclesial forms to facilitate mission, and an embrace of missional ecclesiology. It enfolds a growing body of literature, practitioners, communities, and theologians in the West, networked less by definitions than by a similar assessment of the missional challenges and possibilities of contemporary post-Christendom Western culture. It must be recognized, however, that the diversity of the group and its perspectives makes it a very loose, young, evolving, and complex movement. Some within this group would prefer to call it a "conversation" rather than a movement, yet the idea of it being a movement is becoming more acceptable as it grows in influence and expanse.[2]

The influence of emerging-missional ecclesiology on the shape of the contemporary church, therefore, cannot be ignored. This chapter will briefly examine the primary concerns and perspectives of emerging-missional ecclesiology, which are summarized under the headings "missional and incarnational ecclesiology," "grounding mis-

---

2. In an introduction to their book on emerging-missional churches, Gibbs and Bolger write, "This study of emerging churches represents a determined attempt to identify the key practices of this disparate movement, which is so diverse and fragmented that some observers and insiders do not like to think of it as a movement at all. For insiders, it is more of a conversation. . . . Although the communities they lead may be small in number, the numbers are growing rapidly as their influence spreads through websites, blogs, chat rooms, and conference interactions" (*Emerging Churches*, 29).

sional ecclesiology in local worshipping communities," and "missional experimentation and church planting." From there this chapter will suggest some preliminary implications for denominational leadership and affiliation. The central perspectives of emerging-missional ecclesiology are described in the following few sections of this chapter not to provide a definitive treatment of the topic, but to lay a foundation for considering the future of denominational bodies in a postmodern and so-called post-denominational setting, and for putting issues surrounding denominational affiliation and allegiance into a conversation with emerging-missional ecclesiology.[3]

Missional and Incarnational Ecclesiology

The development of a missional and incarnational ecclesiology is of primary concern in the emerging-missional literature.[4] There is a deep conviction that there must be a concrete outworking of missional ecclesiology in the local congregation. According to the North American "Gospel and Our Culture Network," Michael Frost (Morling Baptist Theological Seminary), and Alan Hirsch (Forge Mission Network), churches that embrace a missional ecclesiology will demonstrate certain "indicators." Frost and Hirsch propose that the first three provide "energy and direction" for the remaining twelve, and they indeed shape the chapters of their book, *The Shaping of Things to Come: Innovation and Mission for the 21st Century Church* (2003), around these first three themes or indicators. For each of these fifteen indicators I begin with quoting the indicator verbatim, and then briefly elaborate on each one, adding insights on missional ecclesiology from other emerging-missional church movement writings as appropriate.

---

3. Summarizing some of my findings in my doctoral thesis, "Examination of Emerging-Missional Ecclesiological Conceptions."

4. See, for instance, the passionate advocating of missional and incarnational ecclesiology, missiological alertness among churches and leaders, theologizing missionally and forming a missiological hermeneutic, incarnational apologetics, and forming concrete missional communities in Moynagh, *Emergingchurch*, 30–31, 146; Drane, *Mcdonaldization*, 9–10, 171–82; Sweet, *Church in Emerging Culture*, 251; McLaren, *Church on the Other Side*, 36, 141–42; McManus, *Unstoppable Force*, 23, 169; Kimball, *Emerging Church*, 17, 68–70, 93–95;Murray, *Post-Christendom*, 251–53, 302–6, 321–22, 337–38; Hunsberger and Van Gelder, eds., *Church between Gospel and Culture*, 14–15, 45–48, 362–69.

In *Treasure in Clay Jars: Patterns in Missional Faithfulness* (2004), edited by Lois Barrett, the "Gospel and Our Culture Network" outline their fifteen key "indicators of a missional church" and describe what each one looks like in practice, as well as providing concrete examples of churches who are genuinely attempting to apply a missional ecclesiology in their local contexts in these ways. It is possible for pastors and denominational leaders to go through this following list and ask probing questions about the present practices and models of pastoral and denominational leadership. It is worth asking how faithful our approaches to pastoral ministry and denominational leadership are to these indicators.[5]

- "The missional church is *incarnational*, not attractional, in its ecclesiology."[6] It incarnates the gospel in contemporary culture, rather than attracts people to sacred or contemporized sanctuaries. Leaders that embrace a missional ecclesiology are sensitive to the current post-Christendom and postmodern context, and are shaping their ministries and evangelistic approaches accordingly.[7]

- "The missional church is *messianic*, not dualistic, in its spirituality." Frost and Hirsch allege that like Jesus the missional church has a worldview that is "holistic and integrated" rather than dualistic. For instance, it seeks to promote the discipleship of the whole person, not just the mind.

- "The missional church adopts an *apostolic*, rather than a hierarchical, mode of leadership." The fivefold gifts of Ephesians 6 are all equally recognized, and a flat rather than hierarchical leadership approach is maintained.

- "The missional church proclaims the Gospel."[8] A faithful, creative, and contextually-sensitive presentation of the gospel narrative is used.

---

5. Barrett, *Treasure*, 159–72; Frost and Hirsch, *Shaping of Things*, 11–12.

6. Again, for clarification, the opening definition of these first three indicators are taken from Frost and Hirsch, *Shaping of Things*, 12; the rest are from Barret, ed., *Treasure*.

7. Roxburgh, *Missionary Congregation*, especially ch. 5, "Toward a Missionary Ecclesiology."

8. Barrett, *Treasure*, 162.

- "The missional church is a community where all members are involved in learning to become disciples of Jesus."[9] Discipleship and learning to live in God's reign are valued, expected, and sought after. Mentoring, training, and nurturing are intentionally shaped so that "the skills and habits of Christian discipleship" are ingrained in individuals and the community.[10]

- "The Bible is normative in this church's life."[11] Knowledge of the Scriptures is complemented by a passion to obey them, processes for hearing and following them communally, and a desire to put them into conversation with the community's context.

- "The church understands itself as different from the world because of its participation in the life, death, and resurrection of its Lord."[12] Therefore, there is an evidenced longing to conform to Christ instead of the plethora of cultures surrounding the church, and a willingness to be different, to take risks, to embody Christ's love, and to suffer.

- "The church seeks to discern God's specific missional vocation for the entire community and for all its members."[13] Missionality is embraced by the whole community and is its clear priority, the community's faithfulness to its particular missional vocation is pursued and recognized by all, and giftings in the community are identified, developed, and released.

- "A missional community is indicated by how Christians behave toward one another."[14] The world knows who their Lord is by their love, generosity, self-sacrifice, and the fruit of the Spirit.

- "It is a community that practices reconciliation."[15] A heterogeneous community intentionally evolves as barriers are removed, conflicts are constructively resolved, difference is valued, and peacemaking and reconciliation are honoured.

9. Ibid., 163–64.
10. Ibid., 163.
11. Ibid., 164.
12. Ibid., 165.
13. Ibid., 165–67.
14. Ibid., 167.
15. Ibid., 167–68.

- "People within the community hold themselves accountable to one another in love."[16] They covenant with each other in this regard, evaluating the quality of their structures, relationships, and community, and seeking honest and transparent unity of spirit.

- "The church practices hospitality."[17] Welcoming strangers into the love and care of the community is pivotal to their missionality and communal values.

- "Worship is the central act by which the community celebrates with joy and thanksgiving both God's presence and God's promised future."[18] Communal worship is culturally asensitive, but also transformational, communally unifying, and eschatologically oriented.

- "This community has a vital public witness."[19] The church's immediate surroundings and social contexts are demonstrably influenced by its public witness, as it seeks practical justice, peace, transformed lives, and the like.

- "There is recognition that the church itself is an incomplete expression of the reign of God."[20] There is an eschatological and providential vision of the reign of God that undergirds the life of the church, and the church's frailties are viewed in the light of the broader realities of the kingdom of God.[21]

Such perspectives, whether we agree with them unreservedly or not, surely have very real implications for our understanding of the nature of the church and, by implication, of the very nature of our ministries (not to mention their concrete forms and approaches). The question emerges, "Do our denominational and pastoral leadership practices and forms reflect and facilitate these fifteen indicators listed above in very concrete and practical ways?"

---

16. Ibid., 168–69.
17. Ibid., 169–70.
18. Ibid., 170.
19. Ibid., 171.
20. Ibid., 171–72.
21. Ward, *Liquid Church*, 8–10.

Grounding Missional Ecclesiology in Local Worshiping Communities

Local worshiping communities and ministries are considered in the emerging-missional literature as the natural context in which missional ecclesiology is grounded, in which the witness of the Christian church is made credible, and in which Christians are disciplined into a radical engagement with people in their culture.

When missional ecclesiology is grounded in such broader communities of faith or pastoral leadership contexts, these communities have the following three features, as well as the previously mentioned fifteen "indicators," according to the emerging-missional works. These features may seem idealistic given the inadequacies and failings of actual Christian communities, yet they are expressed, even if only embryonically, in ministries that embrace and pursue genuine missionality.

First, they are churches and ministries that facilitate transformation within cultures through their constitution as alternative communities. Christian communities in general, and ministries in particular, need to be bonded together as alternative, distinct, and visible communities "offering an alternative form of life," "rediscovering the tradition as a reservoir for transformation," and experiencing "the intersubjectivity of persons formed by a new centre, Jesus Christ as the head of the *communitas*."[22] In this authentic *koinonia* they may also stand in contrast to the disintegration of communality and social cohesion in Western culture.[23]

Second, they are churches and ministries characterized by fluidity and networking, according to Ward, by which he means that they emphasize relationships, commodify religious products in order to enable fluidity and contextualization, communicate through networks, and have fuzzy edges that facilitate growth.[24] However, Ward's location of hope in the commodification of goods and services that circulate through networks seems somewhat commercialized and market-driven, and his reliance on "liquid," self-regulating and -forming groups instead

---

22. Roxburgh, Missionary Congregation, 49-56. This view of the missional church as an alternative community is found in the emerging-missional church movement writings in such passages as Webber, *Younger Evangelicals*, 118-20; Shenk, *Write the Vision*, 16.

23. Hall, *End of Christendom*, 59-61; Webber, *Younger Evangelicals*, 51-52, 101-6.

24. Ward, *Liquid Church*, 40-48.

of "solid" ecclesial structures again seems somewhat culturally shaped, theologically questionable, and too idealistic for most ministries.

Third, they are ministries given definition and direction by the four dimensions of worship, community, mission, and relationship to the wider Body of Christ; therefore, their experimentation and missionality is grounded in a holistic expression and understanding of church.[25]

Murray maintains that they will be simpler than we have known some ecclesiality in the past to be, "recovering friendship . . . as our relational paradigm . . . (which is) non-hierarchical, holistic, relaxed and dynamic"[26] as well as enjoying the rich benefits of being community around meals and laughter. He invites his readers to "imagine" communities (ministries) that are enriched by apostolic and prophetic poets and storytellers, that are characterized by the mission, social action, and contemplation of a monastic missionary order, and that are safe places to pioneer, experiment, and take risks.[27]

Based on his analysis of the works of Newbigin, Hunsberger, the "Gospel and Our Culture Network," and other materials in the field of missional ecclesiology, Hendrick notes the following characteristics of missional congregations (ministries):[28]

- They understand that they exist in a cross-cultural situation.
- They enter into dialogue with their context and culture.
- They provide opportunities for their members to reflect on culture from a biblical perspective.
- They pray for and seek their own transformation.
- They accept the marginal position in which they find themselves.
- They bear witness in their social and cultural situation.

Hunsberger, in the same book, *The Church between Gospel and Culture: The Emerging Mission in North America* (1996), may be considered to add to this list by including some practical shifts congrega-

---

25. Moynagh, *Emergingchurch*, 148–49, 155–56, 166–67.

26. Murray, *Post-Christendom*, 275.

27. Ibid., 277–82. For other emerging-missional passages with similar perspectives see Drane, *Mcdonaldization*, 28; Riddell et al., *Prodigal Project*, 132; Gibbs, *Church Next*, 168–69, 213.

28. Hunsberger and Van Gelder, eds., *Church between Gospel and Culture*, 302–7.

tions and their ministries need to make in order to move from religious vendor to mission:[29]

- From program to embodiment
- From committee to team
- From being clergy dominated to being laity oriented
- From recruitment to mission
- From (the leader as) entrepreneur to missionary

These, then, are some of the features of local worshipping Christian communities that are grounded in missional ecclesiology.

Missional Experimentation and Church Planting

Missional and ecclesiological experimentation are core values in the emerging-missional literature, communities, and missional church plants. The emerging-missional material often cites such innovative communities and experiments as examples of missional ecclesiology in practice, and as evidence of the influence of their perspectives.[30]

Gibbs and Bolger, in their book *Emerging Churches: Creating Christian Community in Postmodern Cultures* (2005), have gathered the stories of numerous emerging-missional leaders and pastors planting innovative missional communities.[31] Murray, attempting to classify the emerging-missional church movement, has demonstrated the vast range of missional and ecclesiological experimentation that they are undertaking in Western culture. He includes such things as contextualized cell churches and churches set in cafes, workplaces, pubs, club-culture, cyberspace, various specific subcultures, youth settings, indigenous neighbourhoods, and marginalized contexts. He also notes the emergence of midweek church, seven-day-a-week church, post-Alpha-course church, "organic church," contextual liturgy, multicongregational church, "menu church," multicultural church, new forms of monasticism and monastic orders, "common-purse" communities, and "boiler rooms" (contemporary communities formed around imaginative prayer). What Murray

29. Ibid., 344–45.
30. See Frost and Hirsch, *Shaping of Things*, 182–200; Moynagh, *Emergingchurch*, 13–14.
31. Gibbs and Bolger, *Emerging Churches*, 239–328.

and others are demonstrating is the extent of the emerging-missional ecclesiological experimentation and church planting developing alongside the emerging-missional church movement literature.[32]

The planting of new missional opportunities is vital if the church in the Western world is going to be relevant to postmodern cultures. Established churches and ministries are often well placed to experiment with missional initiatives, and should be encouraged to plant missional communities and projects for reaching particular subcultures. Kelly comments that "somewhere in the genesis and genius of these diverse groups is hidden the future of Western Christianity. To dismiss them is to throw away the seeds of our survival."[33]

Some Implications for the Future of Denominational Leadership and Affiliation

Having described some of the key perspectives of emerging-missional ecclesiology, this section will now suggest some preliminary implications for denominational leadership and affiliation in a postmodern and so-called post-denominational setting.

Perspectives on denominationalism, ecumenism, catholicity, and unity are evident in the emerging-missional material, but not usually in a systematized or structured way. The texts *Missional Church: A Vision for the Sending of the Church in North America* (Guder, ed., 1998) and *Church Next: Quantum Changes in How We Do Ministry* (Gibbs, 2000) are exceptions to this with regard to denominationalism. *Missional Church* dedicates a chapter to the historic development of denominations; the biblical-theological, historical, sociological, and organisational perspectives on denominations; and proposals for the purposes of such "paralocal" and "parachurch" organizations.[34] The author concludes that "a missional ecclesiology takes seriously the organizational life of the church both in its expressions of local missional congregations and in paralocal missional structures," and goes on to call for a "careful evaluation" of these systems through the lens of missional ecclesiology and our understandings of the unity, catholicity, and apostolicity of the church.[35]

---

32. Murray, *Church after Christendom*, 67–98.
33. Kelly, *Retrofuture*, 185. Also quoted in Frost and Hirsch, *Shaping of Things*, x.
34. Guder, *Missional Church*, 46–76.
35. "The church's nature as both one *and* catholic means that these structures must

Some in the emerging-missional church movement claim that even though we are in an age of post-denominationalism, and though much ecumenical and denominational activity "can seem life-emptying, dull, and bureaucratic," denominations and broader church gatherings are useful as long as they serve particular functions.[36] These functions include practical accountability, encouragement through participation in such events as regional gatherings and worship events, genuine support and resourcing, personal encouragement and care (especially in difficult times), networking of pioneers and missionary initiatives, and coaching and mentoring. While funding emerging initiatives and serving as permission givers, denominations can also fund approaches to selecting and training pioneers, partner with emerging churches in planting, advocate for emerging churches and their leaders, research fresh approaches to church and distribute their findings, facilitate learning networks, create space for theological and ecclesiological reflection, and actively sustain these innovative churches.[37]

Churches seeking to engage missionally with their communities, therefore, will often be looking for denominational affiliations that are relational and missionally productive, and for denominational leadership that serves the missionary activities and nature of the local churches. Such denominational affiliation and leadership will help local churches navigate the post-Christendom and postmodern context while shaping appropriate ministries and evangelistic strategies, will provide resources for discipling the whole as a missionary and in the image of Christ, and will encourage leadership structures that catalyze ministry and mission (rather than inhibit mission through their forms and presumptions). These churches will often be looking for denominational and interchurch relationships (the operative word being "relationships") that offer resources, coaching and help in the complex challenges that confront them as they experiment with approaches to discipling believers in contemporary Western culture, and navigate the tension between

---

exist in a symbiotic relationship with local congregations and their denominational structures. The apostolic character of the church implies a variety of ways in which its mission is carried out, and thus a variety of structures that a missional ecclesiology must address" (ibid., 75).

36. Moynagh, *Emergingchurch*, 158.

37. Ibid., 158–65, 210–42; Williams, *Mission-Shaped Church*, 125–49.

contextual relevance and countercultural faithfulness in their life together and missionary endeavors.

The fifteen indicators mentioned in the first section of this chapter are not easy to implement, and how they might be applied in one context might be quite different from another. Therefore, such churches will be looking to their denominational and interchurch connections for guidance and support. Many of these connections will inevitably be grounded in like-mindedness, geographic proximity, and similarity of church culture rather than denominational affiliation. Instead of being threatened by this, denominational leadership will be honored by many of their churches if they appreciate and broker these connections. Such support will need to help them shape practices of hospitality and community engagement, and design worship experiences that are meaningful and eschatologically oriented. It will facilitate the discovery of forms of public witness that testify to the values of the kingdom of God, and build communities that evidence centripetal force through their attractive love, community, and discipleship, and centrifugal mission into the world around the particular community of faith.

This kind of multilayered support is beyond the scope of most denominational bodies—hence the need for these communities to connect with support groups at denominational, geographical, cultural, and other relational levels. The role of a denomination as broker of relationships is central. The key perspective maintained by such denominations is one of service of the local community, along with the recognition that genuine mission is grounded in local worshiping communities. And these, of course, do not exist in isolation, but are themselves connected to the broader Christian community in concrete ways through denominational, geographic, and other relational ties.

In *Church Next*, Gibbs calls this the movement "from bureaucratic hierarchies to apostolic networks." Beginning with the institutional and cultural problems of mainline denominations in the West, the shift in Western Protestantism toward "super-churches" and "new apostolic networks," and the emergence of "dynamic churches in the majority world," Gibbs goes on to propose the implications for local churches, regional networks of churches, and denominational and ecumenical institutions. His implications and proposals revolve around notions of relationality, flattened organizational structures, permission giving, resourcing and equipping, diversification and decentralization, healthy accountability, and the potential of networks.[38] Such dynamic networks, whether they are formal denominational links or not, facilitate missional experimentation of the kind described earlier in this chapter, innovative church planting, and the healthy dialogue that must exist between established churches, denominations, and missional plants. These three exist in a symbiotic relationship. Not all symbiotic relationships are comfortable or always mutually beneficial. Nonetheless, the particular symbiotic relationship here is far too often antagonistic, inhibiting the lateral thinking, innovation, mutual enrichment, and advancement of the kingdom of God that is possible. Each party gains from the other two, and antagonism must be replaced by cooperation and grace.

Ecumenical cooperation is critical to missional effectiveness in postmodern culture, from an emerging-missional church movement perspective. Globalization, multiculturalism, intellectual pluralism, and the burgeoning dialogue between evangelicals, mainline churches, Catholicism, and Eastern Orthodoxy have facilitated such ecumenical openness in the emerging-missional church movement and among younger evangelicals.[39] However, missional ecclesiology demands that both denominational and ecumenical structures be examined for their "cultural captivity," so that authentic "structures of connectedness" are developed that facilitate the church's mission.[40]

In some forms of evangelicalism, and the ecclesiology of Reformed churches, the unity of the church is primarily of an internal, spiritual character, rather than external. This unity comes through being joined in the mystical body of Christ. Whether or not there is visible fruit to such unity, and without denying the visible existence of the catholic and local church, this unity is an invisible bond that is forged by the Spirit of Christ and our common profession of his death, resurrection, saving and sanctifying work, and lordship.

In emerging-missional ecclesiology, however, there is an emphasis on the visible and concrete expressions of unity and catholicity. All such unity and catholicity must manifest itself in the local community of believers, and any unity of the church universal is objectified and outworked in the unity of the local church. Similarly, catholicity includes communities of faith joining in a shared mission, understanding them-

---

38. Gibbs, *Church Next*, 69–92.
39. Webber, *Younger Evangelicals*, 37–38, 110–12.
40. Guder, *Missional Church*, 248–68.

selves as part of a broader mission and movement. This identification with a broader movement, which is expressed both concretely and particularly in their specific local congregation, is one of the key theological and practical functions of denominational bodies.[41]

Webber notes the wide range of sources for this "recovered" emphasis on the visible unity and catholicity of the church, including the communication revolution, the worship movement, postliberalism, and missional ecclesiology. There is a recognizable intentionality about ecumenical, interchurch, and denominational cooperation and networking—even between diverse and differing communities of the Christian faith—which reflects a genuine desire for practical expressions of catholicity and unity.[42]

This does not mean, however, that denominational distinctives have no place in the current cultural or ecclesial context, or that those who embrace an emerging-missional ecclesiology are unconcerned for such theological distinctives. It should not escape our attention that authors in the emerging-missioanl church movement come from a wide range of theological positions and denominational standpoints and, without relinquishing those distinctives, strive together for a re-missionalization of denominational, ecclesial, and local church structures and practices. Their theological distinctives add texture to the burgeoning literature on emerging-missional ecclesiology, and they lose nothing by embracing their distinctives and their common passion for mission.

Nigel Wright has argued persuasively, for instance, for the attractiveness and contribution of Baptist tradition and theological distinctives in the current cultural context.[43] Many of the values and ecclesiological perspectives espoused by Baptists strike a chord with the emerging-missional literature—liberty of conscience, the separation of church and state, regenerate church membership, the priesthood of all believers, the autonomy of the local church, the lordship of Christ, the supremacy of Scripture, and congregation forms of church government,

---

41. For evidence of these perspectives see Berkhof, *Systematic Theology*, 572.

42. Webber, *Younger Evangelicals*, 107–23. Webber's full list of sources includes secularism, pluralism, globalization, the communication revolution, inter-Christian dialogue, charismaticism, the demise of denominationalism, the worship movement, the interest in ecumenical spirituality and theology, and Vatican II. He also suggests that incarnational, Radical Reformation, and postliberal ecclesiologies have played their part in focusing younger evangelicals on the visible church.

43. Wright, "Post-Denominationalism," 6–11.

for instance. But if those theological and ecclesiological distinctives are to be given fresh expression in established settings and in new communities of faith they must be reclaimed, retold, and reimagined—given new life among a new generation of believers. The same is true, I have argued, for denominational leadership and affiliation. It is my contention that emerging-missional ecclesiology contributes much to this fresh discovery of denominational dynamism and connection.

8

The Little Church That Could

STEVE McALPINE

Introduction

There we were, hundreds of leaders at a mid-week pep talk in one of our city's biggest and most progressive churches. We'd done the sanctified schmooze over coffee. We'd done the church catch up: "How's your church going?" and "Did you hear so-and-so is moving to . . . ?" Now we sat in the black-curtained auditorium. Under the lights, the stage was bare, save for the podium and the drum kit quivering behind Perspex, impatient for Sunday. The speaker walked up. We applauded before tailing off and settling in to the rustle of note taking.

The speaker readied himself and then, leaning into the podium, delivered one of the most memorable and compelling openers ever uttered—memorable and compelling to me anyway. It was just a throwaway, an icebreaker; but I can't remember another word he said, despite the sustained applause when he'd finished. Those initial words have been the catalyst for the last six years of my life. They have seen me uproot my family, move overseas, blow out my mortgage, and juggle several jobs to keep our heads above water.

Here are those words: "I've had heart troubles recently. I wonder what it would say in your newspapers tomorrow if I dropped dead on stage tonight?" I didn't hear the next bit. I was too busy writing a headline for the next day's newspaper. I'd won a headline-writing award at journalism school, so I was fairly confident I could condense the drama of such an eventuality. Here it is: "Person You've Never Heard of Dies in Place You've Never Been To." See it? Right there on page 37. Just underneath "Small Earthquake in Chile; Not Many Dead."[1]

Perhaps I am too generous. Perhaps I should have written nothing. Nothing would have been close to the mark. Why? Because *nothing* would have been written in the newspaper if a Christian speaker dropped dead on the stage of my state's largest church during a leadership conference—nada, nix, nothing. Evangelical church life exists to the blissful ignorance of the vast majority of the population. The population suffers unconscious incompetence. It does not know that it does not know. We do not figure in its life or in its decision-making. The majority of its hatches and matches no longer reference us. Increasingly, neither do its dispatches. It is not pointing out our buildings saying, "If I never go to church, that's the one I am never going to." It is not waiting to discover us. It is not wistfully awaiting an invite to church to hear and see what goes on. If anything, the mere hint of one would steer conversation to safer waters.

This is a fact. The church is not on the radar in the twenty-first century West. I can live with this. My primary concern is not the culture's but the *church's* unconscious incompetence. It is one thing not to be on the radar. It is a another matter entirely to think you are when you are not; to believe that, given the right tweaking, church profile can be increased. Such an assumption has practical implications, costly implications. Millions of dollars and person-hours have been spent under this assumption. Thousands of programs have been implemented, seminars attended, books written, sermons preached, and theological units taught, all under the noble but misguided assumption that if we raise our game the culture will sit up and take notice. Neil Cole remarks,

> The best preachers cannot out-entertain Jay Leno and David Letterman, with their team of talented writers. The best worship band cannot put on a better show than the Rolling Stones, No Doubt, or Green Day. Our buildings are not so nice as the ones that corporate America is constructing; in fact, other religions and cults are outdoing us architecturally. Have you seen any Christian movies? Please! *We are not able to come up against the*

---

1. "Small Earthquake in Chile; Not Many Dead" won a most boring headline competition in the 1920s.

world, play its game, and win. It is a foolish strategy—and a needless one.[2]

I am not suggesting that we think we are up there with Leno, Letterman, and Gwen Stefani. If American churches cannot compete with pop culture's vast array of resources, then what chance the rest? I am not even suggesting that we are trying to entertain. What I am suggesting is this: The common thinking in Western evangelicalism is that we should corner a section of the market and play to our strengths. We never put it as crassly as that, but the sentiment is there. Find a way to propel our message *above* the noise of the marketplace and see what we can catch. But listen to Cole again:

> What we draw them *with* is what we draw them *to*. If they come expecting to be entertained, we had better entertain them if we want to keep them coming back every week. This mentality creates a vicious circle of program upgrades, staff improvements, and building campaigns to feed the consumer monster. The monster is always hungry. Pastors are burned out. Members are marginalized and lost in the programs. The lost community gets a corrupted caricature of the Kingdom of God.[3]

This is an extreme and unattractive end of the trajectory, but it *is* the trajectory. Western churches are scattered along this continuum. Most are not seeking simply to entertain. Most have good motives. None looks to burn-out, marginalize, or corrupt. However, except for extreme fringe groups, almost all are looking for a way to put themselves on a radar. Whether a local, regional, state-wide, national, or international radar, getting your church on a radar is the aim. What is to be avoided at all costs in our market society is to become a "left behind church," one that missed the corporate bus and, with shrinking numbers, funds, and pastor drawing-power, is slowly dissolving in the harsh acids of modernity.[4]

Burn out or rust out. Neither seems a particularly palatable prospect for the future of our churches. Are these the only options? They are if you play the radar game. Maybe not today, or tomorrow, however, the direction of the culture is forcing the church's hand.

But what if the premise is turned on its head? What if our goal was to fly *under* the radar? Not to fly under it in an admission of defeat, but

---

2. Cole, *Organic Church*, 94; emphasis added.
3. Ibid., 95.
4. Tucker, *Left Behind in a Megachurch World*.

to fly under it deliberately and with great purpose. What if, instead of a vain attempt at pitching ourselves *above* the noise of the "Look at me! Look at me!" culture, we pitched ourselves *below* it? What difference would it make to aim for the ground and not the sky? Reveling in our ordinariness? Rejoicing, dare I say it, in how average we are? The title of this chapter used the word "little," it could just as easily have used "average." "Average" is a swear word in our culture. No one describes themselves as average. A below-average number of people self-identify as average![5] Average is the antithesis of what most leaders and congregations desire their churches to be, but which most inevitably and logically are.

This chapter is borne from my conviction that deliberately small churches flying under the radar are far better placed to take God's gospel to the culture than a vast array of large and apparently above-average alternatives. Unless something technologically catastrophic occurs in the world during the twenty-first century the noise is set to increase. Dare we keep trying to pitch ourselves above it?

The communities I am championing are more mongrel than pedigreed. They are robust and adaptive. They will flourish in this century of rapid discontinuous change because they are well placed to accomplish mission, discipleship, and reproduction.[6] They are well placed for mission because they are *average*. They are well placed for discipleship because they are *small*. They are well placed for reproduction because they are *simple*. Average, small, and simple do not guarantee survival, but when infused with mission, discipleship, and reproduction the survival rate of these "mongrel" churches increases exponentially.

Average Church and Mission

Most of life is average. Get up, eat, feed, feed someone else, wash, work, drive, chat, watch TV, SMS, snooze, sleep. Most of life—but not all of life. There is great food, great sex, great company, great achievement. But these are so-defined because they stand out against tasteless but filling food, partially satisfying late-night-when-the-last-kid-is-in-bed-

---

5. Jean Twenge, Associate Professor of Psychology at San Diego State University, conducts studies that indicate the self-esteem movement has given people an over-inflated view of themselves.

6. Hirsch, "Adaptive Challenges."

and-the-dishes-are-done Wednesday-night sex,[7] boring company, and signing off yet another ho-hum report. Average gives meaning to great.

In the world of advertising, however, average is hell. Rescue is dependent upon product purchase. Average is the *other* guy. Hyper-reality—life lived constantly on a higher plane—is pitched as normal. All of life should be great. "The Age of the Understatement," a song on a side-project album by the lead singer of the UK band Arctic Monkeys, is wrong. This is the age of the overstatement. Everything is awesome, amazing, and thrilling. The vacant lot near me is described as a new, "exciting" office development. Concrete tilt-panels never looked so good. In the suburban super hero animated film *The Incredibles*, the villain, Syndrome, racked by jealousy, claims, "When everyone is super, no one will be."

This trend has percolated church. Type the Web addresses of big churches in your region. What does life look like? Average? Hardly! Yet a major report concluded that UK churches are not effective missionally because they do little to connect Christian faith to all of life. It blames

> the pervasive belief that some things are important to God—such as church, prayer, meetings, social action, Alpha—but that other human activities are at best neutral—work, school, college, sport, the arts, leisure, rest, sleep."[8]

Now where would Christians get that idea from, unless from church? The Crowded House missional church movement has stated the following in response to this report:

> We need non full-time leaders who can model whole-life, gospel centred missional living. It means thinking of our work-places, homes and neighbourhoods as the location of mission. We need to plan and pray for gospel relationships. This means creating church cultures in which these are normal, celebrating day-to-day gospel living in the secular world and discussing how we can use our daily routine for the gospel.[9]

---

7. "Business Time," by the New Zealand comedy and musical duo Flight of the Conchords (*Flight of the Conchords*, Sub Pop, 2008), is about exactly that.

8. From a report published by the London Institute for Contemporary Christianity in association with the Evangelical Alliance, sourced from Chester and Timmis, *Total Church*, 35.

9. Ibid., 36.

Note the words "normal" and "daily routine." These are the enemies of "on the radar" churches presenting hyper-reality and beautiful people in ecstatic worship. But for churches under the radar these words are gold. If in our mission we can infuse "normal" and "daily routine" with gospel intentionality we can impact literally millions of people living normal, daily, routine lives. If the bulk of life is average, why not play to your apparent *weaknesses*? Why not focus on the profundity of the mundane? This is hard to get, saturated as we are in thousands of advertising messages per day. There is much we have to unlearn, even for those flying under the radar with stated missional intent. Let me offer a personal example.

Our original household congregation church plant, The Local, is an eclectic mix of evangelicals. One night while discussing and praying how we wanted the Holy Spirit to work in us, some voiced their concern that we were not seeing the Spirit really changing the world. Someone asked why we were not expecting people to be raised from the dead. As we talked I marveled at how much unlearning we needed, despite having been together as a group for a year at this stage, and despite our stated desire to do church differently. So I told two stories.

I told about the young woman I had been working with that year. She had been diagnosed with diverticulitis—a painful bowel problem that often requires surgery. She and a number of the staff had decided to hold a dinner party for a psychic reading. This girl was told by the psychic that her upcoming colonoscopy would prove clear and that nothing was wrong with her. A week or so later, when the colonoscopy proved otherwise, she was upset. She needed major surgery that would require six weeks recovery. As she told us this another staff member offered her a psychic healing. At this point I interjected and said, "How about I pray for you first. I think Jesus is concerned about your condition and he is more than capable of doing something about it—you've had your psychic shot." Later that day in the board room with tears in her eyes my friend allowed me to pray for her. A few weeks later she found out though she still had the problem it could be managed and that the surgery was no longer required. "I think you praying for me worked," she told me later.

The whole group loved story number one. It had the Holy Spirit stamped all over it. But then I told story number two. I told how Paula, a friend of my wife, Jill, whom she'd met at the school gate, had been impressed by the friendliness of the women from The Local when they took Jill out for her birthday. The Local had been praying for Paula and her husband and Jill saw it as a chance for the ladies to meet. Paula was even more impressed when, for her own birthday, Jill reprised the get-together. All the girls turned up at the local Thai restaurant—with presents! As Jill, Paula, and the friend Paula had invited drove home, both ladies remarked to Jill how they'd love to belong to a community like this. Paula told her friend how our church seemed different to what she'd expected church people to be like. So far so good.

Then I asked our group this question: "Were you ladies aware as you sat in that restaurant eating green Thai curry, drinking wine, and chatting, that you were probably the only Holy Spirit community who'd turned up that night, that two women craving good community were with you all evening?" Silence as it sank in. Story number two has the Holy Spirit stamped all over it as well, it just sounds less exciting than story number one.

As the discussion concluded they resolved that next time they go out together with friends who do not know Jesus they will text a prayer to each other before turning up, and will encourage each other to be less self-focused and more other-centred.

They are learning the profundity of the mundane. They are learning that an effective mission strategy is available to them. It does not require an event external to their life rhythms to implement.[10] Paid wait staff saw to the tables, chefs prepared the meal, a business owner supplied the building, the dishes were washed by a university student. All they had to do was to turn up.

In the schema of the kingdom of God, the average is profound. As you can see it is also plentiful. Average does not have to position itself somewhere, it already *is* somewhere. A whole layer of unwieldy, unnatural, and increasingly ineffective programs can be removed from a church's missional strategy when this truth is grasped. If we are fully committed to an eschatology in which *all* of the creation is redeemed, then the mundane is a critical component in God's work in his world. The run-of-the-mill is infused with missional possibilities.

---

10. Chester, "Rhythms."

Small Church and Discipling

Every church group attempts to create an internal plausibility structure; proof that it is on the right track. Fundamentalists define themselves theologically and culturally over and against others. Liberals are moving with the times and cater for a wide range of sociopolitical and sexual variables. And evangelicals? We know we've made it when we are BIG. Size is our internal plausibility structure. For the church's first nineteen centuries congregation size was irrelevant.[11] For a mere five percent of our existence we have slavered over the prospect of being big.

A church growth mantra says that if a small church is an apple and a larger church an orange, the trick is to behave like an orange while still an apple. That makes perfect business sense. Ask any small business owner how much work they knocked back in the early years. Very little. You take the work, do the hours, convince the customer that you can play with the big boys. You act big while you are still small—paddling hard under the surface while trying to look calm above it. One magic day the hard work pays off: you are a big boy yourself now. At this happy juncture you sit back and relax. You wish! To stay in the game you have to up the ante. There is no such thing as reaching the plateau in business. "Plateau" is business speak for "terminal."

It is also church-growth speak for "terminal." The Latin word *terminus* means "boundary stone." A boundary stone marks the outer limit of your reach, your influence. Terminal cancer means the boundary stone is your gravestone—this is as far as *you* come. In church growth a church is at the outer limits of its reach and influence when it plateaus. Once it plateaus questions come to the fore. Have we reached our terminus? Should we push out the boundary stone? Plateau is the point at which the church leadership re-pitches the new (bigger) vision to the congregation. No one wants to go back to apple after tasting life as an orange.

Oranges, however, are not the only fruit. Increasingly there is a movement towards being deliberately small. Books such as *Organic Church*, *Total Church*, and *Left Behind in a Megachurch World*[12] promote apples. Meanwhile the emerging/emergent movement has been self-consciously birthed over and against the church growth movement. The internal plausibility structure of size is under serious scrutiny.

---

11. Pappas, *Inside the Small Church*, 3.
12. See the bibliography under Cole, Chester and Timmis, and Walker, respectively.

History is on the side of the small church. It is indisputable that the small church was the antecedent norm.

> On one point nearly all New Testament scholars presently agree: early Christians met almost exclusively in the homes of individual members of the congregation. For nearly three hundred years . . . Christians gathered in private houses built initially for domestic use.[13]

However, historical precedent is not reason enough to plant churches that fly under the radar.

> Our point is not a slavish adherence to homes as the location for church gatherings, or a denial of the value that purpose-built buildings can bring. The point is that, as they grew, the apostolic churches became networks of small communities rather than one large group, *to safeguard apostolic principles of church life.* It matters little whether these small groups are called churches, home groups or cells, *as long as they are the focus for the life and mission of the church.*[14]

Deliberately doing small church is not an excuse to de-clutter life in the manner of Oprah Winfrey's "The Joys of Letting Go."[15] It is a commitment to apostolic integrity and missional intentionality. I meet many Christians who yearn wistfully for smaller church, but when pressed further reveal they are too busy for big church commitments and that small church would better fit their overscheduled family life. Guess what? They will find this model of church too busy for them as well. In The Crowded House we talk about doing discipleship "life on life, eyeball to eyeball." It is less to do with church size, and more to do with how size serves discipleship.

Let me explain with some *idol* thoughts. The exposure and destruction of idolatry is discipleship's aim. Nothing has exposed my idolatries more painfully than eyeball discipleship from a concerned brother or sister who has been around my life often enough to see what I cannot. At the very end of 1 John the apostle says, "Dear children, keep yourselves from idols" (1 John 5:21). This is not an afterthought to finish the scroll. It is said in the context of a community split apart by various idolatries. In big churches preachers can denounce idolatry. What they cannot do is

---

13. Gehring, *House Church*, 1.
14. Chester and Timmis, *Total Church*, 91–92; emphasis added.
15. Walsh, "Joys of Letting Go."

daily observe how insidiously idols penetrate life, mutating and adapting to their surrounds. Old Testament idols were things of stone and wood. Today's idols are inexorable vines forcing their tendrils into every sinew and organ. Idols cannot be *managed*, they must be *removed*. Idolatry is simply the decision, considered or otherwise, to seek God's kingdom second. Idols do not want first place in our lives, they want every place. Counselors are swamped with idolatry's bitter fruit—adulteries, addictions, anxieties.

My wife Jill confronts idolatry as a clinical psychologist. She is concerned that her practice is being sustained by Christian clients. Idolatry is putting food on our table! She regularly listens as broken Christians explain how their small group knows nothing about their issue. A pastor friend of mine describes the average level of conversation in small groups as "vague sharing." He is right. The secular taxpayer is funding psychologists to Band-Aid the discipleship failures of the church.

How is the type of small church I am describing able to disciple us away from idolatry? First, a "bad" idol example—adultery. "Wait a moment," you might say, "Can you imagine the awkward silence if someone in your lounge room church piped up and told everyone they were having an affair? Some things are better referred to specialists aren't they?" True, but remember, adultery doesn't start in the bedroom, it starts in the heart (Matt 5–7). Church under the radar is a perfect place to open the heart's door in order to ensure that the bedroom door stays locked. Central to the ethos of The Crowded House is the following.

> We often think of pastoral care as something that takes place in moments of crisis. But most pastoral care takes place in the context of ordinary life, as we eat together, wash up together, play in the park, walk along the road. This preventative "care" often averts pastoral crises or helps people cope when they face difficult circumstances. But for these to be occasions of pastoral care we need to be intentional about encouraging and exhorting one another with the gospel.[16]

How does "ordinary life" in a small discipling community stop people from committing adultery? The same way idolatry encourages people to commit it—slowly and incrementally. Gospel intentionality percolates the Word of God into our hearts where it tackles idolatry's roots. In everyday life a Christian brother or sister picks up your scathing tone towards

---

16. Chester and Timmis, *Total Church*, 133.

your spouse, sees the undue attention you may be giving to someone else, or the way you overwork and underplay. The idol can be dealt with early. In the Old Testament Jerusalem was not so much destroyed by the Babylonians as revealed for what it was: a tottering structure at the point of collapse. It is the same with us. Left unchecked, sin eats away at us like white ants to the point where we are pushovers. Life-on-life, eyeball-to-eyeball discipleship is a great preventative treatment.

Now for the "good" idol—busyness. How does "ordinary life" in a small discipling community stop us from over-scheduling? The same way idolatry encourages over-scheduling—slowly and incrementally. Whilst I have met a handful of Christians who have shipwrecked themselves on the rocks of adultery, I have lost count of the number who are shipwrecking their faith on busyness yet who believe that is just how things are, as if it were neutral. Gadgets have not, nor ever will, slow life down.

> Access to a car certainly cuts down the time it takes to *do* certain things, but it also increases people's expectations concerning what they can and should do. The greater availability of the car has resulted in a decline in its use for recreation.[17]

We are being consumed with busyness. The trend in larger churches is to pay professionals to fulfill what were once volunteer responsibilities. We risk nurturing an overscheduled generation towards efficient rather than effective discipleship. While no man is an island, increasingly every family is, as busyness takes a stranglehold. Busyness is killing discipleship and mission in the twenty-first century. The bigger the church the more professional structures are in place to cosset this idolatry. This may not be the intention, but it will be the outcome if busyness is sanctified by our church model rather than challenged by it. The overscheduled life is the idol Christian families are most reluctant to give up. They may not say as much, but when challenged to give their family's time to the community of God's people *first*, they baulk. It is seen as a plausibility issue. Twenty people committing to costly Christian community together can't offer their children the same future that two sports, one musical instrument, a social event, and extra tutoring in maths can offer. Tragically this is the case.

---

17. Banks *Tyranny of Time*, 83. Almost three decades later the issues are just as pressing as Tim Chester's *The Busy Christian's Guide to Busyness* reveals.

Can large churches do effective discipleship? Yes, but read their Web sites. All large churches claim that effective discipleship occurs in the context of small groups! Big churches wants to get 100 percent buy-in for small groups. Missional household churches have it already. If discipleship is critical to Christian communities, and apples are *naturally* better placed than oranges to affect it, one question remains: What is the orange achieving that the apple is not already taking care of?

Simple Church and Reproduction

Vast swathes of suburbs in fifty US cities are set to be demolished to ensure survival. Something is wrong in a rust belt city like Flint, Michigan. Empty suburbs are being bulldozed and left to return to nature. Precious resources have wasted as rubbish trucks have collected a single rubbish bag per week from some streets. Grand hotels have stood empty. Flint spokesman Dan Kildee partly blames America's obsession with size for the city's decline, but, in a positive spin, likened the demolition to the pruning of an overgrown fruit tree to encourage it to bear fruit again.[18]

Such cities have declined as the future has caught up with the US car industry. Cheaper imports, bad management, complicated union deals, and climate concerns over large "yank-tanks" have taken their toll. The world has changed and the industry didn't begin until it was too late. Whole communities have lost their jobs in the knock-on effect.

How different is the Chinese church's response when threatened by the Cultural Revolution. That church movement is now eighty million strong. Alan Hirsch concludes,

> One of the "gifts" that persecution seems to confer on the persecuted is that it enables them to distil the essence of the message and thus access it in a new way . . . in order to survive in the context of persecution, they also have to jettison all unnecessary impediments . . . to condense and purify their core message that keeps them both faithful and hopeful.[19]

The future has caught up with the Western church. One thousand young people walk away from the UK church every week. US church attendance is spiraling, especially in the country's north. Europe is all

18. Leonard, "US Cities."
19. Hirsch *Forgotten Ways*, 85.

but dead. Australia is deeply secular. We need more mongrel churches, churches that follow the lead of the Chinese church, not the US auto industry. We need churches well adapted to any future. Go on, pick an impossibly dystopian future for the West—persecution, financial collapse, social disorder, natural disaster. Now view your church's structure through that prism. How will it fare? The simpler the structure the better its chances, that's my guess. Think that is far-fetched? Take a look at the dystopian future we are witnessing in which Christian underpinnings are collapsing: a future in which humility, once alien to the pre-Christian Roman Empire, is again alien; in which freedom of speech, a concept deeply Christian in its roots, is being brutalized; in which charity, yet another idea foreign to Imperial Rome, is increasingly nonexistent; in which the debate over the sanctity of life is settling in the negative. Is your church ready for this future? It needs to be.

Neil Cole tells of how he shared with his daughter a dream he had about her starting a church with her friends. To his surprise and delight, she did. Neil takes up the story:

> I asked the students what was the biggest church they had ever been to. Living in California there are many options of megachurches, and a number of churches were mentioned, ranging in size from two thousand attendees to more than fifteen thousand. I then told them that I think Satan is more intimidated by this little church of fifteen high school students than by any of those Godzilla-sized churches. . . . I showed them why I thought this way: "How many of you think you could start a church like one of those megachurches?" No one raised a hand. I asked, "How many of you think you could start a church like this one?" and all raised their hands. I asked them to look around the room at all the raised hands, and I said with a newfound soberness, "I assure you, Satan is terrified by this."[20]

Our culture is hurtling towards pride, fear, lovelessness, and killing for convenience. Only well-pruned, stripped-back Christian communities of humility, freedom, love, and life offer strong enough plausibility structures to survive and reproduce. If big church is struggling to do mission and discipleship in the present, what chance the future? The Crowded House founder, Steve Timmis, says that while a big light can shine over a city, it takes little shards of light to infiltrate the nooks and

---

20. Cole, *Organic Church*, 211–12.

crannies. He talks about scattering Sheffield in the UK with "communities of light." By happy coincidence the gospel shards essential to this task are the easiest to produce and reproduce.

My favorite (and only) engineering maxim is "Add lightness and simplicity." The best-functioning machines are the most simple. But you can't add lightness. You can't add simplicity. These qualities require stuff to be *taken away*. Like Flint, Michigan, churches can prepare themselves through a humbling but essential pruning. Derelict suburbs will be returned to nature. Empty homages to the past will be bulldozed. Profligacy will be shunned. All unnecessary impediments jettisoned. What will be left? Ordinary life. Yes, but ordinary life infused with Jesus. Cole says, "It is not the local church that will change the world; it is Jesus."[21] The church has a future because the once dead and buried, now resurrected and ascended Jesus *is* its future.

The church's survival kit is Jesus. So start with him. Gather a group of Christians who know that their survival depends on Jesus and not their pension fund: a group who talks to, with, and about Jesus. That's discipleship and mission right there. When you've done that spend even more time with each other. Serve, love, and forgive each other because Jesus did that for you. Eat, share, and bear with each other just as he did. Spend leisure time, give money, and host unconverted friends with each other. Learn the Bible together. Sing. Break bread and drink wine. Look after each other's kids. Text prayer to each other. Eat lunch in the city with each other. Invite a non-Christian colleague to join. Call sin for what it is just like Jesus did. Offer grace for what it is, just like he did too. Seek the welfare of your suburb. Pray through the stuff of life—relationships, heartaches, directions. Make major decisions collectively—jobs, houses, travels. Don't fill your house with Christians, leave room for those who don't know Jesus yet. Once you have done the above, do it again with other people.

Isn't this a cop-out? Where are the church planting strategies? Where is the networking? Be patient, that stuff will come. But it cannot come *first*. A wise man told me to avoid becoming the church planting expert and to concentrate on planting a few, failing the odd one. Do not bypass talking about Jesus in your rush to talk about talking about Jesus. That will be hard as it is the default mode for those who like to offer solutions. We have talked about talking about Jesus enough.

21. Ibid., xxiv.

If you do all of this and it works, the headlines in the newspaper will still never mention you. The headlines in *Leadership* magazine may never mention you either. If you can cope with this then you are a step closer to belonging to the church of the future.

> The revolution will not be televised, will not be televised . . .
> The revolution will be live.[22]

---

22. Gil Scott-Heron, "The Revolution Will Not Be Televised," *Pieces of a Man* (Hi Horse, 1971).

9

Cyprian and *The Pilgrim's Progress*

EDWINA MURPHY

Introduction

I would like to introduce or perhaps re-acquaint you with two prominent Christians in the history of the church. Cyprian was the bishop of Carthage in the mid-third century and is perhaps best known for his views on the unity of the church and the impossibility of salvation for those outside it. Born sometime between 200 and 210, he was a man of considerable property and wealth, most likely inherited.[1] He became a Christian in middle age under the influence of the aged presbyter Caecilianus.[2] Echoes of his prior career as a *rhetor* remained in his skillful use of words.[3] Within few enough years to be still regarded a neophyte, and possibly not even previously appointed as a presbyter, Cyprian be-

---

1. The birth date is arrived at by working backwards from Pontius's assertion that he was well established in his profession by the time of his conversion, and that neither Cyprian nor Pontius felt it necessary to defend his age as inappropriate to his appointment. See Sage, *Cyprian*, 103–7; Clarke, *Letters*, 1:14–15.

2. Pontius, *Vita Cypriana* 4.

3. One may note, however, a change in style from *Ad Donatum*, with its somewhat overblown language, to a more restrained elegance in his later works. See Bardy, *Christian Latin Literature*, 41–45.

came bishop of Carthage in 248 or 249.[4] His election owed much to the support of the laity, and being opposed by a group of presbyters.[5]

John Bunyan was a dissenting preacher in seventeenth-century England who repudiated the established church, identifying himself as a Baptist.[6] Born in November 1628 in Elstow, Bedford, he became, as his father had been, a tinker or brazier.[7] He had managed to gain but a rudimentary education.[8] Despised both for his lowly status and for his religious views (which some feared were also seditious), his scoffing contemporaries could not have imagined that one of the classic works of English literature would come from his pen.[9]

Thus far, the two men would seem to have nothing in common except the designation "Christian." Yet for all the differences of time and

---

4. Pontius, *Vita Cypriana* 5. The dating of Cyprian's baptism and whether or not he was appointed as a presbyter remains unclear. Jerome, *De viris illustribus*, 67, believes he was a presbyter, albeit briefly. In support for his belief that Cyprian was first ordained as a presbyter, Sage, in *Cyprian*, 135n3, quotes Pontius, *Vita Cypriana* 3.3: "*presbyterium vel sacerdotium statim accepit.*" But see the discussion of this phrase by Bobertz ("Cyprian," 97), who considers that Cyprian had an "immediate rise from novice to bishop." Burns, *Cyprian*, 16, 189n49, depicts Cyprian as being chosen by the people as bishop "without his having passed through the lower clerical ranks," making reference to Pontius, *Vita Cypriana* 5. Eusebius's account is found in *Historia ecclesiastica* 6.29.2–4. The date for his appointment as bishop is based on Cyprian's defense of his ministry in *Ep.* 59.6.1 (dated 252; see Clarke, *Letters*, 1:235–36). He states that "he has been held in esteem by his people for four years now as bishop." As Sage (*Cyprian*, 138) notes, "The quadrennium in the Roman system of counting could signify any period from three years and a day to four years less a day."

5. Pontius, *Vita Cypriana* 5.

6. His church did, however, practice open membership. See Kingsley, "John Bunyan," 6–7.

7. See Wakefield, *Bunyan*, 6. He described his family's background in *Grace Abounding to the Chief of Sinners*: "For my descent then, it was, as is well known by many, of a low and inconsiderable generation; my father's house being of that rank that is meanest, and most despised of all the families in the land" (17). This had not always been the case, however, but was the result of the family's decline from being landowners several generations earlier to living in one of the "humbler abodes in Elstow." See Greaves, *Glimpses*, 3–4.

8. Bunyan, *Grace Abounding*, 18.

9. Hill, *Turbulent, Seditious and Factious People*, 107, writes, "For the Bedfordshire gentry Bunyan's preaching, even if it did not directly incite to rebellion, fanned the discontent that many felt with the restored regime and church. Subjectively, Bunyan could honestly deny subversive intentions. Objectively, his refusal to promise not to preach was threatening. The very claim that preaching was his vocation was subversive; his vocation was being a tinker." See also, Hill, "John Bunyan," 13.

place, status and polity, Bunyan and Cyprian have a very strong, if at first glance unexpected, common understanding of what the Christian life entails. At the most fundamental level, this is because Bunyan and Cyprian were men of one and the same book. Despite his excellent education and prior career, Cyprian gave up almost all classical allusions and replaced them with the biblical text.[10] Bunyan, perhaps with less opportunity to do otherwise, liked to boast that his learning came from the Bible rather than classical sources.[11] Given that he was influenced by a number of authors, however, we should not take his claims of *sola Scriptura* to extremes.[12] Galen correctly states the case: "Bunyan recognized the value of Christian tradition, though he refused to grant it equal authority alongside the Bible."[13] In terms of wealth there was again an arrival at a similar position from different directions. Bunyan was poor by birth, whereas Cyprian demonstrated his commitment to his new faith by selling his property and giving it to the poor, although Pontius tells us that his *horti* were restored to him by the indulgence of God and he remained a person of substantial means.[14]

However, the factor that produces such harmony in the views of two such different men, and distinguishes them from any number of other faithful Christians with whom they share common ground on the first two points, is that both belonged to an essentially gathered church that was not looked upon with favor by the state. Greaves's statement regarding Bunyan could equally be applied to Cyprian:

> For Bunyan, as for his pilgrims, the world is the battleground between good and evil, light and darkness. Ostensibly, he restricted militancy to the spiritual realm, but his willingness to stand firm regardless of penal statutes and persecutory acts was by nature a political as well as a religious act in a society whose rulers claimed and exercised the power to compel obedience to their view of right religion.[15]

---

10. As Clarke, *Letters*, 1:17, notes: "This can only be the result of conscious rejection and restriction." For a detailed account of Cyprian's use of Scripture, see Fahey, *Cyprian*.

11. Greaves, *Glimpses*, 5.

12. Hill, *Turbulent, Seditious*, 69.

13. Johnson, *Prisoner*, 198.

14. Pontius, *Vita Cypriana* 2.7; 15.1. From his place of withdrawal he was able to send his own funds to assist those in need. See *Epp.* 7.2; 13.7.

15. Greaves, *Glimpses*, 250.

Both men knew what it was to live out faith in a hostile world, and they were alert to the dangers that must be faced and overcome in order to achieve the promised hope. The decade of Cyprian's episcopacy in Carthage, which ended with his martyrdom in 258, was a turbulent period for the North African church. The Decian persecution, schisms, and plague raised questions regarding the identity of the community, its place within imperial society, and God's control of history. As bishop, it was Cyprian's responsibility to provide answers, thereby uniting his flock and keeping them on the path to salvation. Likewise, Bunyan was a preacher and pastor who lived in a time when those who desired to worship according to their conscience rather than the dictates of the established church were liable to be persecuted by the state. Whilst not imitating Cyprian's martyrdom, Bunyan did suffer twelve years of imprisonment.[16]

During his imprisonment, one means by which Bunyan sought to stimulate people to embark on the journey of faith, and having begun, to persevere, was through his most famous work, *The Pilgrim's Progress*.[17] By examining the events in part 1 of the work and comparing them with Cyprian's letters and treatises, the similarities between Bunyan and Cyprian in their understanding of the nature of this world, the trials and victories of Christian life, martyrdom, the dangers of wealth, death, and the hope of the life to come will become apparent.[18] Their summary of the terrain may provide invaluable assistance for us in our own pilgrimages.

---

16. Hill, *Turbulent, Seditious*, 109. Bunyan did consider that he might be put to death, he and struggled for many weeks, questioning whether he could die with courage and whether in the end he would indeed be saved, until he came to a realization "that it was for the word and way of God that I was in this condition, wherefore I was engaged not to flinch an hair's breadth from it. . . . I am for going on, and venturing my eternal state with Christ, whether I have comfort here or no" (Bunyan, *Grace Abounding*, 177–79).

17. Recent scholarship tends towards dating its composition in the second part of this main period of imprisonment rather than to the six months he spent in prison several years later. See Hill, *Turbulent, Seditious*, 197–98; Greaves, *Glimpses of Glory*, 210–27; cf. Brown, *John Bunyan*, 239–49.

18. In restricting the discussion to a more manageable text, I am not intending to discount the unity of the two parts, nor the significant reinterpretation of some events in the first part in light of the second. For more on the relationship between the two, see Austin, "Figural Logic."

Following Christ

Bunyan and Cyprian shared a conviction that following Christ means relinquishing this world, a world under judgment. Christian's birthplace is the City of Destruction, signifying, as Stranahan notes, "the realm in which all persons begin their earthly lives,"[19] a city that "will be burned with fire from Heaven."[20] To leave, therefore, represents no enduring sacrifice, given that ahead lies "Life! Life! Eternal Life!"[21] Understanding this, Christian responds to the concern of Obstinate for the loss of friends and comforts with the assurance that "all which you shall forsake is not worthy to be compared with a little of that, that I am seeking to enjoy."[22] The Interpreter similarly shows a picture to Christian in which a man has "the World as cast behind him, and . . . a Crown hangs over his head" to demonstrate "that slighting and despising things that are present, for the love that he hath to his Master's service, he is sure in the World that comes next, to have Glory for his reward."[23]

Whilst Cyprian makes use of pagan commonplaces regarding the old age of the world and its coming end in his apologetics, he sees God's action above all.[24] He warns concerning the inexorable "day of judgment which Holy Scripture announces saying: 'Howl ye, for the day of the Lord is near: it shall come as a destruction from the Lord.'"[25] Cyprian presents hope, as does Bunyan, in the context of a lack of hope in this world. In *Ad Donatum,* one of his earliest works, Cyprian demonstrates

---

19. Stranahan, "Bunyan," 284.
20. Bunyan, *Pilgrim's Progress*, 4.
21. Ibid., 4.
22. Ibid., 5.

23. Ibid., 25–26. The Interpreter also shows Christian two children, Passion and Patience, with the lesson understood by Christian to be that "it is not best to covet things that are now, but to wait for things to come." The Interpreter affirms him, "For the things that are seen are Temporal; but the things that are not seen are Eternal," Ibid., 27–29.

24. Most fully in *Ad Demetrianum* 3–5. Daniélou, *History of Early Christian Doctrine*, 3.253, among others, has noted Cyprian's use of natural reasoning in this apologetic work rather than the scriptural argument which he employs when addressing Christians. Other references to the "decline" of the world are to be found in *De catholicae ecclesiae unitate* 16 and *Epp.* 58.2.1; 67.7. Cyprian is at variance with the ancient traditions in that, as Castagna, "Vecchiaia e morte," 252n23, notes, "in Cyprian, the old age of the world is laden with implications of hope, not of pessimism."

25. *Demetr.* 22.

to his friend the corruption of the world with the goal that he will "rejoice with greater joy that [he has] escaped from it."[26] Even prior to the threat of persecution, Cyprian emphasizes that the Christian hope lies outside the natural realm. True security is to be "released from the snares of the entangling world, to be purged of the dregs of earth for the light of immortality."[27] The dichotomy between the temporal and the eternal is never far from his thoughts.

However, one is not translated from this world to the world to come, from the City of Destruction to the Celestial City, in an instant. The journey that must be undertaken forms the substance of *The Pilgrim's Progress*.[28] There are many trials the pilgrim must overcome.[29] Of the three figurative meanings of "the Way" that Stranahan identifies, the one most similar to Cyprian's understanding is that which represents the "proper and necessary conduct of a Christian: those who leave it for other roads, or who take short cuts to enter on it, never attain the Christian's reward."[30]

If the Christian life is a pilgrimage, it is one in which there are many battles to be fought. Christian meets with the fiend Apollyon in the Valley of Humiliation, from whom he is tempted to turn and flee, but considering "he had no Armour for his back" engages in the contest.[31] Despite almost being slain by his enemy's accusations, he overcomes him and quotes, "Nay, in all these things we are more than Conquerors, through him that loved us."[32] So, too, he passes through the Valley of the Shadow of Death in the dark, with a Ditch on one hand and a Mire on

---

26. It may be his first, as Jean Molager, *Cyprien*, 12, suggests: "[The] *Quod idola* is probably not by him, and the *Ad Quirinum* does not appear to be prior to it. . . . [I]t is the first of Cyprian's truly original treatises." It is usually dated to soon after his conversion. See Sage, *Cyprian*, 380; Cyprian *Don*. 6. Estimates therefore vary from 246 to 248.

27. *Don*. 14.

28. Greaves, *Glimpses of Glory*, 227–28, provides a succinct summary of the plot.

29. Hill, *Turbulent, Seditious*, 201–9, summarizes the discussion regarding possible antecedents for *The Pilgrim's Progress*. Stranahan, "Bunyan," 280, believes that Bunyan's primary written source was Hebrews 11–12.

30. The other two are the span of a Christian's life and the "unchanging sequence of religious experiences that must be encountered by Christians in the present state of things . . . though as individuals they may have different adventures along the Way" (Stranahan, "Bunyan," 289).

31. Bunyan, *Pilgrim's Progress*, 58.

32. Ibid., 63, quoting Rom 8:37.

the other, emphasizing the narrowness of the Way.[33] Fiends threaten to assault him, and it is only when he cries out, "*I will walk in the Strength of the Lord God*" that he is free from them.[34]

When Evangelist again meets with Christian and Faithful on the road and hears the story of their travels so far, he is glad "not that you met with Trials, but that you have been Victors, and for that you have (notwithstanding many weaknesses) continued in the way to this very day."[35] The overwhelming necessity of staying in the Way is again demonstrated when, finding it becoming rough, Christian disregards Hopeful's concern and decides to leave it for a more pleasant path that appears to be going in the same direction.[36] This episode results in their imprisonment in Doubting Castle, owned by the giant Despair. Here they almost lose all hope until, after a night of prayer, Christian remembers that he has the key of Promise with which they gain their liberty.[37] As Furlong notes,

> Whatever [Christian's] weaknesses, however, he is a man armed with one important piece of knowledge; life as he used to live it is no longer tolerable, and the only remedy is to persevere in his difficult journey.[38]

Throughout, Christ is both the entrance to the Way[39] and the means by which the pilgrim gains victory. It is his promises that provide the pilgrim liberty and it is hope in him that sustains Christian in his quest for a glorious eternity in his presence.

This perseverance in hope is a central theme for Cyprian. The one who endures to the end will be saved.[40] The bishop expounds upon Romans 8:24–25:

---

33. Ibid., 66.
34. Ibid., 67–68.
35. Ibid., 96.
36. "The Pilgrims now, to gratify the Flesh/Will seek its Ease; but, oh! how they afresh/Do thereby plunge themselves new Griefs into!/Who seek to please the Flesh, themselves undo" (ibid., 128).
37. Ibid., 125–35.
38. Furlong, *Puritan's Progress*, 106.
39. Bunyan, *Pilgrim's Progress*, 4.
40. Matt 10:22b, cited six times by Cyprian with slight variations in the wording (Farhey, *Cyprian*, 296–97).

> We must endure and persevere, beloved brethren, so that, having been admitted to the hope of truth and liberty, we can finally attain that same truth and liberty, because the very fact that we are Christians is a source [*res*] of faith and hope. However, in order that hope and faith may reach their fruition, there is need of patience. For we do not strive for present glory, but for a future one, according to what Paul the Apostle teaches, saying, "For in hope we were saved. But hope that is seen is not hope. For how can a man hope for what he sees? But if we hope for what we do not see, we wait for it with patience." Patient waiting is necessary that we may fulfill what we have begun to be, and through God's help, that we may attain what we hope for and believe.[41]

Here Cyprian's strong orientation to the future, noted by Studer, is clearly discernable.[42] Hope is reliant upon patience to bring it to its fulfillment, but that same hope of glory is what provides the Christian with the ongoing motivation to endure. This patience is not only a passive virtue, but an active one, as may be seen from the following.[43]

> It is patience that both commends us to God and saves us for God. . . . It is this patience which strongly fortifies the foundations of our faith. It is this patience which sublimely promotes the growth of hope. It directs our action, so that we can keep to the way of Christ while we make progress because of his forbearance. It ensures our perseverance as sons of God while we imitate the patience of the Father.[44]

The importance of ecclesial discipline to Cyprian has been widely acknowledged, but the essential link between "keeping to the way of Christ" and hope has been frequently overlooked.[45] He advises a fellow bishop,

> Accordingly, our dearest brother, you must ensure that the unruly do not die or perish, by guiding the brethren, as best you

---

41. *De bono patientiae* 13; see also 21.
42. Studer, "Hoffnung," 1211.
43. Ayedze, "Tertullian," 214–17.
44. *Pat.* 20.
45. Clarke, "Two Mid-Third Century Bishops," 321, says that "*Disciplina* is this man's favoured word (collapsing doctrinal teaching, church regulation and order, and moral duty)." Dunn, "Infected Sheep," 20, suggests that "The questions of discipline and of maintaining the integrity of the community in the face of both external and internal threats were the primary focus of Cyprian's episcopal activities."

can, with saving advice and by taking counsel for the salvation of each individually. Straight and narrow is the way by which we enter into life, but great, exceedingly great is our reward when we reach glory.[46]

The maintenance of discipline is not an end in itself, but is always presented as a means of achieving the glorious hope to which Christians have been called.

In the often threatening world in which Bunyan and Cyprian lived, the dangers faced were not only metaphorical; martyrdom was a real possibility. In seeking to motivate pilgrims to remain steadfast, their language is at times almost identical. When Evangelist meets with Christian and Faithful on the road, he encourages them,

> The Crown is before you, and it is an incorruptible one; so run, that you may obtain it. . . . Hold fast therefore that you have, let no man take your Crown. . . . Let the Kingdom be always before you, and believe steadfastly concerning things that are invisible . . . set your faces like a flint; you have all power in Heaven and Earth on your side.[47]

He warns them that they are about to reach Vanity Fair, where

> [One] or both of you must seal the testimony which you hold, with Blood; but be you faithful unto Death, and the King will give you a Crown of Life. He that shall die there, although his death will be unnatural, and his pains perhaps great, he will yet have the better of his fellow; not only because he will be arrived at the Celestial City soonest, but because he will escape many miseries that the other will meet with in the rest of his Journey.[48]

As predicted, Faithful is tried and sentenced to a cruel death, but is immediately taken by a waiting chariot "the clouds with Sound of Trumpet, the nearest way to the Celestial Gate."[49] Christian, however, is remanded back to prison and then escapes, the song on his lips honoring his companion's profession and contrasting Faithful's immortality with the punishment destined for his persecutors.[50]

---

46. *Ep* 4.5.1. See also *De habitu virginum* 1; *De dominica oratione* 1.
47. Bunyan, *Pilgrim's Progress*, 96.
48. Ibid., 97.
49. Ibid., 109.
50. Ibid., 110.

As Bunyan used the term "crown" to designate what is the martyr's due, so it is Cyprian's favored way of describing the rewards awaiting those who confess their faith, drawing on Paul's language of the arena.

> This is the contest of our faith, wherein we do battle, wherein we conquer, wherein we are crowned. This is the contest which the blessed Apostle Paul has also revealed to us, the contest in which we are to run and to attain to a crown of glory. "Do you not know," he says, "that of those who run in a race, all indeed run but only one receives the palm. So run that you may win it. In their case their object is to receive a corruptible crown, but ours an incorruptible."[51]

Martyrs are not alone in their struggles, however, for Christ wrestles within his servants. "He joins battle Himself, in the blows of our contest He Himself both gives and wins the crowns."[52]

In *Epistle 58*, his letter to the laity in Thibaris written around May 253, there is a heightened apocalyptic mood.[53] There is a clear sense that the final battle is approaching, and Cyprian uses all his considerable powers to motivate his brethren to withstand the assault. At such a time "we should have no thoughts other than for the glories of eternal life and the crown that is won by confessing the Lord."[54] It is a matter for rejoicing "for it is when persecutions come that the crowns of faith are awarded, that the soldiers of God are tested, and that the heavens stand open for the martyred."[55] As Christian's song suggested, a time is coming when the present order will be reversed. Martyrs will reign with Christ and judge those who are currently putting them to death.[56]

---

51. *Ep.* 10.4.2–3, quoting 1 Cor 9:24–25, omitting verse 25a. See *Epp.* 6.1.2; 6.3.1; 6.4.

52. *Ep.* 10.4.4. Such rewards are, however, reserved for those who, like Abel, have "both the justice and peace of the Lord." The "discordant and dissident" shall not gain entry into the kingdom of heaven, even if they have been slain for the name, reflecting Cyprian's emphasis on the unity of the church, which is sustained by charity (*Dom. or.* 24, quoting 1 John 3:15).

53. Clarke, *Letters*, 3:226.

54. *Ep.* 58.1.2.

55. *Ep.* 58.3.1. Such rewards are available to all those who have stood fast in their confession, regardless of the direct cause of their death (*Ep.* 58.4.2).

56. *Ad Fortunatum* 13. This element is also present in the words of the Shining Ones as they escort the pilgrims to the Celestial City. "When [the King of Glory] shall come with Sound of Trumpet in the Clouds, as upon the wings of the Wind, you shall come with him; and when he shall sit upon the Throne of Judgment, you shall sit by him; yea,

In another inversion of worldly values, *The Pilgrim's Progress* displays what we might call "God's preferential option for the poor"—wealth is depicted as an impediment to salvation. As Hill notes, "Undesirable characters in *The Pilgrim's Progress* . . . are almost obsessively labelled as lords and ladies, gentlemen and gentlewomen."[57] In one demonstration of this, Christian and Hopeful (converted by the witness of Christian and Faithful in Vanity Fair) are joined by By-ends of Fair Speech, who claims to

> differ in Religion from those of a stricter sort, yet but in two small points: First, We never strive against Wind and Tide. Secondly, We are always most zealous when Religion goes in his Silver Slippers; we love much to walk with him in the street, if the Sun shines and the People applaud him.[58]

This attitude is all the more stark for its juxtaposition with the pillorying of the pilgrims in Vanity Fair, where Faithful has given his life for his faith. Christian proclaims,

> If you will go with us, you must go against Wind and Tide; the which, I perceive, is against your opinion: You must also own Religion in his Rags as well as when in his Silver Slippers; and stand by him too when bound in Irons, as well as when he walketh the streets with Applause.[59]

Such a commitment is rejected by By-ends, and unsurprisingly it is not long before he and his companions are lured by Demas and the promise of riches and perish from the Way.[60] Christian and Hopeful, having avoided the danger, then see the "Pillar of Salt into which *Lot's* wife was turned, for her looking back with a *covetous heart*, while she was going from Sodom for safety."[61]

---

and when he shall pass Sentence upon all the workers of Iniquity, let them be angels or men; you also shall have a voice in that Judgment, because they were his and your Enemies" (Bunyan, *Pilgrim's Progress*, 185).

57. Hill, *Turbulent, Seditious*, 215.
58. Bunyan, *Pilgrim's Progress*, 111.
59. Ibid., 112–13.
60. "By-ends and Silver Demas both agree;/One calls, the other runs, that he may be/A Sharer in his Lucre, so these two/Take up in this World, and no further go" (ibid., 122). As Sharrock, *John Bunyan*, 85, notes, "Demas is chosen as the symbol of covetousness because of St. Paul's words about him ('Demas hath forsaken me, having loved this present world', 2 Tim 4:10)."
61. Bunyan, *Pilgrim's Progress*, 123.

It is perhaps unsurprising that a man of humble circumstances such as Bunyan would believe wealth to be a danger to faith, but a similar attitude is held by Cyprian, one of the privileged few of his society.[62] In *De lapsis* he identifies the attachment of the rich to their riches as the cause of their failure to confess, and declares that if they had followed the Lord's admonition to "sell all thou hast and give to the poor" they would have been able to be overcome, since their treasure—and heart—would have been in heaven.[63] He further elaborates on this theme, dwelling on the rich compensation that will be received in return for the "small, insignificant losses of this world."[64] Those who leave property or family for the sake of the kingdom of God will receive "seven times more in the present time, and in the world to come life everlasting." Such losses are not to be feared, but rather desired, because of the great heavenly reward.[65] Furthermore, these treasures are eternal and free from the potential of loss or damage which may be suffered by those on earth.[66] Cyprian urges his flock not to increase their patrimony to the detriment of their standing before God, but to go into partnership with Christ in their earthly possessions, that they may be made co-heirs of his heavenly kingdom.[67]

When Christian and Hopeful arrive at the River separating this world from the next, Death is presented as an unavoidable part of the journey.[68] Christian suffers from the doubts that have plagued him at various times throughout his journey and is almost overcome, but as he is encouraged by Hopeful and, again, recalls the promises of God, he makes his way across.[69]

Cyprian wrote *De mortalitate* in 252 or 253 to exhort his congregation during the plague that was ravaging Carthage.[70] In it, as Scourfield

---

62. Clarke, *Letters*, 1:14.
63. *De lapsis* 11, quoting Matt 19:21.
64. *Laps.* 12.
65. The same pattern, Luke 18:29 followed by 6:22, is found in *Ep.* 58.2.3.
66. *De opera et eleemosynis* 7, quoting Matt 6:19–21; *Hab. virg.* 11 (allusion).
67. *Eleem.* 13.
68. Bunyan, *Pilgrim's Progress*, 181.
69. Ibid., 181–83.
70. It is probable that the plague reached Carthage by 252, and the treatise is often dated to that same year, although Scourfield, "*De mortalitate* of Cyprian," 23, believes it may have been written in 253.

notes, he presents death as something "positive and advantageous."[71] Cyprian does not so much console those who have lost loved ones, as emphasize the advantages of death as a means whereby the Christian is freed from the devil, the storms of the world, and temptations of the flesh to join Christ and those who have gone before in the heavenly kingdom.[72] To die is to "pass by death to immortality,"[73] so one should not fear death but rather dwell on the immortality which follows.[74] This is not true only in this work, but is a constant theme in all his writings. To be summoned from this world is to enter paradise and the kingdom.[75] All the faithful will join the martyrs in living and reigning with Christ.[76] To die is to be reunited with dear ones (parents, brothers, children) who await us, and to enter into "the highest possible and everlasting happiness," celebrating eternity with all the faithful—apostles, prophets, martyrs, virgins, and the merciful.[77]

The Shining Ones present a similar vision to the pilgrims as they ascend the hill beyond the River. In a fairly traditional account,[78] a distinctive note is that "the joys of the city are a relief from suffering—both from the fear of death and judgment that causes the pilgrims to flee from the City of Destruction, and from the perils that they encounter along

---

71. Ibid., 15.

72. *Mort.* 3, 4, 22, 26.

73. Ibid., 22.

74. Ibid., 24. See also *Don.* 14. "[Now] the things of heaven are succeeding those of earth, and great things small, and eternal things, transitory. What place is there here for anxiety and worry? Who in the midst of these things is fearful and sad save he who lacks hope and faith? (*Mort.* 2).

75. *Mort.* 18, 26. See Hill, *Regnum Caelorum*, 145. In reflecting on the hours of prayer, Cyprian gives an insight into his vision of the future of the believers in the kingdom, in which there will be "day alone without the intervention of night." He calls on those "who by the indulgence of God have been recreated spiritually and reborn" to imitate what they are destined to be, not ceasing here also to pray and to give thanks (*Dom. or.* 36). As Hamman, "Le rythme," 172–73, says, by praying day and night "we repeat from here below our role in eternity. Vigilance gives prayer its eschatological dimension."

76. *Fort.* 12. See also *Mort.* 2, 21. Daley, *Hope of the Early Church*, 42, correctly emphasizes the distinctiveness of Cyprian in this respect.

77. *Mort.* 26.

78. Angels, Abraham, Isaac, Jacob, and the Prophets all welcome the pilgrims to the Heavenly Jerusalem where they will wear Crowns of Gold and see the Holy One as he is. Bunyan, *Pilgrim's Progress*, 184–88.

the way."[79] Further, Bunyan emphasizes "the reality of this transcendent community of the blessed who enjoy actual communion with God and express their joy in melodious praise."[80] As Greaves notes, *The Pilgrim's Progress* is predominately about sanctification.[81]

> This is not a period free of recurring struggle, doubt, and even despair. . . . From the moment of justification the believer does not experience perseverance as absolute certainty, but must resolve, as Evangelist tells Christian and Faithful, to run for the crown.[82]

Temptations that may waylay the pilgrim seem to lie at every turn. One of the more subtle, and perhaps all the more dangerous for it, is that of conforming to "this world." The Baptist ideal to which Bunyan bore witness was that of a holy community—men and women regenerated by grace and living in accordance with the hope to which they are been called. Perhaps this is part of our heritage that needs to be reclaimed; to be distinguished by our growing conformity to Christ and alignment with his purposes for the world.

If for Bunyan the Christian life is a pilgrimage, for Cyprian it is a contest. This is not a matter for despair but a cause for rejoicing, as there is no crown without a victory, no victory without a preceding battle.[83] We may not confront the persecution that the North African church faced (and which is still a reality for many of our brothers and sisters around the world), but that does not mean we are not involved in a spiritual struggle. Every challenge of life is an opportunity for the Christian to respond in a way consistent with the gospel.

> Peace also has its crown, by which we are crowned as the victor of many a varied combat, after the adversary has been laid low and subdued. To have overcome lust is the palm of continence. To have resisted wrath and injury is the crown of patience. Triumph over avarice is to spurn money. Praise of faith is to endure the adversities of the world by faith in the future. And he who is not

---

79. Stranahan, "Bunyan," 287.

80. Knott, "Bunyan," 203. The present dimension of the corporate Christian life is more fully rendered by Bunyan in part 2 of *The Pilgrim's Progress*. See Knott, "Holy Community," 208.

81. Greaves, *Glimpses of Glory*, 262.

82. Ibid.

83. *Mort.* 12.

proud in prosperity obtains the glory of humility. And he who is inclined to the mercifulness of befriending the poor gains the retribution of a heavenly treasure. And he who knows not how to be jealous and, being of one mind and kind, loves his brethren, is honored with the reward of love and peace. We run daily in this contest of virtues; we arrive at these palms and crowns of justice without interruption of time.[84]

We tend to be people who seek immediate gratification. Bunyan and Cyprian remind us that the Christian life is a matter of faith and hope. Following Christ and living in accordance with his commands will require us to make difficult decisions in everything—from how we spend our money to how we treat those who we feel have wronged us. The rewards are often not instantaneous, but if we persevere we will experience a reward far greater than we could hope for or imagine.

---

84. *De zelo et livore* 16. Cf. *Demetr.* 18: "But there is no grief from the attack of present evils for those who have confidence in future blessings."

10

Leadership Style and Church Culture

JANICE HOWARD NEWHAM

Introduction

Crossway Baptist Church began as a Bush Sunday School among the orchards on the fringe of Melbourne. Blackburn Baptist Church (BBC), the congregation from which Crossway evolved, joined the Baptist Union of Victoria (BUV) in 1954. Led by four church pastor-leaders, the church became an ethnically diverse, charismatic Baptist "megachurch."[1] It had its main campus in the centre of Melbourne's "Bible-Belt."[2] At the end of fifty years Crossway's average weekly attendance across several congregations was 3,500 adults and children. Adherents tend to come from the well-to-do business and professional groups of society. Traditional Baptist practice has given way to a charismatic emphasis in worship

---

1. Charismatic spirituality is an expression of Christian evangelical, conversionist faith that retains the centrality of the Bible in defining the beliefs and practice of faith, emphasizes a daily personal experience of relationship with God through the Holy Spirit, and expects supernatural guidance and intervention in personal and corporate life. Manley, *Wooloomooloo to Eternity*, 2.716. Evangelical faith is characterized by four core beliefs: conversion, focus on the Bible, activism, and the centrality of the cross. Bebbington, *Dominance*, 3.

2. Historian Graeme Davison explains that in Melbourne "well-to-do Protestants led the march into the eastern suburbs creating a Bible-Belt whose moral atmosphere has survived even the decline of the churches that created it. Camberwell and Nunawading's notorious 'dry area'—a zone bereft of hotels—and Canterbury's spirited resistance to the introduction of the 'Canterbury Tales' brothel suggest the tenacity of this tradition." Davison, "Suburban Character."

and a business understanding of leadership and governance, with subtle shifts in church culture and ministry, and mission emphasis.[3]

This paper focuses on one of the themes arising from a study of Crossway's history. It explores the relationship between the style of each church pastor-leader and significant features of the church culture over the first fifty years.[4] Material is sourced from archival research and the perspectives of Crossway staff, members, and attendees. Interviews have been conducted with forty people who have formed Crossway's identity and been formed by it.[5]

While Crossway's experience and people are unique, Crossway has become a model for some Australian churches aspiring to grow. The interaction between leadership, church culture, and identity at Crossway should be of interest to students of church mission and growth. My thesis is that the personal style of each church leader has influenced Crossway's ministry, culture, and identity. The last two of the four pastor-leaders significantly reshaped the church. At the same time, the organizational culture of the church and the style of each leader arose out of a combination of personal factors and secular-social and Christian influences.[6]

Cultural Reading

Reading a church culture requires a lens, as Pugh has shown in his analysis of transformations in church cultures. An organizational cul-

---

3. See Manley, *Australian Baptists*, 717, 719.

4. The fifth era identified in this paper ends with Stuart Robinson's tenure at the end of 2007. A focus on the church founder and interim pastors (such as J. E. Newnham and K. Forbes) is outside the scope of this paper.

5. Participants in the study (with the exception of church leaders) are quoted anonymously and are identified by arbitrarily assigned numbers beginning with "P."

6. As a Crossway "insider," I have a personal history dating back to 1984, which includes five years on the Crossway board. My interview plan was to ask open-ended questions and check with participants my assumptions about the significance of events and the meaning of the descriptors they used. In my research I have taken critical-realist and social-constructionist positions. Critical realist: on the one hand, I am assuming a partially knowable, undisputed reality about Crossway's history; on the other hand, I believe that the richness of the history depends on the varied perspectives of the people who have shaped it. Social constructionist: documents are viewed as constructs, or artifacts, of culture (rather than "factual"), as are stories from participant observers. The temptation to homogenize conflicting data is resisted.

ture taxonomy offers the ability to differentiate between eras according to certain variables.[7] Schein defines organizational culture as

> a pattern of shared basic assumptions that the group learned as it solved its problems of external adaptation and internal integration, that has worked well enough to be considered valid and, therefore, to be taught to new members as the correct way you perceive, think, and feel in relation to those problems.[8]

Schein explains organizational culture as existing in three levels:

- visible artifacts;
- values, beliefs, symbols, and rituals; and
- underlying assumptions that are subconscious and difficult to change.[9]

Schneider's typology of organizational culture is based on two dimensions. The first is content—what the organization pays attention to: there is either a focus on what is happening in the present time (*actualities*, the practical demands of the day) or on future *possibilities* (a visionary, perhaps idealistic, emphasis). The second dimension is process—how the organization makes judgments and decisions: there is either a task focus (*impersonal*), or a *personal* focus which recognizes subjective aspects and personal values.[10] These dimensions render four types of organizations:

- *Control* (actuality-impersonal): task-focused, attending to tangible reality and practical utility; analytically detached and makes prescriptive decisions.[11]
- *Collaboration* (actuality-personal): people-oriented, attends to concrete reality in which subjective aspects and personal values are

---

7. Pugh, *Fantasyland Faith*.
8. Schein, *Organisational Culture*, 12.
9. Ibid., 16–27.
10. Schneider, *Reengineering Alternative*.
11. The "role church" would be an example. According to BNET Business Dictionary, role culture is "a style of corporate culture, identified by Charles Handy, which assumes that employees are rational and that roles can be defined and discharged within clearly defined procedures. An organisation with a role culture is believed to be generally very stable but poor at implementing change management. Online: http://dictionary.bnet.com/definition/role+culture.html.

recognized; with organic and informal decision-making.[12]

- *Competence* (possibility-impersonal): task-oriented, attending to potentiality, imagined alternatives, creative options, and theoretical concepts; scientific and prescriptive decision-making.[13]
- *Cultivation* (possibility-personal): attends to possibilities, subjective aspects and personal values are recognized; attends to potentiality of persons, their ideas and beliefs, aspirations, and values, inspiration and creative options; people driven, organic and subjective decision-making.[14]

Four Pastor-Leaders, Five Periods of Crossway's History

The four men appointed to lead the church were matched in strength of commitment to their calling. Church growth in each era necessitated a building extension and/or relocation program. For each period, the leadership style, the church's external contexts, and the organizational culture of the church will be described briefly with the aid of Schneider's taxonomy and material from interviews.

1954–61. Early Years: "The Extended Family" under George Ashworth

LEADERSHIP STYLE

> Let us realise that we are living in a day of tremendous opportunity—a day when radically new methods are being used to spread the Gospel—a day when to quibble with the old cry "we've never done that before" or "we have always done it this way"... will surely spell disaster for our cause.[15]

Something from Crossway's senior pastor in recent times, surely? No, the year was 1957, and the writer, George Ashworth.

Out of a sad, short childhood George Ashworth found a strong and simple faith to sustain himself and to inspire others, and at the age of

---

12. The helping professions would be good examples.

13. Advertising agencies and consultancies with strong achievement emphasis would be examples.

14. The "person" culture and religious and therapeutic organizations are examples.

15. Ashworth, *Blackburn Baptist Church News*, 7 Feb 1957.

nine was aware of a call to the ministry.[16] An energetic and caring pastor, he would cycle down unmade roads to visit church folk. He encouraged his people to pray boldly for the work of the Holy Spirit.[17] He continued the work of church founder Reg Jones and interim pastor J. E. Newnham, setting in place the structures needed for a new Baptist church. Unity, loyalty, and allegiance to the Baptist Union were spoken of with pride.

> [The Pastor] brought forward a Master Plan for the Future. This plan was set out in a well produced booklet and suggested methods whereby we could win men and women for Christ and thus build our membership and our church property. It envisaged the Church Committee System.[18]
>
> At a church service, it must have been early '59, when George Ashworth prayed, and he implored the congregation. He said, "Right, let's have a target. Let's have a goal—that next week we want to have a dozen people at the (evening) church service," and there were seven.[19]

The Sunday school was soon overcrowded.[20] To resolve the space problems, Ashworth made his "outrageous" proposal for a costly relocation of the church. After unfavorable initial reactions, the diaconate unanimously approved it to go to the church meeting.[21] Ashworth was positive, self-disciplined, structured, and a concrete, sequential thinker.

---

16. "My dad was gassed in the first world war, died at 35 in 1930, leaving mum with three children 2, 6, 10. It all caught up with Mum a couple of years later, she had a heart attack and died. We were orphaned at 4, 8, 11. My teen years were a sad experience. But someone said, 'God was preparing you for times of tragedy.'" Ashworth, interview, 24 November 2006.

17. He wrote exhorting folk to pray for the power of the Holy Spirit to come on the church at Pentecost (*Blackburn Baptist Church News*, June 1957). This sort of language precedes the era of Pentecostal or charismatic spirituality and might stem from a spiritual perspective of personal surrender, influenced by Keswick or "deeper life" theology and the popular Upwey conventions.

18. Church meeting minutes, 19 September 1956.

19. P22.

20. It went from 71 members in mid-1956 to 118 in 1961, the year Ashworth left. The Sunday school was the greatest source of growth. Ashworth had the church fully embrace the White and Coleman Mission in 1957; 270 children attended and the campaign resulted in a number of "brethren coming to know Christ as Saviour" and wanting to be baptized (*Blackburn Baptist Church News*, June 1957).

21. Ashworth, interview 24 November 2006. The new building was opened after Ashworth's departure, on 17 February 1962.

Both task- and people-oriented, he attended to detail but was never impersonal.[22]

CHURCH CULTURE

The time was booming post-war Melbourne—frugal, politically conservative, and sectarian.[23] BBC joined other churches in opposing the sale of alcohol.[24] A benevolent paternalism was prevalent, inside and outside the church, and the status of being a reverend drew respect everywhere. The churches grew from burgeoning British and European immigration and the 1959 Billy Graham Crusade.[25]

"Church" embraced the whole of life, fueled by an enthusiastic volunteer workforce consisting mostly of the pastor's wife and at-home mothers. The Blackburn church resembled an extended family, part of a close-knit Baptist clan that defined itself over against other churches and the unchurched.

> At least for my family and for many, you judge people not on their socio-economic background but on which church they went. . . . [T]o me the Baptists were the right "way," because it was biblical.[26]

Commitment to the familiar Baptist church model of Sunday worship meetings, clubs, brigades, and committees was expected of every church member. Ashworth wrote a punchy admonition to this effect for the BBC News in September 1956.[27]

---

22. Described in terms of Tomlinson's leadership model. See Tomlinson, *How a Man Handles Conflict*, 73.

23. The sectarian stand-off between Protestants and Catholics was a feature of life in Australia. Evidence of anti-Catholic feeling at BBC is found in the *Blackburn Baptist Church News*, September 1955.

24. P.8 describes aspects of the Baptist moral conservatism of the 1950s and 60s— no drinking, dancing, smoking, gambling (including raffles), Sunday trading, or entertainment on Good Friday.

25. In 1955 Australia's post-war immigration from Britain and Europe passed one million. See Clark, *Short History*, 277–78, 300–301. On 15 March 1959 the Billy Graham Crusade reportedly drew 143,000 people to the MCG. See Doogue, "Billy Graham's pretty faith."

26. P8.

27. "But what a surprise it has been to me to note during my first nine months as Pastor: 1. The Members and friends who do not regularly attend church; 2. the amazing

Despite the pastor's exuberance in drawing up a "Master Plan" and talking about growth targets, these aspects of his leadership do not seem to have been determinative for the church. The church's ministry was shaped by the familiar Baptist pattern of well-defined roles and functions. Current, tangible realities were the focus. When Ashworth talked about introducing an all-age Sunday school he did not find enough support.[28] Perhaps the Baptist "role culture" was stronger than this idea-man without the leadership training of more recent times or the mandate to make any deep changes. He was expected to fit the mould of a preacher and pastor. The relocation project was a practical answer to crowding and did not threaten deeply held values.

In terms of Schneider's model, BBC in this early period was actuality-focused and personal, a "collaboration" culture with Baptist roles and traditions providing stability. The pastor, who was of course not the founder, might have preferred to introduce a more future-oriented "competence" culture, but it appears that his efforts were quietly resisted.

1962–72. Established, Growing Church under David Griffiths: "The Corner Store"

LEADERSHIP STYLE

Very much a teacher-pastor of the flock, Griffiths focused on sermon preparation and home visitation, which he called "boundary riding."[29] He had a quiet way of finding and encouraging those in need of spiritual sustenance. He saw himself as a "pastoral evangelist" rather than a

---

number of folk who only attend one service on Sunday; 3. the heartbreak attendance at our mid-week meeting on Wednesday. . . . Remember above everything else the Church is the Body of Our Lord—and He died for us and depends on us to carry on His work through the Church. We can only have a strong and virile Church if every member faithfully serves and accepts his and her responsibility. Can we count on you?" (*Blackburn Baptist Church News*, September 1956).

28. This may have contributed to his decision to move on after only five years (Ashworth, interview, 24 November 2006; P14, P9). Ashworth's letter of July 1961 to the deacons informing them that he had accepted a call to RAAF chaplaincy came as a shock.

29. Griffiths, interview, 12 September 2006. Griffiths attended the Baptist college in North Melbourne and gained the LTh from the Melbourne College of Divinity in 1956. He was inducted at BBC on 27 May 1962.

"pulpit-evangelist." Griffiths was known for Bible teaching and an understanding of world context.

> There were two kinds of people to preach to—conservative evangelicals, and those who read widely and thought differently from most. I found I could preach three safe addresses and one to stretch them, each month. I liked to push them a bit.[30]

Having produced well-researched notes for discussion and guidance, Griffiths started adult study groups—the forerunner of the church's cell group network. Participants also recall Don Dyer's study group and his exceptional Bible teaching. In 1963 a Christian book stall was opened.[31]

Griffiths talks about his early reading and the grounding for his personal theology, which was perhaps "left of centre" of the evangelical spectrum.[32] He gives an amusing anecdote about an act of disobedience of his strict Sabbatarian father, which ironically ended in an encouragement to a floundering congregation.

> This incident was extremely meaningful for me. It broke my fear concerning practices which were thought to express rebellion against God. So from then on, I had a healthy suspicion of exegesis; some of the interpretations that people used to have are no longer considered correct, for example the women and equality issue; so I listen with half an ear.[33]

Through his experience as a chaplain Griffiths reacted against "infantile religion" built on simplistic, false premises, which he regarded as dangerous.[34]

As a pastor his leadership style was apparently sensitive and values-driven. He was a quiet, deep thinker-feeler with a balance of people- and task-orientation. Those interviewed remember him as non-directive,

30. Griffiths, interview, 12 September 2006.
31. Deacons' meeting minutes, 4 March 1963.
32. "I had one hand on the Bible and one on the newspaper and science" (Griffiths, interview, 12 September 2006). Griffiths entertained the possibility that the theory of evolution might be true, engaged in careful exegesis, and supported tithing only as a kind of standard for giving while warning his readers that it was not a specifically Christian practice (Griffiths' notes on conversion and stewardship, 1967).
33. Griffiths, interview, 12 September 2006. His father was Welsh Calvinist, his mother "liberal."
34. Griffiths speaks of the "infantile religion that was blown out of the water" in both World Wars. "They had been taught 'the Lord will provide' . . . in a sense, the Lord *didn't* provide" (Griffiths, interview notes, 27 January 2009; emphasis original).

wise, and friendly. "David, I would say he was a feeler; avoids conflict; promotes harmony . . . people-oriented definitely. . . . And an encourager. Not end results oriented."[35] Decision-making was still collaborative, which, as well as being the Baptist way, suited his personal style.[36]

CHURCH CULTURE

The 1960s brought anti-war protests and the sexual revolution. Church folk, however, remained morally and politically conservative in this decade. The main external religious influences on BBC were probably Billy Graham, Keswick Conventions, and missionary biographies.

By the time Griffiths was halfway through his pastorship, some thirty-seven sporting clubs, brigades, Bible study groups, and other activities such as religious education were thriving.[37] The metaphor of "the corner store" for the church in this era brings to mind a local community facility where customer service is friendly and people of all ages come several times a week to choose from an array of goods and services—something for everyone. The sense of Baptist identity and commitment remained strong during Griffiths' decade.

The family oriented church grew to 365 members in 1972, with close to 500 worshipping on a Sunday.[38] Members brought along neighbors and their children, and assisted new immigrants—most of whom were already well-disposed towards Christianity—to settle in.[39] Griffiths says, "I had no master plan. I just cared for what came along, and tried to draw more in. The 'church growth' movements came later."[40]

---

35. P11.

36. "Decision-making? The ministry is God's gift to the church, and the deaconate is God's gift to the ministry. Deacons were the rulers of council and creators of recommendations for church meetings, which were not rubber stamps but debating forums" (Griffiths, interview, 12 September 2006).

37. Significant events in the decade were the visit by the Missouri Baptist Convention in 1964 and BBC's participation in the Billy Graham Crusade of 1968.

38. A weekly church attendance of 500 made BBC already one of the largest Baptist churches in Melbourne. The auditorium was extended and on Sundays two morning services were held, to better utilize the 300–350 seating capacity.

39. The typical pastor's wife led women's or children's activities in the church. Ruth Ashworth and Kay Griffiths were no exception. Under Kay Griffiths' presidency the BWA meetings grew up to 100 women. Home Cheer and Project Compassion were started and migrant families from Britain were sponsored.

40. Griffiths, interview, 12 September 2006.

In the last two years of Griffiths' pastorship there is evidence of declining commitment of church folk to church activities.[41] The evening service had never really worked well. Looking back to what he now calls their "salad days" at Blackburn, Griffiths' one regret is that he failed to appoint any staff to share the load.[42]

Recollections from the 1960s about sensitivity and flexibility at the leadership level suggest a strengthening of "collaboration" culture through Griffiths' time. As the congregation grew, like the wider society, it was diversifying, and Griffiths' progressive perspective was well suited. Griffiths speaks about difficult pastoral issues, which he faced not with pat answers but with a listening ear and a desire to find approaches that were valid even if they came from outside sources. His personal tendency to focus first on people and values, his erudition and openmindedness, prepared the diaconate and the congregation for the era of Rowland Croucher.

1973–82. Expanding Regional Church under Rowland Croucher: "The Life-Saving Centre"

LEADERSHIP STYLE

Warm, non-directive, and comfortable with ambiguity, Rowland Croucher respected people and dignified their values.[43] Also, like Griffiths, Croucher had a strict upbringing, and his ministry style grew out of a love of reading. He was not afraid of affirming social justice in an evangelical context which warned against liberal theology and "social gospel."[44] Croucher was open to women in leadership positions and had Claire Wilkinson appointed as an elder. Croucher was seen as an inspir-

---

41. Secretary's report in the BBC's annual report for 1972.

42. Griffiths, interview, 12 September 2006. Griffiths and his wife Kay experienced a form of burnout.

43. He was educated at Bathurst Teachers' College, the Universities of New England and Sydney, the Baptist Theological College in New South Wales, and Fuller Seminary in California.

44. Croucher could not see the point of trying to argue biblical inerrancy (Croucher, interview, 13 September 2006). Those who would label Croucher a "liberal," however, have been taken in by his creative ministry style, which did not necessarily reflect an unorthodox theology.

ing and adventurous preacher who liked to challenge people to think about their faith.

> For the average person that isn't really easy . . . to know what you believe and be able to communicate. Just to say "I asked Jesus into my life, and he came and saved me" wasn't enough for Rowland. He was incredibly intellectual, and he wanted to kind of impart those things to the congregation. So, he would open up the evening service to *all* sorts of creative panels, discussions, visiting preachers, anything to broaden our understanding of how we can relate to the world around us.[45]

Croucher permitted a diversity of creative interpretations of the church's purpose and identity, especially care and respect for outsiders.[46]

> Alan Marr came (in 1974) . . . and revolutionized our little staid church. . . . I would say we were not reaching out into the community, and he was a community-minded person, and he started all the youth pathways, the women's refuge, the half way house for youth, and he got a program going in the church where he would get the homeless, and the marginalized, and put them in church families.[47]

CHURCH CULTURE

The external context for such adventurous diversity was the euphoria of the Whitlam era and the decline of social stability and conservatism in Australia.[48] In the Christian context, BBC folk began to read Pentecostal and renewal literature.

---

45. P3. A number of participants mentioned Croucher's Sunday evening debates, which dealt with contentious topics. One particular evening recalled by many involved a Palestinian Arab and a Jew.

46. Community outreach and social justice was taught and modeled by Pastors Croucher, Tom Keyte, Alan Marr, and Hal Bissett. Church members have commented that each of the pastors had their own ministry areas and tended to work without much reference to each other. Rather than being seen as indicating disloyalty or disunity, theological differences were also celebrated.

47. P3.

48. Features of the social paradigm shift included the contraceptive pill, the women's movement, no-fault divorce, the first casino in Australia, *in vitro* fertilization, and the inaugural Gay and Lesbian Mardi Gras in 1978.

BBC's conscious focus on community outreach under Croucher prompts the metaphor of a "life saving centre." Churches were feeling the brunt of the sexual revolution, the increase in family breakdown, and experimentation with drugs.[49] With an understanding of youth and being at home in the intellectual university environment, Croucher was up to the task.

> [People were] so excited, we could see the church growing.... It was absolutely not to be missed, and the fact that you could see people's lives being changed and see people come to the Lord, and see people walk in there that had never been in church before . . . and have a part of that and their discipleship, that was amazing for me.[50]

Christian "refugees" from Pentecostal, Baptist, and mainline churches were also attracted to BBC.[51] Through the 1970s BBC had a thriving discipling small group culture. The cell groups led by Tim Costello and Bill Hallam brought in many young people. BBC youth were involved in a coffee shop.[52]

Several participants speak of the church's central message of love and compassion. A refreshing theology of grace opened a door to "those of us who've come from a judgmental upbringing."[53] The church structure was decentralized, a "network of constellations," as Croucher sees it.[54] It was an "anyone can do it" climate. The church's espoused values included respect for one another despite differences. A basic assumption was probably that "Baptist churches are fair and egalitarian and everyone must have their say," although the practice of consensus led to

---

49. "We had a people struggling with drugs, and with alcohol, and the down and outs, we had them in our church. It wasn't all just power, and glory, and wonder" (P3).

50. P3.

51. Transfer growth occurred as BBC became a home for those fleeing the excesses of Pentecostal churches and for others who tired of the "fairly rigid Bible teacher kind of approach" in the more traditional churches (P15).

52. Management of the coffee shop project in a nearby shopping centre and a drop-in centre on the church property reflected permission-granting, experimental style of Croucher.

53. Church members observed leaders treating each other with mutual respect, forgiving each other. They mention the openness and vulnerability of the pastors and their wives.

54. Croucher, interview, 13 September 2006.

difficulties even for Croucher.[55] He talks about three proposals he could have pushed, but decided not to place his vision for the church above the views of others.[56]

Participants clearly saw Croucher's facilitative personal style and non-prescriptive Bible teaching as the primary influence on church culture. However, prominent church folk prepared BBC for the groundbreaking challenges and changes that Croucher brought. A crucial appointment early in Croucher's time was that of Robert Colman, who began to introduce contemporary songs.[57] Colman understood worship as entry into God's presence, and he impacted the lives of church folk in worship, in pastoral care, and prayer for physical or emotional healing. He was seen as the heart of the church. In 1980 Rod Denton became youth pastor. Having no theological training but with a business background, Denton revised the youth group structures to reflect a greater emphasis on spiritual disciplines and study techniques. He disbanded sporting clubs.[58] This approach initially led, predictably, to the number of young adults on the events mailing list dwindling from 120 to 6. A new culture of youth ministry began.

> The biggest hallmark was bringing on Rod Denton. A major change in youth with Rod, he took youth and young adults to a new level, brought another level of spiritual maturity, at our age

---

55. In Griffiths' day, there were the "fundamentalists," the "liberals," and the "sherry drinkers." Croucher talks about a social justice stream, a contemplative stream, university students from all persuasions, progressives, and fundamentalists. To this must be added the budding charismatics (Croucher, interview, 13 September 2006). A couple of participants felt that although Croucher had the capacity to embrace diversity, he was "juggling" social justice, charismatic, and conservative Baptist interests and eventually would have had to go in one direction or the other. The beginnings of the charismatic renewal were potentially divisive, so Croucher produced a booklet on it entitled "Charismatic Renewal: Myths and Realities" (reproduced online at http://jmm.aaa.net.au/articles/12475.htm).

56. The three proposals were: to buy property between the church site and Canterbury Road, to lead the congregation into open membership, and to add a woman to the pastoral team.

57. Robert Colman was not ordained or "Baptist." At the height of a stage career Colman had an experience with the Holy Spirit. He brought to BBC the contemporary praise and worship choruses in *Scripture in Song*, by David and Dale Garrett. He produced several "BBC at Worship" audiotapes for sale, and began the current "media ministry" of providing weekly programs for radio.

58. Denton says that the cricket and the football teams were originally effective for outreach, but by the time he arrived the church they had "compromised, and handed over leadership to the community" (Denton, 12 December 2008).

> we can be leaders too, he invested in people's lives.... We used to joke, "Rod Denton has a wonderful plan for your life!"... Rod had this great ability to pin point your gifts.[59]

However, some parents reacted against the changes.

> Decisions are now "dictated," the leadership style... for example, Rod Denton. Some students didn't react well to being told what to do! These were the social action ones—if Jesus came back to earth, what would they be doing?... Rod changed everything in the youth; things were fun and serious under Alan (Marr), but with Rod it was all serious, all the sports went.[60]

As for the church's identity, in Croucher's time a strong sense developed that BBC was different, something special. When Croucher resigned in 1981 to pastor a church in Canada, BBC had a staff of 25 and between 1,000 and 1,500 attending on Sunday. A personal, therapeutic "cultivation" culture with a future, "possibility" focus had replaced the more immediate emphasis of "collaboration." While Croucher would see the quality of relationships rather than buildings or numbers as the indicator of church vitality, he "was always envisioning something different from what was actually here." In the eighteen months before Robinson arrived, the beginnings of a "competence" subculture were introduced. Ironically, Croucher's open leadership style and encouragement of diversity permitted Denton to trial his highly structured, disciplined approach.

1983–97. Church in Transition under Stuart Robinson: "The Battlefield"

The characterization of this era as "the battlefield" reflects the views of BBC people—those who supported Stuart Robinson's changes and the smaller group who opposed them. This period was a time of conflict. The prospective relocation, preparatory changes, and leadership style alienated some church folk and resulted in problems of disunity and low morale in the pastoral team.[61]

59. P24.
60. P9.
61. Participants mention these indicators of conflict. Crossway statistics show that from a "high" of 772 members in 1982 (the year before Robinson's appointment) the membership numbers remained about the same for Robinson's first nine years, with 743

LEADERSHIP STYLE

Robinson heard a different call from that of his predecessors, a more strategic one: to relocate BBC to prepare it for its role as a major regional church.[62] Although ordained as a Baptist and working for the Baptist mission, Robinson was later to identify with Peter Wagner's corporate, visionary "new apostolic reformation pastors."[63]

Robinson's mission background would have appealed to the "more conservative mission-minded evangelicals."[64] He had been leading a groundbreaking mission project in South Asia in a time of great turmoil and danger. He had shown entrepreneurial ability in visioning and managing a fundraising project for the Baptist College in Queensland.[65] Robinson had already some affinity with charismatic spirituality; a friend in Asia from an American Assemblies of God church had mentored the Robinsons regarding the "baptism in the Holy Spirit" and spiritual gifts such as prophecy."[66]

More directive in management style than his two predecessors, Robinson would tend to "see things in more black and white" than they would.[67] His leadership was authoritative, deliberate, structured, task- and goal-oriented. Participants describe him as persuasive and competitive, a thinker rather than feeler, and one who "takes charge." He did not have Croucher's or Colman's ease in social situations, and compounding this, he was new to pastoring a Western church. Behind the scenes, how-

---

in 1991. Then in 1992 the membership fell to 645 and it took until 1999 (four years after the relocation) to build up to 770 again. In 2007, Robinson's last year as senior pastor, Crossway's membership had climbed to 1379. Similarly, the average weekly attendance hovered around 1100 in the early 90s—less than it had been in Croucher's time—until the relocation, when in 1996 it jumped to 1356 and then to 1532 the following year. Disunity in the pastoral team was also a factor, with painful staff departures continuing to occur during the twelve years after the relocation.

62. "I believe that in 1982 the Lord showed me that B.B.C. would become a 'great' church. From its position within the south east corner of Australia, its influence would radiate out as rays of light throughout Australia and continue on in a north western arc to particularly minister in the south east and southern Asian regions" Stuart Robinson, 17 May 1984.

63. Wagner, *Churchquake!*

64. A phrase used by p.26.

65. Nickerson and Ball, *For His Glory*.

66. Robinson, interview, 24 Aug 2009. One of Robinson's books is dedicated to "Cal, my mentor in matters of the Spirit. A faithful friend"—Robinson, *Mosques and Miracles*.

67. P.30.

ever, Robinson took time to care for certain people in deep difficulty or grief.

The language to encourage the church was no longer "unity in diversity," but "with God nothing is impossible" and "faith is spelled R-I-S-K." Robinson was known for his exegetical preaching and engaging, dramatic presentation. His sermons on the annual "Vision Sunday" aimed to inspire the people to seek and follow what new things God was doing among them.[68] He devised a church vision statement: "A caring community of prayerful people empowered and ministering in Melbourne and beyond."

"Faith targets" were regularly updated for each aspect of this statement.[69] Robinson preached on commitment to tithes, offerings, and the mission "faith promise," which would be needed for the church to move towards its calling.[70] Speaking about a radical faith in Christ, the senior pastor attempted to allay any rational concerns people might have.[71] Robinson is remembered for teaching on corporate, targeted prayer and

---

68. In the church archives and Robinson's personal files are the copies of each "vision" sermon from 1996 to 2007, and other notes and sermons on faith, risk, or vision. Typically the vision sermon began with a sober dossier of calamities, deception, and injustices around the world; next, some uplifting examples of the missional possibilities of a faithful, strong church. They end with a compelling call to the task of transforming the lives of those estranged from God or otherwise without hope.

69. A document dated 1993 from the senior pastor's "vision" file is an overhead projector presentation of 3 pages, "Vision" 9/3/93. The "Faith Targets' by 2000 A.D. were: "2000 members, 1600 (80%) in small groups, 300 (15%) in weekly corporate prayer, 100 (5%) deployed cross culturally, 3 new daughter churches, All facilities built and debt free." Page 3 is headed "Process by Stuart" and lists strategies for communicating the vision to each sub congregation.

70. A fundraising strategy, involving the dinners with all church members, took place to encourage pledges to the building and property fund. Color brochures were produced and circulated, titled "Building the Vision," and T-shirts were designed with the "building the vision" logo.

71. For example, this exhortation to pray: "that we will *know the mind of Jesus Christ*, the head of the body and not concentrate on what others think. That each will be able to separate clearly *the vision* that God has for us from the problems and pressures which may emerge in realising this vision. That with Godly vision, together we will *exercise bold faith* and that we will decide not on the basis of our inabilities, but upon God's abilities"—Robinson, letter to the church, 1 July 1984, (emphasis aoriginal). A favorite theme of Robinson's is God's way of working outside human reasoning, and he often repeats William Carey's 1792 proclamation, "Expect great things from God; attempt great things for God!"

fasting, and for leading by example.[72] He was both admired and criticized for his hard-line, "politically incorrect" positions on controversial social issues, which he based on literal scriptural interpretation.[73]

The ministries of Denton and Colman prepared fertile ground for the new senior pastor's priorities to seed and take shape.[74] Within a few years Denton had trained a generation of national youth leaders.[75] From 1989 the vibrant Youth Alive rallies and Pentecostal emphasis on the miraculous, fostered by new youth pastor Steve Roggero, attracted youth from across Melbourne. Pentecostalism injected a sense of anticipation and excitement—almost an unpredictability—into the church culture, which confirmed in the minds of many church folk Robinson's teaching on faith and risk, and his prophetic "charisma."

CHURCH CULTURE

Counseling had already been popularized, and with Robinson's endorsement BBC established "Barnabas House," first as a holistic healing centre, and later focusing on inner healing and deliverance. Meanwhile the church growth movement, the increasing popularity of small groups, and the "metachurch" model undergirded Robinson's vision.[76]

So as to cover a larger, growing congregation, Robinson reconceptualized the role and skill mix of pastors to be "ranchers"—coaches,

---

72. The relationship between prayer and church growth was the subject of his first book and his doctoral thesis at Fuller Theological Seminary—Robinson, Praying the Price. Some regarded the introduction of morning prayer meetings to be one of Robinson's most significant legacies.

73. Issues such as divorce, remarriage, abortion, *in vitro* fertilisation, women in leadership, and homosexuality. Manley, Australian Baptists, 760, notes that Baptist conservatism was assisted by links with conservative bible colleges. Robinson had become pastor of BBC at a time when gender equality in leadership was being addressed in government and business. He was ambivalent about the scriptural mandate for women becoming pastors and board members. Crossway Policy Manual, 1 Jan 1997, 18.

74. Denton's ministry was influenced by his visit to David Yonggi Cho's Yoido Full Gospel Church in Korea which was strong in cell groups, prayer, and leader-training. Colman's approach suited Robinson's vision to build bridges between the Pentecostal and traditional denominational churches.

75. One avenue of training was the annual Summer School of Youth Leadership which Denton started, attracting youth leaders from across Australia. There are several former youth leaders who grew up at BBC under Griffiths and Croucher who have become prominent in the wider Christian church and across the nation.

76. The "metachurch" concept is from George, *Prepare Your Church*.

trainers, and equippers—rather than one-on-one "shepherds."[77] Some saw the changes as a threat to the very identity of the church. They believed that the caring, worshipping family would be destroyed by a distant and uncaring leadership, non-consultative governance, and relocation. However, other participants of all ages supported the senior pastor's rationale that consensus and "democratic" government would not work in a large church. Inspired by the leadership, a strong contingent looked forward to the move and handed in their financial pledges.

Apparently, Robinson considered that some narrowing of Crossway's theological direction was called for, to counter what he saw as "chaos and freewheeling disunity."[78] The tighter discipleship training introduced by Denton was one area he was comfortable with, and refocusing would be easier since the more "progressive" pastors departed.[79] In 1992 a control on teaching was discussed at council level, apparently to ensure a unified message from the pulpit.[80] During the late 80s and early 90s it could be said therefore that the church was driven intentionally towards a "competence" culture, future- and task-oriented. The therapeutic "cultivation" culture of the 70s was no longer sensed by the people.

1995–2007. Megachurch under Stuart Robinson: "The Flagship"

The chosen new church location was appropriate for a high-profile centre, "the flagship" of a vibrant, outwardly reaching Christianity. Meetings began in September 1995 with the loyal members proud of their achievement, which was seen widely as evidence of the hand of God.[81] The move

---

77. See George, *How to Break Growth Barriers*, 91–92.

78. Robinson, paper, 17 May 1984.

79. Alan Marr, Tom Keyte and Hal Bissett had left, and Kevin Forbes, who was seen as people-oriented and community-minded, was "sent out" to assist Steve Addison with BBC's Knox church plant. Eventually, most of the social justice and community ministries set up under their oversight were closed down.

80. "Preachers [are] to be held more accountable for the content of their messages; so that the church hears more systematically what it needs to hear rather than what a particular preacher may feel; basic topics to be finalised by the senior pastor toward the beginning of each year"—memo, Robinson to council, Sept 1992.

81. The decision to take the "step of faith" and commit to relocation had coincided with the recession of the late 80s. It had succeeded in spite of warnings and criticisms from other churches.

signaled the birth of a new era, and in some senses, a new church. The new venue and the apparent blessing of God attracted many new attendees, and some disaffected members returned. With the demand for professionally produced programs from increasing auditorium and radio audiences, up-to-date multimedia facilities were installed.[82]

LEADERSHIP STYLE

Strong centralized authority, with the pastor casting the vision for the church, is an aspect of Wagner's teaching on becoming a "New Apostolic Reformation church."[83] One participant reflects on Robinson's visionary leadership, his ability to wait for the right time, "read the rhythms" and present to the church a well-thought-through plan, the details of implementation already in place.[84] In 2003–4 the church was incorporated and a board of directors replaced the church council, a further step away from Baptist congregational governance.[85] Board members are now more likely to be from the professional and highly educated ranks of society, satisfying secular competence criteria.[86]

---

82. By the mid 2000s the weekly hour-length Crossway program recorded from one of the morning services was being run by over 100 radio stations.

83. Wagner, *Churchquake!*, especially chapter 4, "The Pastor Leads the Church." The most radical change in the New Apostolic Reformation is the "recognition in the amount of spiritual authority delegated by the Holy Spirit to individuals" and the pastor in particular.

84. P.24.

85. The adopted governance model was greatly influenced by Geoff Holdway, a former AOG pastor from Queensland, who assisted Crossway in the role of executive pastor 2001–2002. Holdway and Robinson were working from a booklet produced by Paul D. Borden, "Issues and Principles Underlying Denominational Change." This publication champions "true change that will produce friction," a strong visionary leader, willing to take risks and give strong leadership, and the changing of pastors' roles from "chaplains" to "leaders," and from "comforting" to "coaching."

86. For some leadership positions Crossway still includes the qualifications for elders and deacons found in 1 Tim 3:1–13. However the qualifications for the positions of pastor and church board member now borrow heavily from the language of job descriptions in the business world. Some participants interviewed here question the validity of a performance-oriented business model for a covenant community. See Guinness, *Dining with the Devil*, 52–53.

Church Culture

Australia under the Howard government became more prosperous and conservative.[87] Young Asian professionals have been attracted to the eastern suburbs, which are increasingly affluent. Non-Caucasians now comprise around half of the English-speaking congregation at Crossway Central. Mandarin, Cantonese, Indonesian, and Korean-speaking congregations also meet there.[88] The Chinese, in particular, respond well to a clear organizational structure and a lively but conservative evangelical Sunday service.

Strong uniform culture. After the move to East Burwood the church has become more unified in purpose and in acceptance of the vision, direction, and administrative decisions of the leadership, centred in one charismatic individual.[89] Only three formal church meetings are held a year and these are times of worship and thanksgiving rather than decision-making.[90] Each congregation and campus reports centrally. Crossway's "Baptist" title is no longer an adequate description.[91]

The pastors develop and pass on a Crossway style of doing things. An "assimilation pastor" has responsibility for newcomers. Leaders talk about replicating Crossway's ecclesial model by transplanting "the Crossway DNA."[92] If seeking a social justice emphasis, contemplative spirituality, traditional worship, or relational, "missional" church, attendees have often chosen to go elsewhere.

---

87. For one analysis of the religious, political and social conservatism of the late 1990s and 2000s, see Maddox, *God under Howard*.

88. Due to experience in Asia, Robinson encouraged Asian ministries at BBC and later, at Crossway. In the 1980s he predicted that at least one pastor of the church would be of Asian ethnic background. Through much of the 1990s and 2000s the church council has been chaired by a Malaysian. By 2000 Robinson had appointed a pastor for Crossway's Cantonese and Mandarin speaking congregations and by 2007 Crossway staff included pastors for Indonesian and Korean congregations.

89. Robinson, interview, 24 Aug 2009.

90. So that low attendance will not delay business at a church meeting, the quorum is now only seven members, down from the 1990 requirement of 20 or 25% of the members.

91. These trends are becoming common amongst Baptist churches in Australia. A list of ten Baptist convictions, many of which are being challenged, is found in Manley, *Australian Baptists*, 8.

92. The concept of Crossway DNA refers to home-grown pastors and leaders who have been trained in Crossway's style of worship and ministry.

Popular youth culture is reflected in worship to the extent that it is now "cool" for young people to be at church, and even to aspire to enter the ministry. Some young adults, however, appear to have experienced a sense of alienation. The launching of small group leadership training and newcomers' courses have not always been successful in linking people socially and spiritually. The introduction of transformational "Recovery" groups attracted hundreds of participants over a few years until the resignation in 2001 from the pastoral team of their facilitator-teacher, Beth Davies. Complaints were received about a need for pastoral care in all areas of the church. One participant reports, "I think the heartbeat of Crossway . . . has been lost . . . the heartbeat of caring for people. . . . We're supposed to be a caring church and I don't see that we are."[93]

Professionalism. Meanwhile, business and information technology provide the means to promote accountability and "best practice." The mood of the contemporary-charismatic praise and worship time on Sundays is enhanced by "critical mass," professional, multimedia presentation, and singers on stage who have been "called" and trained.[94] Easter and Christmas shows are designed particularly for the "unchurched."[95] The annual Crossway Conference (since 2003) showcases Crossway's ecclesial model and proven growth strategies. Some participants, however, claim a marketing approach makes the attendee, as "client" or "consumer," the focus instead of God. Strategic planning and performance management are a necessary part of the new legal, incorporated structure.[96]

The "competence" culture of professionalism has a down side, even for participants strongly committed to Crossway. One expressed it this way:

> I think there's a culture at Crossway of professionalism and excellence . . . even on the staff, very performance driven. . . . I actually

---

93. P.6.

94. As a constant reminder of the church's identity, Crossway's new mission statement is projected in moving images on the stage backdrop in Sunday meetings: "Crossway . . . following Jesus, transforming the world."

95. Others use the term "seeker-service."

96. To be accountable, each department of the church proposes annual quantitative goals for approval by the senior pastor. Crossway's weekly attendance target for 2005 was 4000, and that year the 2010 target was set at 10,000.

never felt that it's ok to fail. [T]here's more of a focus on leadership, rather than pastoring.[97]

The church associates with other contemporary megachurches rather than with Baptist churches.[98] Crossway weekly attendance was averaging 3516 adults and children across all congregations by the end of Robinson's 25-year term.[99]

Risk-taking and giving. Part of the mythic identity of Crossway, a legacy of Robinson's leadership, is that "we are a giving church and we are blessed when we give."[100] Robinson's language of risk-taking, radical faith has continued into the pastorship of Dale Stephenson. In February 2009 Stephenson commended church board chairman Dr. Quay for his "Holy Spirit power," faith, and wisdom in exhorting the church to build in times of economic downturn. Whether the mantra "faith is spelled R-I-S-K" will continue to shape behavior in a mature "competence" culture of goal-setting, accountability, and rational action—where "charisma" has been routinized—remains to be seen.[101]

Conclusion

The four pastor-leaders all influenced the church culture of Crossway, but more so Croucher and Robinson. Each leader suited his context and

97. P.35. Another participant was bothered by a poster in all the Crossway offices picturing a rock climber with the caption "failure is not an option."

98. Crossway has been identified with the other large churches in Melbourne. Church leaders are invited to share the pulpit at each other's churches. Robinson has mentioned his communications with megachurch leaders such as Bill Hybels and Rick Warren in the USA. Wagner, *Churchquake!*, 101, suggests that "apostles" tend to relate in depth to their peers who lead other apostolic networks. See also, Manley, *Australian Baptists*, 719.

99. This figure reflects something of a plateau in numbers during the last half of 2007, but in 2008 there was a marked increase in attendance.

100. P.12, p.24. Robinson explains this lasting core value as coming out of the 1990s when the church had to make quarterly bank payments for the East Burwood site. The funds always came, but often it was a close call. During this time Robinson felt led to ask the church to give $15,000 to a nearby church struggling with the cost of relocation and the loss of members. The BBC folk grasped this opportunity to be generous and, according to Robinson, this led to God's blessing on BBC and thereafter he never had to worry again about bank payments.

101. The "routinization of charisma" is Weber's way of describing the institutionalized authority that follows the charismatic stage—Weber, *Economy and Society*, 212. Charisma has operated as a cohesive, directional force at Crossway.

was shaped by it. Each one encouraged elements of the internal culture that suited his vision. Croucher was able to extend and challenge an already open "collaboration" culture to look towards an exciting and diverse future by building on personal relationships. Robinson's approach, however, ran up against deeply held values of the "cultivation" culture built by Croucher.

In the 1950s and 60s the church culture mirrored Baptist traditional structures and the social conservatism of post-Second World War Melbourne. In the fast-growing eastern suburbs the new church led by George Ashworth and David Griffiths was energetically engaged in responding to immediate needs. In Schneider's terms, the church was then an actuality-focused, personal "collaboration" culture. Baptist roles and traditions were breaking down as the church profile diversified.

In the 1970s the creativity, warmth, and intellect of Rowland Croucher inspired creative expressions of faith and outreach. The way for a people- and possibility-focused "cultivation" culture at BBC was prepared, however, by dramatic shifts in external social and Christian contexts.

The vision and determined, task-focused, strategic leadership of Stuart Robinson drove the next stage of Crossway as a vibrant megachurch. The ground for a "competence" culture was enabled by a weak Baptist ecclesiology, the advent of discipleship and leadership training, the church growth movement, economic prosperity, the secular business environment, and multimedia technology.

11

Baptists in Mission to and with the Poor: What Do We Need to Learn?

SCOTT HIGGINS

Introduction

One of the remarkable features of recent Australian Baptist history has been the recovery of the biblical call to seek justice for the poor.[1] This is vitally important both for a biblically shaped discipleship[2] and for the practice of Christian mission. The stark reality is that some 2,561 million

---

1. This reflects a widespread trend among Australian and other Western Christians, and evangelicals in particular. The history of evangelical discussions around evangelism and social justice can be found in Baileys, "Evangelical and Ecumenical Understandings." Three popular examples illustrate the point: (1) Rick Warren's 2005 speech to the Pew Forum, in which he confesses he had been blind to the Bible's concern with the poor, and the launch of his P.E.A.C.E Plan (Warren, "Myths"). (2) Jim Wallace's comment on ABC's Lateline program in the leadup to the 2007 Australian Federal election that "I think Christians are definitely concerned about the levels of poverty overseas" (Wallace, "Tony Jones"). Wallace is director of the conservative evangelical lobby group The Australian Christian Lobby, and his comment was in response to a question about issues important to Christians in the federal election. (3) Baptist World Aid Australia, which derives its financial support predominantly from Australian Baptists, saw donations rise from $4.5 million in 1998 to $411 million in 2008. Research commissioned by Baptist World Aid showed that in 2006, 80 percent of attendees in Baptist churches had made a donation to an overseas aid charity in the previous 12 months, and 37 percent sponsored a child through an overseas aid charity.

2. See for example, Wright, *Living as the People of God*; Van Til, *Less Than Two Dollars*; Costello and Yule, *Another Way to Love*.

people, representing 47 percent of the world's population, live on less than US $2 per day.³ If we are to engage in mission to the world we must then engage in mission to people living in poverty. For some this means chronic and extreme poverty—they are permanently unable to meet some or all of their most basic needs such as nutritious food, clean water, adequate shelter, decent work, and effective education; they have very few choices about the direction of their lives; and they are vulnerable to exploitation, violence, and abuse. For others it means the inability to access sufficient resources to open up life options and safeguard against extreme poverty—a sick child, a dowry, a theft can consume all their resources and push them into extreme poverty. For yet others it means a very modest range of life choices, poor access to assets and services, and marginalization from power.

In this paper I do not intend to argue the biblical mandate to seek justice for the poor. That has been defended elsewhere.⁴ Rather, I seek to explore what the "development sector" has to teach us about effective mission to and with people living in poverty. Since the end of the Second World War there has been much attention to the issues of poverty and development by multilateral bodies (for example, World Bank, United Nations), governments, academics, NGOs, and, more recently, some large corporations. These members of government, civil society, and business constitute what can be called the "development sector." They have discussed and debated the factors that enable communities and countries to increase their material well-being, expand their citizen's life choices, and lift their populations out of poverty.⁵ While many issues

3. Chen and Ravallion, "Developing World." Figures are expressed in terms of 2005 "purchasing power parity," meaning that someone living on $2 a day in Cambodia earns an income that equates to $2 per day in the United States in 2005. The more commonly cited $1.25/day figure is 1,376 million, or 25 percent of the world's population. These figures may underestimate the true extent of global poverty. Peter Edward argues that if life expectancy is used as a proxy for poverty, the international poverty line should be set closer to US $3/day, as life expectancy falls away dramatically in countries with GDP per capita below this (Edward, "Ethical Poverty Line," 14–16).

4. See the references in note 2.

5. These discussions take place against ongoing experiences of "development" that can be masked by static snapshots of poverty. Since the end of WWII some countries have virtually eliminated extreme poverty. In the early 1960s South Korea had well-being indicators akin to those of many of today's most impoverished nations. Per capita income was just US $4/day, life expectancy was 54 years, and 15 percent of children died before their fifth birthday. Today per capita income is around US $20,000/year, life expectancy is 76 years, and less than 0.5 percent of children die before the age of five.

remain the subject of vigorous dispute, I believe that by listening to discussions within the development sector and reflecting on them in light of Scripture we can broaden and deepen our understanding and practice of mission with people and communities who are poor.

Key Concepts in Development

"Development" in its broadest terms refers to the processes by which a community enables its members to enjoy increasing levels of well-being. As might be expected, contestability emerges in defining "well-being" and in identifying the processes that lead to its increase. Nonetheless, there is an emerging consensus around some key themes, depicted in the diagram below.

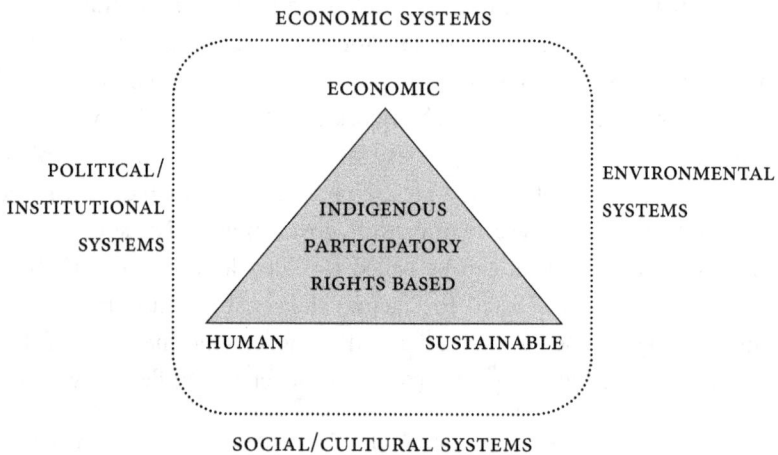

The Nature of Development

In the 1950s and 60s mainstream development discourse focused almost exclusively on economic development. The aim was to increase the per capita income of poorer nations, under the assumption that rising national income would lead to declining poverty and increasing levels of

---

Even in countries with high levels of poverty there have been substantial gains: in East Asia the proportion of people living on less than US $2/day fell from 93 percent in 1981 to 39 percent in 2005, and in South Asia from 87 to 74 percent; and between 1990 and 2005 child mortality was reduced by almost 75 percent, in Bangladesh by 50 percent and in Tanzania by more than 25 percent.

well-being. Development was equated with economic growth and debate centred on the most appropriate ways to facilitate it.

Development as economic growth was subject to vigorous critique. It was argued that the focus should be human development, with economic growth a necessary but not sufficient means to this end.[6] Many questioned the assumption that "a rising tide lifts all boats," pointing out that economic growth leads to improved well-being for people who were poor *only* if it brings employment marked by decent work and just remuneration, and if governments use tax revenues to provide services to poor communities. Moreover, there are factors constraining the well-being of people that economic growth cannot address, such as gender values, violence, and public voice. This led to a new discourse around the theme of "human development" that focused on people having the freedom and capacity to lead lives they value. On this construction development focuses on issues such as health, education, participation in society, freedom from discrimination, and expansion of life choices. It demands that people who are poor set the agenda for their own development and prioritizes human development over economic development, insisting the latter should serve the former and not the other way around.[7]

Critique was also offered around the theme of "environmental sustainability." Economic development was usually associated with industrialization, which brought with it levels of pollution, destruction of habitats, and loss of biodiversity that compromised the ability of future generations to be sustained by the earth's resources. The issue remains live. Writing just one year ago, Jeff Sachs commented that

> The world's ability to combine long-term economic growth with environmental health is heavily debated. Yet one thing is certain: the current trajectory of human activity is not sustainable. If we simply do what we are doing on the planet with unchanged technology—but on a much larger scale as China, India, and other

---

6. Thus the title of Amartya Sen's highly influential *Development as Freedom*, in which he describes development as the process of enlarging people's freedoms—for example, freedom from hunger, freedom to participate and have their voices heard.

7. The human development approach was championed especially by the United Nations in its Human Development Reports that drew heavily on the work of economist Amartya Sen. An important recent development is the emergence of rights based approaches. These frame human wellbeing in terms of realization of rights and highlight the obligations of "duty-bearers" to respect the rights of people who are poor.

large population centres experience rapid economic growth—the environmental underpinnings of global well-being will collapse. The limits of the environment itself will defeat our global aspirations for prosperity.[8]

These critiques have led to widespread agreement that the world must pursue sustainable human development that leads to the improvement of people's well-being. Economic growth may be necessary to achieve this end, but it must be "pro-poor" and it must be environmentally sustainable.

Vigorous debates continue as to the best ways to achieve these ends. For example, there has been strident disagreement about the place of "free" markets in achieving pro-poor economic growth. Similarly, there is strong disagreement as to the constraints that environmental sustainability places on economic growth. Nonetheless, sustainable human development supported by pro-poor economic growth characterizes the nature of "development" as widely understood within the sector.

The Context for Development

Sustainable human development does not occur in a vacuum. The choices available to people are constrained by the social, institutional, economic, and environmental systems within which they live, systems that are commonly shaped by the more powerful to serve their own interests. Amartya Sen, for example, argues that famine results not from a decline in food supply but from lack of entitlement to food. That is, sufficient food always exists to meet the nutritional needs of famine struck communities; the problem is that some people have lost the capacity to access it, due to factors such as loss of land, loss of income, or decline in their income relative to the price of food. Consequently, Sen claims, famines are relatively easy to prevent. Countries simply need to ensure that the poor don't lose their entitlement to food, which they can do by providing public employment programs that preserve the purchasing power of the poor. These are usually enacted in liberal democracies, where political leaders suffer loss of power if they allow famines to occur, but are not enacted by illiberal, non-democratic regimes where there is no political incentive to prevent famine.[9]

---

8. Sachs, *Common Wealth*, 57.

9. Sen, *Development as Freedom*, 161–88. Sen points out that many of the severest

Sen's argument is borne out in the recent history of Malawi. Rapid population growth led to overuse of farmland, which in turn caused substantial declines in soil fertility and crop yield. Too poor to purchase fertilizers or food, millions of Malawians went hungry and malnourished. Under pressure from the World Bank and other international financial institutions, the Malawian government had eliminated subsidies for fertilizer and seeds. After a disastrous 2005 harvest, however, the Malawian president, Bingu wa Mutharika, reinstated farmer subsidies for fertilizer and grain. The subsequent years have seen bumper crops and a massive increase in food security.[10]

Such an example demonstrates how political and economic systems, both nationally and internationally, can subvert development. Other examples abound: social custom may demand payment of dowries that consume a poor household's resources; gender values may see a devaluing of the education of girls; caste systems may exclude lower castes from participation in society; absence of effective credit markets may see poor households dependent upon moneylenders who charge exorbitant rates of interest; corruption may impose costs on the poor and deprive them of public services; imperfect and unregulated labor markets may enable multinational firms to pay poverty level wages for goods produced in poorer countries; population growth may make traditional farming practices untenable and lead to a degradation of the environment; climate change may increase the prevalence and intensity of drought, storm, and flooding; and so on.

These systems occur at the level of the household, the local community, the nation, and the international community. If people living in

---

famines have occurred in countries where food production was rising or where food was being exported. He continues, "The causal connection between democracy and the non-occurrence of famines is not hard to seek. Famines kill millions of people in different countries in the world, but they don't kill the rules. The kings and the presidents, the bureaucrats and the bosses, the military leaders and the commanders never are famine victims. And if there are no elections, no opposition parties, no scope for uncensored public criticism, then those in authority don't have to suffer the political consequences of their failure to prevent famines. Democracy, on the other hand, would spread the penalty of famines to the ruling groups and political leaders as well. This gives them the political incentive to *try* to prevent any threatening famine, and since famines are in fact easy to prevent . . . the approaching famines are firmly prevented" (180). This is why, Sen claims, there have been no famines in post independence India.

10. Dugger, "Ending Famine."

poverty are to achieve sustainable human development, these systems must be transformed so that they serve their interests.

The Process of Development

One of the most important lessons of the development sector is that development cannot be imposed. Long-term, sustainable transformation involves far more than the injection of new forms of capital into a community. It is an inherently human process that requires the building of community capacity, transformation in relationships and power structures, and engagement with deeply rooted values. It can then be nothing less than an indigenous process in which all members of a community participate in making and implementing decisions that will affect their lives.

Mission with the Poor in Light of Developmental Wisdom

Having overviewed some key development concepts, we are in a position to reflect on them theologically and consider the implications for our mission to and with the poor. I will argue that a developmental perspective calls us to reframe our discussion of mission, such that our understanding of the mission of the church is related to the wider mission of God to and with humanity and the earth.

A Biblical Vision of Development

Theologically, the Baptist movement in Australia has, on the whole, moved beyond the spirit/matter dualism of the past. Nonetheless, our individualistic culture and our concern with the church mean we have not always operated with a robust and holistic vision for the whole earth community.[11] Yet such a vision is integral to the biblical narrative.

The Scriptures are bookended by a striking vision of the earth community (Gen 1–2, Rev 21–22). Over against alternate narratives told by the nations around Israel, this is no barren world on which humankind and the animals eke out a miserable and violent existence subject to the

---

11. I deliberately use the term "earth community" rather than "human community" as this includes the earth and all its creatures. I will not, however, focus on eco and animal theology in this paper.

whims of capricious deities. Rather, God creates a productive, abundant, and beautiful earth that sustains its creatures and provides the environment within which communities marked by loving service of the Creator, one another, and the animals can thrive.

In the creation narratives this community is nascent, ready to emerge as the creatures "multiply and fill the earth." By the end of the Book of Revelation the earth has been populated to become an abundant, just, and good garden city in which righteousness and the presence of God prevail. The story that unfolds between creation and new creation tells of the tragic unraveling of this vision and the work of the Creator to redeem the earth community.

Central to the realization of the biblical vision is humankind fulfilling its calling to image the Creator (Gen 1:26–28). Although this has been understood as referencing particular human characteristics such as rationality or relationality, it is more likely Genesis is thinking of humankind as representative of God on the earth, much as ancient Near Eastern culture thought of idols and kings as physically representing gods on the earth.[12] This explains the close relationship in Genesis 1:26–28 between bearing the image of God and ruling the earth. Kings and idols, as the representation of their gods on the earth, were the vehicle by which the gods exercised dominion. It was through them that the gods established their presence and exercised their will. Genesis 1 dramatically "democratizes" this concept. Humankind, "male and female," functions as God's representative on earth, responsible to exercise God's dominion by "ruling" and "subduing" the earth in a manner consistent with the character and purposes of God. Thus the central human mission is to steward the earth and its resources such that all creatures are able to enjoy its productivity and beauty, enjoy just, equitable and participatory communities, and engage in loving, faithful relationship with the Creator.

The first major redemptive move after the "fall" is the call of Abraham and the promise that through him and his descendants "blessing" will be restored to "all families of the earth" (Gen 12:1–3). This is

---

12. Middleton points out that while theologians have long debated alternative meanings of the "image of God," among biblical scholars there is a widely held consensus that "sees the image of God as the royal function or office of human beings as God's representatives and agents in the world, given authorized power to share in God's rule over the earth's resources and creatures." Middleton, "Liberating Image?"

given greater shape when his descendants, the Israelites, are liberated from slavery and called to a new land where they are to live as the people of God. With strong echoes of the garden experience (a beautiful and abundant land belonging to God in which God fellowships with the people), the Israelites are to craft a community in which God's vision for the earth community is embodied. All Israelites are to enjoy the productivity and beauty of the land, the community is to be just, equitable, and inclusive, and provision is made for people to engage in loving, faithful relationship with their Creator who dwells in their midst. As they do so they will be the vehicle by which the world's nations are drawn into a similar relationship with Israel's God (Exod 19:4–5).[13]

Just as the first humans failed to enact God's vision and were expelled from the garden, so Israel fails to enact God's vision and is expelled from the land. To explain this dramatic action the Prophets repeatedly call attention to the twin failings of refusal to worship Yahweh alone and refusal to create a community that is loving, just, and equitable. Yet they also speak of a time when Israel will be restored, the creation vision will be enacted, and Yahweh's reign will be realized through his people.

This is the essential framework for understanding the story of Jesus and his declaration that "the kingdom of God is near" (Mark 1:14–15).[14] Jesus is the One who truly images Yahweh, brings near the presence of God, and calls people into a just, equitable, and inclusive community centred around himself.[15] In fulfilling this mission Jesus challenges the prevailing powers of both Israel and Rome, leading to his crucifixion. Yahweh, however, vindicates the mission of Jesus by raising him from the dead and calling all humanity to follow in his way. Upon his return the vision for the earth community expressed (to varying degrees of perfection) in creation, Israel, Christ, and the church will be fully realized across the entire earth.

Scripture then has a robust and consistent vision for the earth community: humanity and the animals sharing a beautiful, productive, and abundant earth, living under the gracious reign of their Creator in loving, peaceful, equitable, and just communities, enjoying robust

13. See Wright, *Living as the People*, and his more recent expansion of this work, *Old Testament Ethics*, for a superb elaboration of these themes.

14. A point forcefully made by Wright in *Jesus and the Victory of God*.

15. Jesus presents himself as replacing the functions of the temple—it is in Jesus that people find the presence of God, forgiveness of sin, and instruction in the ways of God.

physical, emotional, and mental health and with human beings fulfilling their calling to represent God on the earth by stewarding the earth and its resources in a manner that enables the biblical vision to be realized. This, I argue, is a biblically framed understanding of development against which alternate articulations of development should be measured. Australian Baptists should repent of a vision for the earth community that is anything less than the one outlined here and for failing to live it out to the full. In this respect the development sector's call for environmentally sustainable development and a just international order remind us of obligations we have sometimes neglected in favor of a highly individualized faith that focuses on restricted dimensions of "private" morality and conversion. On the other hand, we bring to the sector a conviction that human well-being is complete only when people are able to enjoy right relationship with God through Christ and that other dimensions of well-being must be framed in a fashion consistent with the lordship of Christ.

The Mission of God, Humanity, and the Church

While the biblical story line focuses on God's work in and through Israel, Christ, and the church, Scripture does not see God's work as restricted to these. As Lord of the whole earth God is continually working toward the fulfillment of the creation vision for the earth community. On the one hand, the Creator sustains the creation so that its productivity and beauty can be enjoyed by all his creatures (e.g. Gen 8:21–22; Ps 104; Matt 5:45; Acts 14:17). This goodwill towards his creatures is poignantly expressed in Paul's words to the Lystrans: "He has shown you kindness by giving you rain from heaven and crops in their seasons; he provides you with plenty of food and fills your hearts with joy" (Acts 14:17).

On the other hand, God is involved in the history of nations in a fashion akin to his involvement with Israel. Amos, for example, makes much of the parallels between the history of Israel and the nations around it. The first two chapters of the book recall God's acts of judgment upon the surrounding nations called forth by their violence. It then makes the provocative claim that Israel will be treated in the same way for its acts of injustice. In the closing chapters Amos challenges the notion that Israel's rescue from slavery in Egypt is indicative of a privileged status before God, for God had also been active in the history of Israel's neighbors, bringing the Philistines from Caphtor and the Arameans from Kir (Amos 9:7). The book of Daniel likewise insists that Yahweh is sovereign over the kingdoms of the world, active in both judging the hubris of kings and in establishing their thrones when humbly fulfilling their calling to acknowledge Yahweh and do justice (Dan 4). Particularly significant is Daniel's assertion that God's sovereign power over kings sees him deposing those who act oppressively (4:25–27), a theme also developed elsewhere in Scripture (e.g. Ps 10:12–18; Ps 74; 82; Ezek 16:49–50; Luke 1:46–55). Yet God's response to oppression is not first and foremost to punish, but to call to repentance, as evidenced in the book of Jonah and its poignant closing words:

> But the LORD said, "You have been concerned about this gourd, though you did not tend it or make it grow. It sprang up overnight and died overnight. And should I not have concern for the great city Nineveh, in which there are more than a hundred and twenty thousand people who cannot tell their right hand from their left—and also many animals?" (4:10–11).

The difference between Israel and the nations is not that God is present and active among the Israelites but not among other nations, but that Israel has been the subject of redemptive acts and revelation that carry significance for the entire earth community. Through Israel they may come to know the identity of the one true God who is at work in their midst, and in knowing Yahweh more fully appreciate the nature of righteousness and justice.

A similar case can be made for the relationship between the church and other human communities. Paul sees God's wrath unfolding in the experiences of the Gentiles (Rom 1:18–32); recognizes the hand of God's Spirit when Gentiles show the works of the Law written on their hearts (Rom 2:14–15);[16] affirms that "in him we live and move and have our being" and declares to the Athenians that he knows the identity of the "unknown God" who gives life to all things and has shaped the history of nations (Acts 17:21–29); and sees governments as the servants of God called to restrain evil and reward good (Rom 13). As for Israel, the difference between the church and other human communities is not that God works only in and through the church but that the church bears

---

16. Note the way this passage evokes the imagery of Jer 31:33 and 2 Cor 3:3, making Paul's assertion quite remarkable.

witness to the redemptive act in Christ that bears significance for every community.

It is quite appropriate then for Baptists to think of:

- a *missio Dei* in which God works for the well-being of the entire created order and which includes God's work to bring people under the acknowledged lordship of Christ; to sustain a productive and beautiful creation; and to create justice, peace and equity;[17]
- a *missio terrae* in which the earth yields its beauty and productivity for the pleasure of God and the nourishing of its creatures;
- a *missio humanitatis* in which human beings worship the Creator, steward the earth so that it fulfills its mission, and utilize their God-given capacities to build loving, just, peaceful, and equitable communities;
- and a *missio ecclessiae* in which the church witnesses in its life and words to Christ as the Lord who embodies, defines, and will bring to completion the *missio Dei*, *missio terrae*, and *missio humanitatis*.

This has several implications for mission to and with the poor, two that I wish to explore here.

A Dual Role for the Church

First, the church has a dual role toward the world. It offers something no other group can—witness to Christ and the call to repentance, faith, and salvation. In this capacity the church is right to emphasize its distinctiveness and safeguard the uniqueness of its message. On the other hand, the church participates along with the entire human community in the *missio humanitatis*. The knowledge that Christ works through individuals and institutions outside the church to bring about justice enables the church not only to call them to repentance where they fail to act justly, but to partner with them in constructing communities of peace and justice.

---

17. The concept of the *missio Dei* has been vigorously debated. In order to preserve the unique redemptive focus of the church some have argued for a distinction between God's work as creator and God's work as redeemer. This seems an unhelpful distinction to me, as it suggests a split in the work of God that I don't think measures up to the much more fluid biblical descriptions.

Confusion of these dual role is common. Collapsing the *missio humanitatis* into the *missio ecclesiae* sees the church lose its distinctive witness, a critique perhaps not unjustifiably made of some "ecumenical" approaches to mission.[18] Conversely, collapsing the *missio ecclesiae* into the *missio humanitatis* sees the church assume to itself responsibility for the entire *missio humanitatis*, something it is neither called nor equipped to do.

A good example of this confusion is found in Rick Warren's P.E.A.C.E. Plan, which identifies spiritual emptiness, self-serving leadership, extreme poverty, pandemic diseases, and rampant illiteracy as five "global giants" confronting the world, then claims, "There is no organization or government that can effectively eradicate these giants. The only successful solution is the global Church of Jesus Christ."[19] In proffering the church as the only solution Warren assumes to the church responsibility for the *missio humanitatis*. His solution is to mobilize a billion Christians in short-term church-to-church partnerships in which skills and knowledge are transferred.[20] As admirable as the P.E.A.C.E. Plan may be, and whatever good may be achieved, it is blind to the developmental realities described in this paper. In particular it fails to recognize (1) that human development requires much more than the injection of new forms of capital; it is a difficult, long-term process involving transformation of human communities with all their strengths, weaknesses, ambiguities, power structures, entrenched values, attitudes, and customs, etc.; (2) the necessity of groups other than the church for the realization of the *missio humanitatis*—for example, a "medical clinic in a box" will never provide the health system required to provide decent medical care; and (3) the systemic factors such as unjust international economic structures that keep people trapped in poverty.

In recent years a similar confusion of roles has seen Australian Baptist churches forming often unhelpful partnerships with local churches in the developing world. The partnerships are unhelpful because the leaders of these developing world churches often themselves constitute something of an elite within their communities—a status

---

18. By "ecumenical" I refer to the distinction between the so-called "ecumenical" and "evangelical" conceptions of mission that became apparent following the Willingen conference.

19. "What is the P.E.A.C.E. Plan?" Online: http://www.purposedrivenchurch.com/en-US/PEACE/PEACE_Plan.htm. See also http://www.thepeaceplan.com.

20. See http://www.thepeaceplan.com.

reinforced by the funds flowing to them from Australia—and in their efforts to assist the development of their communities they function out of a *missio ecclesiae* paradigm rather than as participants in the *missio humanitatis*.

The church will become a positive agent in transformative development only when it recognizes it has a dual role to play in the world, offering both its unique witness to Christ, and itself in love as partner with the rest of humanity in the *missio humanitatis*.

Poverty as Injustice

The second area I believe needs to be explored concerns the way we conceptualize poverty. For many people poverty is viewed as deprivation, which in Australian Baptist churches frequently and rightly evokes strong compassion and generous acts of giving. Yet behind this generosity lie unstated or unquestioned assumptions as to why people are poor. Some blame the poor, attributing their deprivation to laziness, lack of faith, or moral failure. Others attribute poverty to misfortune. The human development movement, and especially the emerging human rights approach to development, invites us to see poverty as an injustice in which the rich and powerful maintain economic, social, and political systems that marginalize, exploit, and impoverish those who are poor. As noted earlier, these systems extend from the local (for example, corrupt police and gender discrimination), to the national (for example, an elite capturing the bulk of public funding), to the international (for example, exploitation of cheap labor, unfair trade practices, climate change).

Such an approach resonates with the teaching of Scripture. The Scriptures insist that both God and the earth are "good." The "fall" may have made it more difficult to access the earth's productivity, but this does not alter the fact that the earth remains good, fit for the purpose of sustaining its creatures (for example, Gen 8:22; Ps 104; 1 Tim 4:4). Similarly, God may at times withhold blessing as an act of judgment that restrains the progress of evil, but the normal functioning of the Creator is to show kindness to humankind in maintaining the earth's productivity (Matt 5:43–48; Acts 14:17). The root cause of poverty then, lies in the failure of human beings to fulfill their calling to steward the earth and its resources such that God's purposes for the world are realized. Scripture recognizes that at times the fault may lie with the person falling into poverty (for example, Prov 10:4; 20:13; 21:17; 23:21), but this is a very minor theme. The dominant note in Scripture is the failure of the richer and more powerful to respect the rights of the poor (for example, 1 Sam 8:10–18; Prov 13:23; 22:16; 29:7; Isa 1:10–31; 58:1–14; Amos 1–2; 4:1–3; 5:11–12; Jas 5:1–5).

Critical to a biblical approach is the insistence that the earth belongs to the Lord and is gifted to humankind and the animals for their sustenance and as an environment in which they might experience rest, enjoyment of the earth's beauty, and participation in community. Social, political, and economic systems that militate against rather than serving these outcomes are manifestly unjust and an abrogation of the essential human calling to image God.

This understanding is given clear expression in the laws of Israel— the land belongs to God and is to be redistributed every fifty years to ensure all households have access to the means of production (Lev 25); the temporarily landless are to be offered work and a share in the harvest (Lev 19:9–10; Deut 23:24–25); loans are to be offered interest free whenever needed and the outstanding portion to be forgiven after seven years (Deut 15:1–11). Such laws gave shape to the socioeconomic systems of Israel and provided a collective means of guarding against individual household vulnerability. If followed, they would ensure all Israelites maintained access to the abundance of the land and participation in the community.

This biblical framework also provides the context within which Jesus' challenge to the powerful and wealthy is mounted (for example, Luke 6:20–26; 7:36–5; 12:13–34; 16:19–31; 18:18–30; 19:1–10). The failure to include those on the margins and share wealth with them is not merely a failure to be charitable; it is a failure to respect the rights of the poor to sustenance, inclusion, equity, and rest, and to follow the provisions made in the Law. When Jesus challenges Simon the Pharisee over his response to an "unclean" woman, he challenges the sociopolitical system from which Simon benefits and which as a community leader he perpetuates. Or consider the story of the rich ruler (Luke 18:18–30). In popular Baptist preaching the problem is that the rich ruler loves his wealth more than Jesus and thus Jesus challenges him to give up the thing that holds him back from complete devotion. The logic is that there is nothing wrong with being rich per se, but with loving riches more than Jesus. Such an interpretation is difficult to sustain in light of both Jesus' constant call for the rich to divest themselves of their wealth and the Old Testament approach to economics. In calling the rich ruler to give his wealth to the poor Jesus draws his attention to the Law's insistence that the wealth of the land belongs to God and is therefore to be shared among all Israelites. Jesus exposes as false the ruler's claim that he has kept the commandments. In fact he has failed the basic test of a ruler, which is to defend the rights of the poor and needy (Prov 31:19), and is called to recover his humanity by following Jesus into a lifestyle of justice. Indeed, the continual call for the wealthy to share all they have with the poor appears to be part of the way Jesus sees himself enacting the Year of Jubilee (Luke 4:19), and, given the social location of the wealthy as the elite of society, constitutes nothing less than a call to fulfill the Old Testament vision of a just socioeconomic system.

Poverty then should be seen not merely as deprivation, but as the fruit of marginalization, exploitation, and oppression. This reinforces the notion that development involves much more than the simple transfer of skills and resources. It involves transformation of social, economic, and political systems that marginalize and exploit people. For Baptists there are at least two dramatic implications.

First, we must refuse to support development programs that entrench rather than address the social, economic, and political systems that entrap people living in poverty. Examples of these are legion—church-based programs that entrench the power of pastors acting as "big men" in their communities; orphan homes that remove children from their communities and their inheritance; schools for AIDS orphans that, by further separating AIDS orphans from their community, exacerbate the discrimination against them. These kinds of activities are very appealing to our churches. They are driven by well-motivated people and inspired by godly compassion, but we have been largely unaware of their systemic ramifications.

Second, we must recognize that the causes of poverty are not something external to us. When we spend more on our holidays and home electronics than we do on assisting the poor we are robbing them of what is rightfully theirs. When we buy clothing made in sweatshops for which workers have received a wage insufficient to meet their needs, let alone their full participatory rights, we are the beneficiaries of exploitation. When we sustain lifestyles that deplete the world's fisheries, drive up the price of food, and spew unsustainable greenhouse gas emissions into the atmosphere, the consequences are borne by the world's poor in the form of increased vulnerability and decreased food security. When our governments conduct foreign policy on the basis of narrow national interest and fail to work toward a just international economic order, we collectively fail in the basic human calling to steward the earth and its resources in a fashion that achieves justice for all.

"Doing justice" then calls Baptists to far more than opening our wallets to occasional appeals or supporting mission activities in foreign lands. It demands we construct lifestyles in which we give vastly more, consume ethically, and become involved in advocacy campaigns around issues such as aid, trade, debt, and climate change. Mission to and with the poor must not be something that happens only "over there" but also among us. At this point the *missio ecclesiae* and the *missio humanitas* surely overlap as we take up the challenge to construct communities of faith that witness to the lordship of Christ in a world of immense poverty.

12

Baptist Witness to New Testament Baptism beyond 2009

RICHARD K. MOORE

Introduction

At their best, Baptists do not regard their tradition as the only authentic form of Christianity. They do, however, feel compelled to witness to the church worldwide and to humanity in general certain aspects of the Good News of Christ that have become obscured by the way in which Christianity has developed since apostolic times. In fact the term "Baptist" seems best defined as referring to a discrete set of core beliefs or "distinctives" shared by people who have identified themselves with the Baptist movement since its beginnings in 1609.

These distinctives are by no means to be regarded as the most significant beliefs for authentic Christianity. Rather, they arose in a historical context among Christians who, while acknowledging that the Protestant Reformation had achieved many very valuable reforms, considered it had not gone far enough in several important respects. Further, in varying degrees (according to time and circumstance), these concerns, or distinctives, have continued to be relevant over the 400 years of Baptist history.

One of these distinctives concerns the supreme authority of the Bible for all matters of faith and conduct ("Bible" here referring to the 66 writings making up the Scriptures in the Protestant tradition). This belief was inherited directly from the Reformers' catch-cry of *sola Scriptura*.

A second distinctive is the claim that authentic Christian baptism consists of the baptism of believers by immersion. It is arguable that this is not the most important Baptist distinctive, nor do Baptists insist that baptism is necessary for salvation—as some denominations do. Yet baptism continues to be important for Baptists. Of the several reasons why this is so, the two most compelling are that baptism is a dominical command (Matt 28:18–20) and it was clearly normative in the apostolic church. Baptists therefore feel called to witness to the form of baptism they embrace, not least because of the widespread theological distortions other forms of Christian baptism have created. Basing their convictions primarily on the evidence of the New Testament, but also on the lessons of church history, Baptists do not regard these alternative forms as authentic.

When we ask what the New Testament actually tells us about the theology and practice of baptism in the apostolic church, the response is likely to take one of two forms:

1. The first approach examines what the New Testament has to say when it uses the Greek words for baptism, baptize, and cognates. In short, it takes into account only explicit baptismal vocabulary.

2. The second approach considers not only the word usage in (1), but also endeavors to set the question in the wider context of New Testament theology (or theologies), including ecclesiology.

At first sight the second alternative may appear to be the more attractive. It does, however, suffer from a major drawback, namely, that when texts that do not contain explicit baptismal vocabulary are appealed to, there is often considerable disagreement among New Testament scholars as to whether or not they do, in fact, refer to Christian baptism. That is, such texts introduce an element of uncertainty into this approach. On the other hand, the first approach sets out to listen to the New Testament on its own terms.

This paper divides into two parts. The first consists of observations arising from an examination of the explicit baptismal vocabulary in the New Testament, that is, approach (1) above. The second examines a text that contains no explicit baptismal vocabulary at all, yet arguably it is the text that has had the greatest influence on the theology and practice of baptism in the Western church, namely, Romans 5:12, as it was understood and applied by Augustine of Hippo.

New Testament Baptismal Theology and Practice

A picture of baptismal theology and practice emerges from a consideration of the explicit baptismal vocabulary in the New Testament. The picture is established by the word family with the stem βαπτιζ- or its variant form βαπτισ-. It is represented by four words, one a verb, three nouns. In order of frequency they are βαπτιζω (76x), βαπτισμα (19x), βαπτιστης (12x) and βαπτισμος (4x). These 111 occurrences are distributed among 12 of the 27 New Testament writings.[1]

The single occurrence in the longer ending of Mark (Mark 16:16) is excluded from our considerations, as on text-critical grounds it is to be regarded as a later, non-Marcan addition to the original Gospel. Also falling outside our considerations, on the same grounds, is Acts 8:37; although it contains no baptismal vocabulary, it clearly was added later to Acts 8:26–40, the baptismal narrative concerning Philip and the Ethiopian eunuch.

In our quest for the theology and practice of baptism in the New Testament, not all 111 occurrences impinge directly on our topic, as some are used figuratively, while others are used in secondary senses.

The 12 New Testament writings containing explicit baptismal vocabulary may be grouped into four broad categories, as follows: the letters attributed to Paul, the Gospels, Acts of the Apostles, and the non-Pauline letters.

The Letters Attributed to Paul

The letters attributed to Paul fall into two subcategories: (1) those that are widely regarded as authentic, of which three (Gal, 1 Cor, Rom) contain explicit baptismal vocabulary; and (2) those whose authenticity is in doubt; two of which (Eph and Col) contain explicit baptismal vocabulary. Note the following:

- It is probable that Galatians 3:27 contains the earliest use of explicit baptismal vocabulary in the New Testament.
- With 10 occurrences, 1 Corinthians has by far the most among all the New Testament letters. Six of these occur in chapter 1, where Paul is discussing his personal involvement in baptisms during the formation of the church at Corinth. Two (in ch. 15) refer to a prac-

1. See appendix A.

tice in the apostolic era of baptizing on behalf of those who had died, presumably unbaptized.

- Among all the letters, Romans, with three occurrences (in ch. 6), is second to 1 Corinthians.
- Thus, with only 19 of the 111 New Testament occurrences (17 percent), baptismal vocabulary in the letters tends to be under-represented.

The Gospels

In considering the Gospels, there is value in treating the Synoptic Gospels together for a number of occurrences, while respecting their unique contributions in others.

a. Although Mark is by far the shortest of the Synoptics, it actually contains the highest number of occurrences (19x; vs. 17x in Luke 17x and 16x in Matt). Mere statistics can be misleading in this case, as six of Mark's occurrences are in a single pericope, where they are used figuratively (10:38–39) in a passage not paralleled in the other Gospels.

b. John's Gospel has fewer occurrences (13x) than any of the Synoptics , but contributes unique material by describing Jesus' baptismal ministry contemporaneous with that of John the Baptist; it is administered not by Jesus himself, but only by his disciples.

Acts of the Apostles

Of all the New Testament writings, Acts has the highest count of explicit baptismal vocabulary (27x). In Acts this vocabulary is used in two ways: (1) to describe actual instances of baptism, and (2) to refer to baptism in cases where the baptismal vocabulary does not have this descriptive function.

Actual instances of baptism are described for nine different occasions: the Day of Pentecost; the Samaritan converts, including Simon Magus; the Ethiopian eunuch; Saul (Paul); Cornelius, with his household and friends; Lydia and her household; the Philippian jailor and his household; Crispus, with his household and other believers at Corinth; and the disciples of John the Baptist at Ephesus.[2]

Associated with these accounts is a cluster of phenomena, most of which are not found in all accounts. However, some form of proclamation of the Christian message is common to all. The Holy Spirit's activity is mentioned in five, faith/belief in four or five, and the laying on of hands in three. As is universally acknowledged, the *order* in which these elements appear in the baptismal process is quite varied.[3]

Contrary to a strong Baptist tradition (recently Stein), I have not found any explicit evidence to support the view that the essence of Christian baptism is the public confession of one's faith. Some of the evidence is distinctly against it, for example the case of the Philippian jailor who, with his household, was baptized in the early hours of the morning. The tradition may have arisen from Acts 8:37. As noted above, however, that is not part of the original New Testament, but a later insertion. In any case, the Ethiopian eunuch's baptism seems to have taken place in a very isolated location.

The baptisms of whole households in Acts are noteworthy. Four in number, they occur in a block, from the fifth to the eighth descriptions of actual baptisms. Against those who have contended that households would have included babies and/or young children, the data of three of these household conversions indicates that those in each household were capable of listening meaningfully to the message, and/or of believing, and /or of rejoicing. In the fourth case, that of the business woman Lydia, there is no evidence that any males were associated with her household, making it highly improbable that any babies and/or young children were present.

The Non-Pauline Letters

Of the eight non-Pauline letters in the New Testament, two contain explicit baptismal vocabulary: Hebrews (2x) and 1 Peter (1x).

---

2. See appendix B.
3. See appendix B.

The Semantics of New Testament Baptismal Language

An examination of all occurrences indicates that semantically they fall into five categories, the first of which has two subcategories: John the Baptist's baptism, his name and his ministry; Jesus Christ's baptism (with the Holy Spirit); Christian baptism; figurative uses; and secondary uses.

John the Baptist's Baptism

With 54 occurrences, John the Baptist and/or his ministry have more occurrences pertaining to them than any other area.

- Fifteen of these occurrences function to identify that the John being spoken of is John the Baptist. These include all 12 occurrences of βαπτιστης, to which we need to add three uses of βαπτιζω in its participial form, "John the baptizer." The use of βαπτιστης is confined to the Synoptic Gospels. Although Luke makes use of it three times in his Gospel, he does not use it at all in Acts.

- The other 39 occurrences all refer to the ministry of John the Baptist. This exceeds even the 37 occurrences pertaining to Christian baptism.

Jesus Christ's Baptism (with the Holy Spirit)

Closely associated with John's baptismal ministry are four occurrences in the Gospels (one in each) and one in Acts that refer to a baptism Jesus Christ was to conduct, in which the medium is not water (as in John's baptismal rite) but the Holy Spirit (to which Luke and Matthew add "and fire"). A further occurrence in Acts (11:16) looks back to that baptism as having occurred on the Day of Pentecost.

One of the features of the language Luke uses in Acts to describe the activity of the Holy Spirit in relation to the believer is its *variety*. This variety is already evident in the first two chapters, but when Peter participates in and witnesses the conversions of Cornelius, his household, and other non-Jews (10:44–47) and later, when recounting his experience to the Christians of Jerusalem and Judea, *links the Cornelius experience with the phenomenon of Pentecost* (11:15–16) the varied language is seen to refer to the common experience of Christian conversion. The supporting data is as follows:

- *baptism in the Holy Spirit* clearly refers to both the Pentecost experience and the Cornelius experience (Acts 1:5 cf. Luke 3:16; Acts 11:16)
- *empowerment from on high* (Acts 1:8; cf. Luke 24:49) clearly points forward to the Holy Spirit's role at Pentecost
- *being filled* with the Holy Spirit (Acts 2:4; 9:17)
- the *pouring out* of God's Spirit (Acts 2:17, citing Joel 3:1 LXX; Acts 2:33; Acts 10:45)
- the *gift* of the Holy Spirit (Acts 2:38; 8:20; 10:45; 11:17)
- the Holy Spirit *falling upon* someone/people (Acts 8:16; 10:44; 11:15, where it is applied to 2:4)
- *receiving* the Holy Spirit (Acts 8:17; 10:47)
- the Holy Spirit *coming upon* someone/people (19:6)

These statements make it clear that in Luke's understanding the predictions of John the Baptist that Jesus would baptize in the Holy Spirit find their fulfillment in his account of Pentecost, but also in an ongoing sense in his accounts of actual baptisms in Acts, even though the Holy Spirit's role in those accounts is described in varied terminology.

This position is supported by the only other reference to baptism in the Holy Spirit in the New Testament: Paul's statement at 1 Corinthians 12:13. There the apostle clearly understood baptism in the Holy Spirit to apply to all who are in the body of Christ, irrespective of their ethnic origin or social status. For Paul it was no secondary or later phenomenon limited to some Christians, but constituted the essence of the Christian experience itself (cf. 1 Cor 12:13b; Rom 8:9b).

The evidence discussed up to this point justifies subsuming these seven references to baptism in the Holy Spirit under Christian baptism (discussed below).

It is noteworthy that although baptism in the Holy Spirit was understood to be integrally related to Christian conversion, this did not lead the apostolic church to abandon the practice of water baptism (cf. Acts 10:47–48). At the same time the evidence of Acts 8:14–15, 17 makes it clear that water baptism in and of itself does not automatically (*ex opere operato*) confer the gift of the Holy Spirit.

Christian Baptism

The 37 occurrences referring to Christian baptism are drawn from Acts (15x), the undisputed Pauline letters (12x), the Gospels (John, 4x; Matt, 2x), the disputed Pauline letters (2x), and one each from Hebrews and 1 Peter among the non-Pauline letters of the New Testament.

Included in this statistic are the two occurrences in Matthew's Gospel. In the first John says to Jesus, who has come to him for baptism, "I have need to be baptized by you," (Matt 3:14); the second concerns the Great Commission (Matt 28:19). The latter is of interest because it is Jesus' only command in the whole of the New Testament for his disciples to practice baptism. Further, again unique to this passage, Christian baptism is to be carried out in the name of the Father, Son, and Holy Spirit. Elsewhere, specifically in Acts, it is only in the name of Jesus ("in the name of Jesus Christ" and "in the name of the Lord Jesus" each occur twice).

Also included in this statistic for Christian baptism are the four occurrences in John's Gospel that describe how Jesus' disciples conducted baptisms on his behalf—*prior to* Jesus' passion. This information is limited to John's Gospel.

Figurative Uses

The figurative use of explicit baptismal language accounts for nine occurrences in the New Testament. Six of these are found in Mark, two in Luke, one at 1 Corinthians 10:2.

The occurrences in Mark form a single block. They comprise Jesus' response to the request of James and John for special status in the kingdom of God. His allusions to a future "baptism" he is to undergo—in parallel to another figure of speech, a cup he will be required to drink—are generally understood to refer to suffering he anticipated, and very probably suffering culminating in death. The Lucan occurrences, though in a different context, are strikingly similar in wording to those in Mark.

At 1 Corinthians 10:2 Paul uses baptism as a figure for Israel's experience of being under the supernatural cloud and passing through the Red Sea during the exodus: they were all "baptized into Moses, in the cloud and in the sea."

Secondary Uses

Twice in Mark, once in Luke, the verb βαπτίζω is used in the secondary sense of everyday washing. The occurrence at Hebrews 9:10, referring to various aspects of Old Testament ritual ablutions in order to emphasize their ineffectiveness, constitutes the fourth and final secondary use of explicit baptismal vocabulary.

It will be seen, then, that if we set aside the figurative and secondary uses of baptismal vocabulary just discussed, which account for 13 occurrences, the remaining 98 of the 111 occurrences (88 percent) refer either to John's baptism (54x) or to Christian baptism (44x) (in which, for the reasons given above, we include Jesus' baptizing in the medium of the Holy Spirit).

In fact, the New Testament mentions only these two forms of baptism that, while distinct, have a close relationship. John's baptism was preparatory, foreshadowing a greater baptism, associated with the coming Messiah. It evidently came to an end with John's imprisonment and subsequent execution. Notwithstanding, it is John's baptism that has the greatest prominence in the New Testament documents.

In spite of the fact that the New Testament mentions only these two baptismal rites, considerable energy has been expended in exploring their possible antecedents as well as baptismal practices contemporary with the New Testament. In terms of establishing causal connections, this research has proved to be largely an exercise in futility, simply establishing that the rites considered explain little about the origins of either John's rite or Christian baptism and in some cases highlighting the uncertainty of the periods during which these other rites were practiced.

In each of the nine accounts of actual baptisms in Acts, mention is made of the Christian message being proclaimed in some way. While only four or five of these accounts make explicit mention of faith as the response to the message, in each case faith precedes baptism and in *every* account those being baptized have clearly accepted the Christian message *prior to* their baptism.

While the NT evidence precludes an insistence on the necessity of baptism for salvation (1 Cor 1), it is clear on the other hand that *baptism was the norm*. When Paul wrote to churches he did not know personally, such as Romans, he could assume that those he addressed had been baptized.

Quite apart from the lexical evidence pointing to "dip, immerse, submerse" as the primary meaning of βαπτιζω and cognates, there are four passages in the New Testament that make virtually no sense unless their baptismal vocabulary is understood in this way:

- Romans 6:3-4: Here Paul's imagery is dependent on the act of immersion, entering the water as a symbol of dying and burial, and rising from the water in newness of life.

- Mark 1:9 indicates that Jesus was baptized into (εἰς) the Jordan River, clarifying Mark 1:5, which states that John baptized in (ἐν) the Jordan. This is potentially ambiguous if meanings other than "immerse" are claimed for βαπτιζω.

- John 3:23: We are informed that at one stage John the Baptist was exercising his ministry at Aenon near Salem "because there was a lot of water there." A lot of water is necessary for immersion, but not for other forms of baptism.

- 1 Peter 3:18: Peter, assuring his readers that baptism saves them, immediately points out that he does not have in mind the removal of dirt from the body that occurs in baptism, but rather "the answer of a good conscience to God" or "the appeal to God for a good conscience" (however the Greek is to be understood). The incidental reference to the removal of dirt from the body makes sense in the context of immersion, but not with other forms of baptism practiced later. A sideways glance at the baptismal practice of the Greek Orthodox Church, which involves the threefold immersion of an infant, provides a salutary reminder that the primary meaning of βαπτιζω in the Greek language was, and remains, to "immerse."

Romans 5:12

Romans 5:12 is the single most important text in the development of baptismal theology and practice in the Western church, until the Radical Reformers of the sixteenth century and Baptists of the seventeenth century. In the discussion that follows I will use the term "brephobaptism" rather than "paedobaptism" for the practice of infant baptism. It is, after all, concerned with the infant (βρεφος), not merely the child (παις), who may, within that definition, reach an age of religious awareness and readiness, with the potential to have a genuine faith.

Given the brevity of this paper, it would be easy to convey the impression that I hold that the adoption of infant baptism as the norm in the Western church was a simple linear development running through Augustine and Rom 5:12 to the Middle Ages and beyond. Nothing could be further from the truth. A study such as the massive one by Everett Ferguson[4] is a reminder of the complexities of baptismal understanding and practice in the first five centuries alone. Rather, my goal is to focus on *the major influence* that, in time, worked like leaven throughout the Western church. It established a baptismal theology and practice that came to dominate the Middle Ages and was not abandoned by the magisterial Reformers of the sixteenth century. To the present day it continues to be widely influential and in many denominations it remains the dominant model. Historically, that understanding derives from Augustine of Hippo, for whom Romans 5:12 provided the key text. In the Greek Rom 5:12 reads:

> Διὰ τοῦτο ὥσπερ δι' ἑνὸς ἀνθρώπου ἡ ἁμαρτία εἰς τὸν κόσμον εἰσῆλθεν καὶ διὰ τῆς ἁμαρτίας ὁ θάνατος, καὶ οὕτως εἰς πάντας ἀνθρώπους ὁ θάνατος διῆλθεν, ἐφ' ᾧ πάντες ἥμαρτον·

> For this reason, just as sin entered the world through one person [Adam] and through sin death [entered], so too death came upon all people, *because* all sinned. (my translation)

In spite of its dominant role, the verse contains no explicit baptismal vocabulary. Further, the Latin text from which Augustine worked contained a mistranslation from the original Greek. For the Greek ἐφ' ᾧ ("in that, because") the Latin reads *in quo* ("in whom"). This was the case whether Augustine was working from Old Latin manuscripts or from the Vulgate of his contemporary Jerome, since Jerome in his revision failed to correct the mistranslation. Augustine, then, understood Romans 5:12 to be saying:

> For this reason, just as sin entered the world through one person [Adam] and through sin death [entered], so too death came upon all people, *in whom* all sinned.

---

4. Ferguson, *Baptism in the Early Church*.

Augustine took the antecedent of "in whom" to be Adam. He understood it to be a reference to what he termed "original sin." In succeeding generations the term "original sin" has come to be overlaid with such a variety of meanings that it is important to understand what Augustine meant by it, namely, that the *guilt* or *penalty* of Adam's sin was visited on every one of his offspring.

As to infants, Augustine was quite clear: they have no personal sin, which is self-evident from observing them.[5] However, because the guilt of Adam's sin is inherited by every human being, that guilt should be removed as soon as possible. The means of removing guilt is baptism, since it is by baptism that the benefits of Christ's death are applied, and therefore a person should be baptized as soon as possible—that is, as an infant.

Should an infant, innocent in its own right, die without baptism, it nevertheless faced the consequences of the guilt and penalty of "original sin." While in one place Augustine spoke of them as "damned, but most lightly,"[6] elsewhere they faced the prospect of "darkness,"[7] of being left "more destitute and wretched than orphans,"[8] and "the wrath of God abides on them."[9] This prospect makes baptism essential for all infants, even those of believing parents.

As we evaluate Augustine's view of "original sin," two observations are in order. In the first place, in *de peccatorum meritis et remissione, et de baptismo parvulorum* (412) Augustine creates the impression that his argumentation is based firmly on the authority of the Scriptures, whereas his Pelagian opponents either misunderstand or misuse them. When discussing infants and young children, however, he completely ignores the evidence of the Lord's quite extensive teaching in this area. The issue at stake here may be summed up in the title of a paper I once read to a gathering of pastors: "Forming Our Infancy and Childhood: Shall We Be Informed by Augustine of Hippo or Jesus of Nazareth?"[10]

---

5. Augustine, *Treatise* I.22; I.28; I.33; I.39; I.65; I.66.
6. Augustine 412, I.21.
7. Ibid., 412, I.35.
8. Ibid., 412, III.22.
9. Ibid., 412, I.28.
10. Moore, "Justification by Faith."

Secondly, Augustine charged Pelagius and his associates with making God unjust.[11] According to his own doctrine of original sin, however, Augustine held that God imposes on every human being the guilt and penalty of Adam, their progenitor. This is true even of infants, who, on Augustine's consistent testimony, have no personal sin. Yet had not God already punished Adam for his sin (Gen 3:17–19)? What kind of God would require the guilt and penalty of the guilty to be applied to the innocent? Certainly Ezekiel (ch. 18) ruled this out as completely contrary to the character of God—the God of absolute justice. It is surely quite incredible that so little objection has been raised to this far-reaching Augustinian distortion of God and his justice.

Although infant baptism had been practiced since around AD 200,[12] even in Augustine's day some two centuries later it was by no means the norm in the Western church. For even though his mother Monica was a Christian, Augustine himself was not baptized as an infant, but in adulthood, by Ambrose of Milan. And the historical record attests that many of his contemporaries were not baptized until their mature years.[13]

Augustine's arguments in favor of brephobaptism proved persuasive, and, due primarily to his influence, in time this practice became normative in the Western church. As Barth suggested, in the post-Constantinian era the infant baptism practiced by national churches has typically functioned to cement church-state alliances by making church membership and citizenship coterminous.[14] The effect of this has been to perpetuate infant baptism, even when the evidence legitimating it has come to be recognized as wanting.

One of the corollaries of Augustine's theology of baptism is that baptism came to be regarded as *essential for salvation*. So seriously was this taken that during the Middle Ages the practice of intrauterine baptism developed, whereby if there was reason to fear that the life of an unborn child was at risk, a form of baptism was used even before it left the womb.[15]

---

11. Augustine, *Treatise* 412, III.3.
12. Aland, *Did the Early Church*.
13. Wright, "Infant Dedication" 352.
14. Barth, *Teaching of the Church*, 52–53.
15. Whale, *Protestant Tradition*, 56.

Reflections

My closing observations concern those branches of the Christian church that still practice brephobaptism. They fall into two broad categories Protestant and Catholic (Anglicans fall somewhere in between, depending on the individual!). While the Radical Reformers of the sixteenth century and Baptists from the early seventeenth century based their baptismal rite on the New Testament (in the Reformation tradition of *sola Scriptura*) the magisterial reformers retained the practice of brephobaptism they had inherited from the medieval church, along with the essence of its theology. Luther, formerly an Augustinian monk, provides a clear example of this approach, an approach endorsed by his spiritual heirs. On the one hand he insists that justification is "master and chief, lord, ruler and judge above every kind of doctrine, which preserves and directs every doctrine of the Church" (preface to 45 theses drawn up 1 June 1537), on the other his statements on brephobaptism pose the dilemma as to whether justification really is by faith or by baptism.[16]

Yet since Erasmus's printed Greek New Testament appeared (in 1516, one year before the "formal" commencement of the Reformation on 31 October 1517!) the evidence regarding Romans 5:12 had been out in the open. For the Vulgate's *in quo* ("in whom"), Erasmus's Latin translation read in eo quod *omnes peccauimus*. The original Greek reading was also being reflected accurately through Protestant vernacular translations (based on the Greek) from 1522 (Luther).

Only in the twentieth century did the attitude of the Roman Catholic Church as to what constitutes the Bible undergo a major change.[17] For over 1500 years the Vulgate had been regarded as the official version of that communion. The Vulgate perpetuated the mistranslation that lay at the heart of the Augustinian (and subsequently Western) theology and practice of brephobaptism. However, in 1979 the Catholic Church issued the *Nova Vulgata*, in which the text of the Vulgate had been aligned

---

16. Moore, "Justification by Faith."

17. When Msgr Ronald Knox completed his English translation of the entire Bible in 1949, he was obliged to work from the Vulgate, even though he had a good command of New Testament Greek. Only with *La Bible de Jérusalem*, first completed by French scholars of L'École biblique et archéologique française de Jérusalem in 1955, did Roman Catholic translators work from the original languages. This hallmark translation signalled that at last Catholicism was coming to accept the findings of modern scholarship.

more closely with that of the "original" Greek. Among the revisions was Romans 5:12, where the text was altered from *in quo* to *eo quod* (cf. Erasmus above).

Given the influence of the mistranslation of that text as interpreted and applied by Augustine, is there no responsibility, once the translation is corrected at an official level, to revisit the whole theology and practice of brephobaptism, of which it is the primary foundation?

The New Testament scriptures constitute the common ground between Christian churches practicing brephobaptism and the increasing proportion practicing believer's baptism by immersion. It is my personal conviction that anyone approaching those Scriptures with an open mind will find that the evidence unambiguously leads to the conclusion that apostolic baptismal practice consisted of the immersion of believers. Historical theology is able to explain how differences in baptismal theology and practice developed, but it can hardly be used to justify a mistranslation of the New Testament and the baptismal theology and practice based on it or, once the mistranslation has been acknowledged and removed, the perpetuation of such theology and practice. For the Reformers this took place as far back as the first quarter of the sixteenth century, for Catholics in 1979. Not only the New Testament, but also the lessons of historical theology invite, indeed demand, a serious review by those branches of the Western church that have inherited their baptismal theology and practice from Augustine, namely, Catholics, Anglicans, and those Protestants who practice brephobaptism.

In contrast to the Lord's Supper, which is repetitive in character, baptism, ideally at least, is to be administered only once to an individual. This view is expressed strongly in the World Council of Churches' *Baptism, Eucharist and Ministry*:

> Baptism is an unrepeatable act. Any practice which might be interpreted as "re-baptism" must be avoided.[18]

Such a stance sharpens the issue as to which baptismal practice is the more appropriate and elevates it to one of major significance.

In the twentieth century one of the most vocal advocates of believers' baptism was Karl Barth—even though he belonged to the brephobaptist tradition. Barth felt so strongly about this issue that the final published part of his unfinished *Church Dogmatics* concerned baptism,

---

18. World Counsel of Churches, *Baptism* §13.

even though it meant bringing it forward in his planned presentation. In this "Fragment" Barth made a strong case for believers' baptism. However, for us as Baptists, among whom religious liberty is the most distinctive of our "distinctives," it is Barth's earlier critique of 1943 (*ET* 1948) that cries out to be taken seriously. There he characterized brephobaptism as an "act of violence."[19] It is strong language, but he was arguing that if Christian baptism is indeed to be administered but once to an individual, then brephobaptism, by forcing the rite on infants unawares, deprives them of the liberty of being fully and consciously involved in their baptism. It does so by depriving them of the opportunity of exercising personal faith prior to their baptism—with all the benefits that conscious identification with Christ in baptism brings, including the joy that often accompanies it (Acts 8:39; 16:34).

The protest against brephobaptism, rooted in the very beginnings of Baptist history, is surely an ongoing responsibility of Baptists to the wider church and the wider world. That responsibility will continue into the future, until that day when all branches of the Christian church return to what was clearly the practice of the apostolic church.

---

19. Barth, "Christian Life (Fragment)," 47.

13

An Immodest Proposal for the Practice of the Lord's Table

IAN PACKER

Introduction

When Luther and Zwingli met at Marburg castle in 1529 to discuss areas of mutual understanding, they discovered that they held most important points of doctrine in common. However, toward the end of the meeting in discussion of the Lord's Supper the division between them on this matter alone led to a dramatic schism, such that Luther declared Zwingli to be "of a different spirit" to him. On this matter, it seemed, a vital alliance for the Reformation of Christendom was worth jettisoning or at least jeopardizing.[1] Such strong feelings are not likely to be universally shared by Christian groups in the West today; nevertheless the diversity of practice and theology of the Lord's Supper has grown, and this diversity raises a vital question: Are Christians participating in variants of the one practice or in very different practices?

---

1. Again, regarding the Lord's Supper strong words were by no means the extent of the reaction to diverse belief as many Anabaptist martyrs were burned at the stake declaring that they "knew nothing" of the "baked god" of the Roman Catholics. The Eucharist caused so much controversy in the Reformation because, being at the centre of medieval social life, to challenge the form of the Mass led inexorably to "dissipation of religious consensus" and "consequences for social and political life unforeseen by the designers of religious life." According to Elwood, *Body Broken*, 3, "virtually everywhere the reforming ideas took hold, traditional hierarchies were called into question, existing social arrangements undermined, and both ecclesiastical and political institutions laid bare to attack."

Baptists hardly lead the way in significant ecumenical contribution to questions over the Lord's Table. What is needed is some kind of biblical and theological account that can embrace many differences while critiquing some Eucharistic practice and without reducing everything to some minimalist common core—in this sense an "immodest proposal" in that it provides some unification and normative proposals amidst the diversity. This paper is both an abridgement of a larger study toward that end and a promissory note on further research and constructive theology.

Reading through the relevant literature of recent decades, one is struck by an increasingly marked difference between the approach to and understandings of the Lord's Table emerging in New Testament studies, on the one hand, and that of systematic theology on the other.[2] While no interpreter is free of presuppositions, some New Testament scholars feel confident enough in their exegesis and analysis to accuse many theologians of serious *eisegesis* when it comes to their systematic discussions of the Lord's Table. These scholars argue that systematic theologians often tend to operate with a set of questions inherited from earlier conversations about the Lord's Table and frequently without querying the legitimacy of those questions. As Markus Barth has remarked, "If one asks the wrong question, one is sure to get a wrong answer."[3]

Snapshots from the New Testament

Jesus and the Gospels

So, what picture has emerged in some New Testament studies? It is customary to focus on the sacrificial language of the Passover and relate this to the Last Supper and Jesus' death, understandably so. However, perhaps we also ought to pay attention to the way that Jesus, as an enigmatic Jewish prophet, was subversively transfiguring messianic expectations in his ministry to Israel, particularly through table fellowship.[4] Whether in deed, parable, or story, Jesus returns time and again to the centrality of the table. He returns to the need for welcome, generosity, and equality to all those who are of the house of Israel. Luke's Gospel, in stories such

---

2. See Hays, *First Corinthians*, 192–206; Fee, "History as Context," 10–32.
3. M. Barth, *Rediscovering the Lord's Supper*, 2.
4. See Bartchy, "Table Fellowship"; Reumann, *Supper of the Lord*, 4–5.

as that of Zacchaeus or the sinful woman at Simon the Pharisee's house, "makes clear that these occasions of table fellowship were used by Jesus as events in which he both proclaimed and demonstrated forgiveness and salvation."[5] Hospitality to those formerly on the fringes of society—the "sinners"—was a sign and practice of the inbreaking kingdom, part of the apocalyptic "great reversal" that the covenant God of Israel was working in his people and his world. As the centre of the household, the table was the perfect place to inaugurate submission to and celebration of the kingdom.[6]

The forgiveness of sins as entrance into the new covenant and the coming kingdom is central to Jesus' message. Further, however, eschatological forgiveness raises the issue of Jubilee. The language of "'debts' (rather than 'sins') . . . suggests that economic liberation was one goal of Jesus' mission."[7] Jesus quotes from Isaiah rather than Leviticus when preaching in Nazareth (Luke 4:16), indicating he is using the imagery of Jubilee rather than the legislation.[8] Is it then "just vivid imagery, a highly charged metaphorical way of speaking about a different sort of reality (say, a 'spiritual' one)?"[9] "Must we choose between whether all Israel observes Jubilee or that it is a spiritual reality?"[10] N. T. Wright suggests that Jesus, like other leaders, could well have intended "his people . . . to form cells, groups or gatherings . . . to live by the Jubilee principle among themselves."[11]

---

5. Bartchy, "Table Fellowship with Jesus," 55. "In a culture in which symbolic action meant far more that it usually does in the Western world, Jesus' contemporaries immediately understood his acceptance of outcasts into his table fellowship as a claim of authority to forgive them and to grant them worth before God," placing them on the "same level with the righteous." Special thanks to Scott Bartchy for sending a copy of this hard-to-get paper.

6. Chilton, *Jesus' Prayer*, 53: "A willingness to provide for the meals, to join in the fellowship, to forgive and to be forgiven, was seen by Jesus as a sufficient condition for eating in his company and for entry into the kingdom." Jeremias, *Eucharistic Words*, 204, adds, "After Peter's confession [at Caesarea Philippi] every act of eating and drinking with the master is table fellowship of the redeemed community with the redeemer, a wedding feast, a pledge of a share in the meal of the consummation."

7. McKnight, *New Vision*, 225.

8. At no other point in his ministry do we find a repeat declaration or an attempt to bring it about. See Ringe, *Jesus, Liberation*, 33–49; Yoder, *Politics of Jesus*, 60–75; Wiebe, *Messianic Ethics*, 128–29.

9. Wright, *Jesus and the Victory of God*, 295.

10. Ibid.

11. Ibid. Not only does the messianic age imply a radical restructuring of Israel,but

In this context we come to the Last Supper, which was probably a Passover meal. The significance of the violent end of Jesus' life was poignantly and powerfully dramatized by his final meal with his closest disciples, the beginning of Yahweh's renewed Israel, the core of Jesus' *ekklesia*. The Passover meal was the memorial or remembrance of the exodus event and had an unparalleled significance among Jewish festivals and feasts. It was the "freedom meal," a celebration of the mighty acts of Yahweh in delivering the tribes of Israel from their Gentile oppressors and forming them into a holy nation with an inheritance.[12] The memorial was not mere recollection of history but a powerful symbolic connection with those past events through a dramatic partial re-enactment or "recital" of the original meal, making the *significance* of those events contemporary.[13] Markus Barth urges that the proper English equivalent for the Hebrew concept actually is not "remembrance" but "*celebration.*"[14]

On this particular Passover, following the "Triumphal Entry" into Jerusalem, ostensibly in fulfillment of the Scriptures and with messianic expectations running high, one can only imagine the tension in the air as the disciples thought of the subversive, perhaps even explosive meaning of *this* Passover. Jesus' inference of covenant—a *new* covenant?—at the Supper along with this exodus context must also have resonated strongly with expectations for Israel's full "return from Exile," that is, the removal of pagan oppressors and the establishment of a renewed kingdom community.[15] But the words of Jesus were shocking: referring to his own *broken body* and *blood* poured out for the forgiveness of sins. These are hardly the words of the victorious Messiah who had earlier

---

also an invitation to the wider (Samaritan and Gentile) world to share in the blessings of God's kingdom: "Many will come from east and west, and feast with Abraham, Isaac, and Jacob in the kingdom of God" (Matt 8:11/Luke 13:28, 29). This imagery of a banquet, drawn from the Old Testament (see Isa 25:6), was "used to represent the happiness of the coming Messianic kingdom" (Smalley, "Banquet," 120). Roughly contemporary with this, the sectarian community at Qumran also shared a common meal that "seems to have been a ritual anticipation of the Messianic banquet (cf. 1QS 2)" (ibid).

12. Wright, *Meal Jesus Gave Us*, 16–18.

13. Eller, *Could the Church Have It All Wrong?* This is based upon his earlier work, *In Place of Sacraments*.

14. Barth, *Rediscovering the Lord's Supper*, 12.

15. See Evans, "Jesus and the Continuing Exile of Israel," 77–100; Wright, *Jesus and the Victory of God*, 203–9; idem, "Jesus, Israel and the Cross."

enacted a symbolic judgment of the temple system and was expected to defeat the Gentile occupying forces.[16] This Suffering Servant motif is further accentuated in John's reading, which incorporates the foot-washing episode.[17] The meal itself was followed by his betrayal, arrest, and the climax of Jesus' vocation as the suffering Messiah.[18]

Not only was there an orientation to making the past contemporary, the Passover meal at this time incorporated a future orientation, captured by Jesus' own words: "Until . . . the kingdom of God."[19] In the post-resurrection appearances Jesus gathered his scattered followers together around him and ate together with them. In the "Emmaus account," Jesus goes unrecognized—even during his exposition of the Scriptures—until he takes up his previous "head of household" role at the table, gives thanks, and "breaks bread."[20] The notions of identification and inclusion feature in the gathering of Jesus' failed disciples to himself. Jesus reinitiates the common meal as the centre of his *ekklesia*, the community of God.[21]

---

16. See Evans, "Jesus' Action"; Wright, *Jesus and the Victory of God*, 413–28; Sanders, *Jesus and Judaism*, 61–71. This is challenged by Chilton, *Jesus' Prayer*, 60–70, who argues that Jesus sought to occupy the temple to restore it to its true vocation as a house of prayer for all nations.

17. In the Fourth Gospel, it is a shocking saying of Jesus about eating (literally, "chewing") his body and drinking his blood that drives away many erstwhile followers. Scholars have debated the presence or absence of sacramentality in this Gospel; but leaving aside the questions of sacraments for the moment, we are nonetheless struck by Johannine differences from the Synoptic accounts of Jesus' feeding of the multitudes. What is especially striking is the "flesh" and "blood" reference in the context of this event. It is difficult to see this as anything other than an allusion (at least) to the Lord's Table and to the death it signifies and celebrates. This is further confirmed by the similarity of Jesus' action with the bread ("breaking") to the Synoptic accounts of the Last Supper. (Further, he gives the prayer of thanksgiving (*eucharist*) although this narrow relevance can be challenged, as we will see.) This account is all the more interesting since, later in the Gospel John does not describe the actual meal at the Last Supper.

18. Significantly, Jesus mentions that the one who will betray him is *with him at his table* (Luke 22:21).

19. See Stein, "Last Supper," 448–49. According to Smalley, "Banquet," 120, "Jesus tells the disciples that the meal which they were sharing was a foretaste of the true Messianic glory to come, made possible by his death (Matt 26:27–29; cf. Luke 22:29f; Rev 3:20; 19:9)."

20. Yoder, *Body Politics*, 16.

21. The disciples do not need here to be reinitiated (baptized) but are drawn back to the table and therefore reconfirmed as part of the household of Jesus.

The connection of this story to the Last Supper is unmistakable, but the question arises as to the meaning of the "breaking of bread" and its relationship to Jesus' words of institution, "as often as you do *this*, do it in remembrance of me." What is Jesus referring to? Clearly it is not the annual Passover meal, as the disciples' practice illustrates. In this context, it does not seem that Jesus is doing something odd to give thanks and to break bread *at this time*—rather, it was "customary Jewish practice attested in the early rabbinic period."[22] It implies that the breaking of bread is strongly connected to, if not identified with, the daily shared meal and its prayer of thanksgiving. If we no longer see such significance in shared meals, it is important not to downgrade the significance in this original context.

The Breaking of Bread in the Acts of the Apostles

The summation of life in the early Jerusalem messianic community is clearly set in Luke-Acts as a model for Christian common life.[23] Remembering to keep it in connection with the preceding Gospel of Luke, it becomes clear that its thrust is that *the messianic age has dawned*. As part of this, table sharing has been connected with some kind of "community of goods." Why? Economic sharing is an expression of a *theology*—not merely of enthusiasm, spirituality, or values. It is the outworking of Jesus' good news of the kingdom (Luke 4:18) and the true "restoration of Israel" (Acts 1). It is the logic of the image of Jubilee.[24]

But what of the breaking of bread? Is it the *normal* eating of food? Is it a *sacred* meal? Is it a sacralizing of *every* meal? Certainly Paul's later

---

22. Painter, "Bread," 84.

23. This clearly *normative* dimension has led various scholars—even those sympathetic to its message—to ask whether this was in fact a historical reality or simply an idealization. For a nuanced defense of historicity, see Bartchy, "Community of Goods." For those who stress history, there is the temptation to set it aside as an interesting—even exciting—account of *what happened* but with no strong relevance to today. Nevertheless, a historical moment can act as a program and theological paradigm, and the literary placement of this text (Acts 2:42–45) seems to affirm this. Capper, "Palestinian Cultural Context"; Lindemann, "Beginnings of the Christian Life."

24. We cannot discuss here how the community of goods should translate in other situations precisely, but we can at least note the recurring New Testament theme of generosity *within* communities, *among* them, and the significance of the Jerusalem apostles' concern for Paul to remember the poor, something he himself held strongly (Gal 2:10). There are undoubtedly other analogues in Palestine or across Asia Minor.

breaking of bread and giving thanks (Acts 27:33–36) is not one's usual thought of the Eucharist but rather a sacralized meal (cf. 1 Tim 4:4–5). Yet it is difficult to imagine that Christians breaking bread together saw this as a completely separate activity from the *act of significance* instituted at Jesus' Last Supper.

The Lord's Meal in Corinth

Paul claims in 1 Corinthians that he shares a common Christian tradition of the Last Supper. His accusation toward the Corinthians is that when they gather together (for the worse), despite confessing Christ and having food (including bread and wine), this scandalous affair is in fact *not* the "Lord's meal." A long line of New Testament scholars continue to argue on strong exegetical grounds—and contrary to dominant, historical Christian concerns—that the problem at Corinth is emphatically *not* a failure to treat the "elements" properly or to recognize properly the spiritual meaning or means of the sacrament, but that the wealthier believers act contrary to the character of whatever the Lord's Meal is supposed to be. It is in their perpetuation of social stratification based on the norms of the passing age that nullifies the event *as* the Lord's Meal.[25] Those behaviors, attitudes, or ideas toward which God appears to be exercising judgment should be a key to us as to what issues are important here.

This meal is made possible only by the common confession of the crucified and risen Messiah in whom God gathers people from mixed backgrounds together as one new people. To have the Lord's Supper required that

> the church members should welcome one another when they came together for their meal. That is to say, the rich should welcome the poor and treat them (as indeed all members of the church should treat one another) courteously and graciously; the occasion was still to be a meal, but the implication may be that there was to be sharing of the food . . . so that nobody felt disadvantaged.[26]

---

25. On the nature of the Corinthian situation, see Hays, "Conversion of the Imagination."

26. Marshall, "Lord's Supper," 571–72. See the debate on whether the issue was waiting for arrivals or sharing equally in Bartchy, "Table Fellowship with Jesus"; Witherington, "Making a Meal of It," 97–99; Thiselton, *First Epistle to the Corinthians*,

Paul does not counsel the Corinthians to cease eating together as their normal mode of gathering. Neither does he distinguish between the meal and a sacrament.[27] It is doubtful that Jesus or Paul ever intended that the Lord's Supper should become what it did—what I. H. Marshall describes as a "token consumption of a morsel of bread and a sip of wine."[28] There is no suggestion that this is what Westerners may regard as "just a meal," for in both Jewish and Gentile contexts in the first century there was immense significance in eating together and *even more* significance when eating together with or before one's god.[29]

The Ethics of Eating Together in Galatia and Rome

The table issue is at the centre of the Galatian dispute between certain Jewish Christians who urged compliance with Jewish food laws as constituting proper identification in the people of God, and Paul, who argued that faith in Christ (and *his* faithfulness—*pistis Christou*) was the defining mark, confirmed by the giving of the promised Spirit.[30] In Galatians 2:11–14 withdrawal of table fellowship on the basis of Jew/Gentile distinctions was a *betrayal* of the gospel.[31]

---

863. Also, compare with Rom 15:1–7 following from the table question in preceding chapter 14.

27. Blue, "Love Feast," 579, comments, "The separation of the meal/*agape* from the Lord's Supper, or Eucharist, was made in the second century. Justin Martyr (c.150) indicates that by his time the common meal and Eucharist (as sacrament) were separate observances. He speaks of the Eucharist without referring to a meal. Accordingly, a portion of bread accompanied by the water and wine constituted the Eucharist (Justin Martyr, *Apology*, 1.65–66)."

28. Marshall, "Lord's Supper," 572. Paul apparently had more instruction to give them on this matter but this is lost to us.

29. It is clear then why Paul can take the "strong" at Corinth to task for eating meat sacrificed to idols *in pagan temples* due to the identification with demons this implies—one cannot share the table of demons *and* the table of the Lord (1 Cor 10:21). While sacrifices are in the background of temple eating, the sacrifice and the sacrificial fellowship meal *are not the same thing*; and neither should one see "bread and wine" as corresponding to a sacrifice behind the *agapē* meal. The complete and unrepeatable sacrifice of Christ, himself our "Passover" (1 Cor 5:7), lies behind the community's sacred, common meal (cf. Heb 9:10). To share in the Lord's "cup" is to be at his table and to share his lot and cause.

30. See Hays, *Faith of Jesus Christ*, 141–83; Longenecker, *Triumph of Abraham's God*, 95–107.

31. See Baker, *Religious No More*, 83; Hansen, *Galatians*, 62–67.

It is often said that if it were not for the Corinthian problem we would not have any information of the Lord's Supper in the Pauline churches. Surely this is a serious problem for an understanding of the Lord's Supper as a vital means of conveying (in some sense) grace, new life, and/or forgiveness. Why does the Lord's Supper not appear in Romans or Galatians, the "pillars" of Paul's gospel?[32]

I want to suggest that this may not be the case. Although not corresponding clearly (or at all) with the sacramental conception of the Lord's Supper just mentioned, it is plausible on the model we are developing here that the Lord's Supper as the common meal of the community *is* present in the Galatian crisis. Likewise, the last chapters of Romans, an occasional epistle again dominated by the Jew and Gentile issue, concern the unity at the table as critical for ecclesial life in the kingdom of God (chs. 14, 15).[33] The kingdom of God is not about the food they are eating or refusing when together but rather about "righteousness, peace, and joy in the Holy Spirit." It is about their mutual edification and a common life expressing righteousness—so, the character of this shared meal is important.[34]

Summing Up—a Synthesis

- The Lord's Table follows in the Jewish tradition of common meals celebrating the acts of Yahweh.

- The importance of these meals lies in their centreing in and recital of Yahweh's acts, making their significance contemporary to participants.

- These meals *socially enact* (and don't merely symbolize) obedience to Yahweh by providing an occasion for right response to Yahweh's

---

32. O'Grady, *Pillars of Paul's Gospel*, 1.

33. See Moo, *Romans*, 826-33; Williams, "'Righteousness of God'"; Wright, "Romans and the Theology of Paul"; idem, "Letter to the Romans," 730-51. For an outline of the structure and a defense of the coherence of Romans, see Grieb, *Story of Romans*, with support from Hays, *Echoes*, 34-83. I was pleased to find my view supported somewhat by Koenig, *Feast of the World's Redemption*, 131-38. We leave open the controversial suggestion of Jewett, "Are There Allusions," to references to *the agape* (common meal/love feast) in Romans 13 as a fulfillment of the Law.

34. It is further backed by an eschatological orientation toward the Lord's judgment seat—compare the overlap with 1 Corinthians 11, especially in the wider context of chapters 10-15.

acts: hospitality, solidarity, and reaffirmation of Israel's identity—*especially* the Passover meal.

- There is both continuity and radical reinterpretation in Jesus' table practice and its culmination in his last Passover-time meal with the disciples as part of the inauguration and demonstration of the messianic age—a meal that signaled the new covenant through Jesus' death.

- The table of the common meal, with the traditional practice of breaking bread trans-signified by Jesus' words of institution, was seen as the centre of the messianic community where hospitality, welcome, and the beginning of the holistic benefits (*shalom*) of the messianic age were to be enjoyed and encouraged, including its economic implications.

- This early practice and understanding was perpetuated in the Pauline communities though the quality of "performance" varied.

Analyzing Historical Developments and Deviations

Based on this sampling of some biblical material, we might intuit that the approach developed is somewhat at odds with much of the mainstream Christian traditions, East and West. If it is an accurate portrayal, it seems that many developments in the post-apostolic age entailed a radically altered view of the meaning of certain Christian doctrines and practices. This is not a unique claim. The Reformers were unafraid to challenge the authority of the church and the fathers where they saw a contradiction of Scripture, and Baptists have certainly not been shy about raising such concerns over ecclesiology and sacraments. The change in practice of the Lord's Supper might be tied to a problematic recontextualization of Christian thought from predominantly Jewish soil (even if Hellenistic Jewish) to that of the pagan Hellenistic world. The shift from a more relational understanding of practices to an engagement with a Greek philosophical worldview very much concerned with ontology and "substance" was probably one factor in shifting the meaning of Jesus' words of institution, "this is my body . . . this is my blood."[35]

Everett Ferguson has traced much of the development of sacramental understanding of rituals and ceremonies, that is, as conveying

---

35. Ferguson, "Lord's Supper in Church History," 23.

spiritual or divine power or grace, and there is no space to rehearse that troubling history here.[36] Thomas Aquinas is best known to Protestants for his formulation of the doctrine of transubstantiation: "We could never know by our senses that the real body of Christ and his blood are in this sacrament but only by our faith which is based on the authority of God."[37] Yet it was just this question of the authority behind this belief which was to come under attack in the Reformation. The Reformers argued powerfully against the medieval ideas, scholastic or popular, given their firm grasp of the authority of Scripture over tradition, Christ's once-for-all atonement, and their articulation of justification by faith. Yet the Reformers were still very Catholic.[38] They were able to critique the more fanciful ideas surrounding the Mass, yet, it seems, were bound by some variation on the medieval symbolic praxis. The Reformation argument largely concerned how Christ was present or grace conveyed in these bare symbols of bread and wine, still removed from their original context of the common meal.

Signs, Social Practices, and Sacraments—Where Is the Significance?

The Reformers were united in their desire to reform the Latin Mass and replace it with a service in the common vernacular that would simultaneously confer to the "receivers" the truth of the gospel as proclaimed by Protestant preachers. Of special importance to all of these reformers was the idea of God's gracious condescension to the weakness of humanity to communicate his truth in a powerful, symbolic but also multisensory way, not limited to those with intellectual prowess. Yet they were unable to agree not only on what to call this reformed practice, but the meaning and nature of the practice.[39]

Calvin opposed what was supposedly the "mere memorialism" of Zwingli and believed in a form of special grace or activity of God through

36. Ibid. Happily, John Chrysostom, *Homilies*, 370, provides a moment of relief—theologically, at least—when he reflects back on the now broken custom of true table fellowship: "a custom most excellent, and most useful; for it was a foundation of love, and a comfort to poverty, and a corrective of riches, and an occasion of the highest philosophy, and an instruction of humility." Quoted in Bartchy, "Table Fellowship with Jesus," 61.

37. Aquinas quoted by Ferguson, "Lord's Supper in Church History," 43.

38. See the generally positive assessment of this by Senn, "Reform of the Mass."

39. McGrath, *Reformation Thought*, 160–61.

the means of "receiving" the "elements."⁴⁰ He set the scene for Reformed theologians referring to the practices as "sacraments," as "signs and seals of faith," and as existing specifically for "strengthening faith" and "confirming Christ's benefits." Calvin's and Bucer's instincts that there was supposed to be more going on were right, as were Zwingli's in his later, more developed theology, yet they looked for significance in the wrong places.

What was it that these Reformers *did not* question? They each rightly denied the concept of *ex opere operato* (the "understanding that God works simply through the act or deed of administering the outward element")⁴¹ but instead narrowly connected the efficacy of sacraments with their mediation of gospel truth *and* its "being received with faith." With regard to their own Reformed clergy, the Reformers "compared 'sacramental efficacy' closely to that of the ministry of the word, which enabled them to ascribe power to the ministry of the sacraments as being akin to the ministry of the word."⁴²

The evangelical Swiss Anabaptists had a different take on the meaning of the Lord's Table. Originally among Zwingli's students, they believed he had not taken the work of reformation far enough.⁴³ Zwingli, initially reluctant to use the word "sacrament," took its Latin meaning of "pledge" to refer to *God's* covenantal pledge to us, but then later to *our* covenantal pledge to God (faith) *and to one another* (love). The Anabaptists, in their restoration of the fellowship meal, were able to see more clearly these dynamics of the Lord's Table and its "one-another" dimension—far beyond the "due administration of the sacraments" of the Reformers.

The Anabaptists' greater freedom from the priestly emphases of Roman Catholicism (ministry of sacrament) or the quasi-priestly em-

---

40. See the excellent discussion of Calvin by Tinker, "Language, Symbols, and Sacraments."

41. Buchanan, "Sacrament," 607.

42. Ibid., "The more rigorous Reformers confined the ministry of both to the ordained ministers of the church because they saw correspondence between the two kinds of ministry of God's grace or found them linked in Matt 28:19–20. And the Reformers generally retained a 'high' view of the benefits conferred by God in his sacraments, varying from the medieval and Counter-Reformation authors not so much in this question as in the setting out of the conditions under which God might be expected to confer that grace" (ibid.).

43. See Murray, "Anabaptists," 14.

phases of Protestant church officialdom (ministry of word and sacrament)—and the *political* ties associated with both—allowed them more liberty from the passive, receptive mode of Christians sharing in the Lord's Table.[44] While the "body" and "blood" symbols sacralized this meal around the death of Christ and the promise of his coming, the meal was not reduced to individualistic receipt of elements—whether as means of special grace, or merely instruction—but was a genuine brotherly and sisterly interaction "in the Spirit" at the table designated as Christ's.

The confusion surrounding the *meaning* of "sacrament" is a serious problem. If defined as "means of [conveying] grace," some have said that it is *Christ himself* who can only be truly called the "sacrament"—Luther's early preference in his *Babylonian Captivity of the Church*.[45]

In the twentieth century, perhaps one of the greatest challenges to "sacraments" from within the Reformed tradition has come from the later writings of Swiss theologian Karl Barth, who, with Luther, also declared Jesus Christ *alone* to be "*the* sacrament."[46] In one respect, Barth is "neo-Zwinglian"[47]—"affirming that baptism and the Lord's Supper are human actions, denying that they are sacraments (means of special grace)."[48] He rather moves beyond his earlier divine-monergistic view of baptism to greater emphasis on covenant as "free and responsible" partnership between God and humanity in and through Jesus Christ.[49] This is most clearly seen in his bold, definite aside in the last fragments of his unfinished *Church Dogmatics*:[50]

---

44. See Kreider, *Given for You*, 65.

45. "If I wanted to speak according to scriptural usage, I would have but one sacrament, [Jesus Christ,] and three sacramental signs . . . [baptism, penance, and the Eucharist]," quoted in Wainwright, "Church and Sacrament(s)," 90. Sadly, the habitual sacramental language, dubious in its use from the outset, unclear and attracting so many conflicting meanings, has stuck. To apply George Orwell's comments on the English language to the ongoing use of sacramental terminology: "It becomes ugly and inaccurate because our thoughts are foolish, but the slovenliness of our language makes it easier for us to have foolish thoughts"—and this despite the quality of our piety (Orwell, "Politics and the English Language," 143).

46. Barth, *CD* IV/4:102.

47. Ibid., 130.

48. Buckley, "Christian Community," 195.

49. Barth, *Christian Life*, 42. See Migliore, "Reforming Baptism," 496.

50. Partly because of the unfinished nature of the work, but surely also because of the highly controversial challenge to virtually all Christian traditions, Barth's later

> In dealing with baptism and the Lord's Supper . . . [the decision] regarding their basis, goal, and meaning . . . is as follows . . . , [negatively] baptism and the Lord's Supper are not events, institutions, mediations, or revelations of salvation. They are not representations and actualizations, emanations, repetitions, or extensions, nor indeed guarantees and seals of the work and word of God; nor are they instruments, vehicles, channels, or means of God's reconciling grace. They are not what they have been called since the second century, namely, mysteries or sacraments.

Is the Lord's Supper a "sacrament"? The notion of "sacrament" must be *justified* (and not assumed) as an adequate description for particular practices (especially baptism and the Lord's Supper) whether it be as a comprehensive designation or as a partial descriptor. So, in what other ways can we describe our core practices? Barth continues with this affirmation:

> With all that the community of Jesus Christ and its members are and say and do, they belong to something that God has permitted and entrusted and commanded to Christians, namely the answering, attesting, and proclaiming of the one act and revelation of salvation that has taken place in the one Mediator between God and man (1 Tim 2:5), who himself directly actualizes and presents and activates and declares himself in the power of his Holy Spirit. Like the Christian life in invocation of God, they are actions of human obedience for which Jesus Christ makes his people free and responsible. They refer themselves to God's own work and word, and they correspond to his grace and commands. In so doing they have the promise of the divine good pleasure and they are well done as holy, meaningful, fruitful, human actions, radiant in the shining of the one true light in which they may take place and which they have to indicate in their own place and manner as free and responsible human action.[51]

Barth's theological formulation represents a compelling analysis that is consistent with our biblical exposition but remains strongly at odds with much of Christian tradition.[52] What remains is to vindicate

---

understanding of these "commanded . . . actions" has not been fully grappled with. For various recent and constructive views, Buckley, "Christian Community"; Webster, *Barth's Ethics of Reconciliation*, 116–32, 156–58, 170–73; Hunsinger, "Baptized into Christ's Death."

51. Barth, *Christian Life*, 42.

52. See, also, Barth, *CD* IV/4:ix–x, where he speaks of the influence on him of his

these claims in relation to Reformational emphases on the uniqueness of Christ and his atonement and the Calvinist instinct for greater-than-memorial-significance in the Lord's Supper—but without "sacraments" as "mysteries." In this respect, we will seek to vindicate Barth and move beyond him to include a dimension of the Lord's Table not clearly spoken of here but consistent with his approach—the significance of social processes.

The Presence of Christ—the Spirit, Faith and Communal Praxis

What does it mean for Christ to be present in this *anamnesis*? Is there, in fact, a scriptural or even *theological* requirement for Christ to be *specially* present in this ceremony at all? As Zwingli continually urged against Luther, Jesus the man, the ascended Lord, remains "at the right hand" of God "in the heavens" until "the time of the restitution of all things"—and so, in a vital sense, is *absent*. Additionally, the consistent witness of the New Testament writers is that Christ is indeed also *present* in and with his community *by the Holy Spirit*.

So, in what ways do we see the Spirit at work amongst us? Is there ever a biblical emphasis or even reference—explicit or implicit—to the work of the Spirit imparting some special grace particularly through this practice of receiving the symbolic elements? Or do we connect this idea theologically with Calvin's assertion that Christ is in some sense especially present with us during the preaching of the Word? According to Calvin,

> As often as Christ calls us to the hope of salvation by the preaching of the Gospel, he is present with us. For not without reason is the preaching of the Gospel called Christ's descent to us.[53]

In this case, the Word is vehicle of Christ's presence and, it seems, the symbolic and didactic action of *aspects* of the Lord's Supper is also, derivatively speaking, a vehicle.

But can we review this idea of the work of the Spirit and apply it differently to the Lord's Table? According to Paul, God is at work through the different members of the body of Christ, the gathered people of God.

---

son Markus's work on baptism and the Lord's Meal.

53. Calvin in his commentary on John 7:33, quoted in DeVries, "Incarnation and the Sacramental Word," 386.

So, in Romans 12, for instance (let alone the Table and "Open Meeting" contexts of 1 Cor 11–14),[54] the Spirit is at work (and thus Christ is present) as one teaches, another leads, another shows hospitality, another encourages, another prophesies, another shows mercy, and so on. In this respect, as the Lord's people gather around his Table in remembrance of him, declaring his death until his Parousia he is at work by his everpresent Spirit.

We cannot restrict the work of the Spirit to didactic gospel actions nor do we have any good reason to single out a special presence in the midst of the community's total gospel-shaped common life when one takes specific elements at the common meal—especially because such a theological focus is only possible in an abstracted practice.

Is the Lord's Supper, biblically speaking, "a sign and seal of faith"? Bearing in mind the Galatian controversy, I contend that Paul's consistent reference is to *faith*, as our sign of being in the New Covenant and of the presence-at-work of the Holy Spirit, which is the one seal of our faith, the deposit of our eschatological inheritance. An understanding of the significance of the Table consistent with traditional sacramental concepts is yet to be demonstrated exegetically.

The Benefits and Blessings of Christ—on Serving, Giving, and Receiving

Does the Lord's Supper exist for the purpose of strengthening faith? The piety is impeccable, though the reasoning is unclear. In what sense or senses does this occur? Is it perhaps a mental assurance or increased understanding via a didactic function, or a psychological comfort through expressive identification? Indeed, there is no reason to say that these effects are not sometimes part of the richer, variegated practice (or complex set of practices) evident in the New Testament, but:

- these effects in particular do not require a special presence or grace not *also* and/or *otherwise* available through other means;
- so, this is not unique to the Lord's Supper apart from other pedagogic practices, the mutual encouragement of the believing community, or the perpetual witness of the Spirit of Christ in us (Rom 8);

54. See Yoder, *Body Politics*, ch. 2; idem., "Sacrament as Social Process," 363–66.

- it is by no means clear that benefits take effect no matter how one group performs the Lord's Supper (or a *simulacrum* thereof);
- further, it is not clear as to how one exercises faith in the Reformed (*simulacrum*) context. Is it by generally being a believer? Is it by a certain quality of faith relationship with God? Is it by having a theologically informed faith regarding Christ's "power" in the sacrament?

Not that anyone should necessarily be blamed for failing to provide answers here. Dare I say, this is a rather fruitless line of enquiry, carried along by the traditional language, into things unknown or unreal. Systematically speaking, all of these are unclear explanations, without clear guidance from Scripture. How is it that sharing in the elements is "confirming Christ's benefits"? Again, as above, it is the Spirit who makes present for *us* as the people of God the deposit of the Abrahamic promise (Gal 3:14); and is it not the testimony of the gospel, expressed verbally and, yes, in symbolic action at the Lord's Table that reminds and assures us of God's fidelity in Christ (Rom 3).

Furthermore, surely it is incumbent upon us to recognize our responsibility as subjects of the kingdom of God to embody faithfulness to that kingdom. The very practice of Christian love in the egalitarian fellowship shaped by Christ is surely part of the realization of the salvation of Christ—the process of establishing an authentic community.[55] In this case, the example of Jesus' foot-washing as well as Paul's admonition to the Corinthians to be truly hospitable to one another highlights for us again that the Table is not a place of passive reception, even in faith, but of identification with the Lord in faith, hope, and love.

Sin, Fellowship, and Discipline—the Piety and Politics of the Eucharist

Much could be said about the question of authority and access to the Lord's Table, particularly practices such as the fencing off of the Lord's Table, and various forms of use and abuse of the Table as a religious tool of exclusion and coercion rather than restoration. In light of the Corinthian letter, it seems clear that it is the community that is to examine itself such that it does not tolerate social behavior that contradicts the very meaning of the gospel. Certainly, this community dimension

---

55. See Grenz, "Salvation and God's Program."

does not nullify the need for judging ourselves *in all of life* nor even for some times apart from the business of life for meditative introspection; but this is not by any means a necessary part of the Lord's Table.

So, if we see the Lord's Table as the normal centre of Christian practices, where there is sharing in food and drink, and edifying conversation under the signs of the Lord's death for our redemption, discipline can certainly be connected with that Table—but not as a denial of access to the grace of God. To be excluded from the Table is to be excluded from the community, not denied a special favor or feeling. The politics of the Lord's Table is not about scrutinizing whose piety is particularly worthy or unworthy of receiving sacred elements but of welcoming all sinners to the table of forgiveness to share in the journeying community of discipleship. To share at that table is to focus on the share we will have together in the eschatological gift of the heavenly city—which is itself anticipated in the faithful gathering of the messianic community now.[56]

While allowing for some variation in the *habitus* of the Lord's Table, I argue that there is a normative shape to this ecclesial event, which we can either ignore or affirm. Here, then, are our immodest normative claims:

- The Lord's Table is the sacred common meal of the Christian community.

- The sacred common meal as participation in Christ: To gather together at the Lord's Table is a focal recapitulation of the Christ event comprehending his life of service and his death, resurrection, and future Parousia in which the followers of Jesus identify with their Lord; and this is especially brought to light in this context by the poetic symbolic actions of breaking bread.

- The sacred common meal as gospel embodiment: To gather at the Lord's Table does not merely point to the work of God in Christ but embodies the result of that work, the "working out of salvation" in God's household, including the very material benefits of messianic age inaugurated among us.

- The sacred common meal as Spirit-led community formation: To gather at the Lord's Table is a focal event of the community, which

---

56. For more analysis on the connections of the Lord's Table with our future destiny, see Wainwright, *Eucharist and Eschatology*, 75–116.

is indwelt by God's Spirit in order to practice the fellowship of the Spirit in brotherly love, and to provide occasion for *all* the Spirit's gifts in the community to be expressed as he wills, including works of mercy, encouragement, and hospitality. It is expected that teaching will also be frequently present.

- The sacred common meal as *Eucharist*: To gather at the Table hosted by the Lord is an occasion of thanksgiving to God and appreciation for the work of Christ.
- The sacred common meal as *sacramentum*: To gather at the Lord's Table is to enact a pledge to God to serve him faithfully by his grace and to love one another as Jesus commanded.

Without these features, we may have a derived practice of some kind even if unique and interesting; or worse, some deviation that expresses a theological point, though not necessarily what God intended.

We may also make the following suggestions based on this practice:

- As the centre of Christian community life, the Lord's Table as the sacred common meal should be practiced as often as possible.
- As a focal practice of the community, the trans-signification of "breaking bread" also "intrudes" into the profane or everyday world and provides an example of how to live well at other meals, gatherings, and settings, thereby extending its influence.
- The community "presides" at the meal under Christ's authority and can designate whatever representative person it sees fit to pray, speak, or perform symbolic acts in the meal.
- As the common meal of the community, there seems to be no reason why children could not participate at the Table and learn the public truth of Christ's lordship expressed there as welcome observers and even potential participants in the making of disciples.
- Derived symbolic practices are valid to the extent that they are understood to be such and that they do not supplant the regular fullness of practice we are called to express.

On the Way to a Conclusion[57]

The debate over the Lord's Table has historically ranged over the "nature of symbols and symbolization, patterns of change in symbolic worlds, conceptions of power, and the social location of the sacred."[58] Alongside these debates, we have sought to argue for the meanings of the Lord's Table that recover its social and ethical along with symbolic-poetic meanings. The various areas of significance we have uncovered go far beyond the narrow debates over signification, render speculative metaphysics irrelevant, and reconnect the modes of Christ's presence with pneumatology and wider ecclesiology.

We are left now with the practical challenge of imaginative implementation of some of our proposals. I leave the final question in Scott Bartchy's words:

> What is it, then, that prevents Christians in the twentieth century from practicing again such an excellent and useful custom? Are the hindrances, of whatever sort, really of greater importance than the need in our time to demonstrate table fellowship with Jesus?[59]

---

57. I welcome your dialogue, criticisms, and suggestions. Email me at iangpacker@hotmail.com.

58. Elwood, *Body Broken*, vii.

59. Bartchy, "Table Fellowship with Jesus," 61.

14

Church as (Covenant) Community—Then and Now[1]

MICHAEL PARSONS

Introduction

We live, in the West at any rate, in a fast-changing culture and society, and in an age of changing paradigms or core metaphors of meaning and imagination. This is self-evident. However, as Baptists we have always argued that some things (not everything) should remain unchanged—they are best left as they are—and that appears at variance with the prevailing mood or spirit of the time. For example, generally, as Baptists we maintain an understanding of church as associated with both the idea and the experience of covenant, of church as committed community. Indeed, more than that, we have always held that the covenant is essential or integral to our ecclesiology, and by that we intend both the divine overarching covenant and the more localized covenant between committed members of a particular church. We have held on to this particular belief fairly consistently and almost tenaciously at times since the beginning of the seventeenth century—400 years—so it is well rooted in our denominational and theological DNA.

However, the question is whether it ought to be. Some are arguing that commitment and close relationship are not very postmodern con-

---

1. This essay is a reworking of the short article "An Understanding of Covenanted Church: Is There a Contemporary Relevance?" which appeared in the *Journal of European Baptist Studies* 7 (2007) 5–15.

cepts and are asking whether the church ought to refashion its ecclesial understanding to suit the times in which we live. The present short chapter is a brief exploration of this question, meant merely to be suggestive for further reflection. It begins by outlining early Baptist thought on covenant and the local church, and moves to contemporary expressions and development of that theology. Then it calls into question those who want to dispense with covenant/relational models of church community, suggesting key theological ideas that need to be addressed and to be taken into account if we are to be both true to our past and true to the kerygmatic call of Jesus Christ to be contemporary and relevant in the world in which we live and serve.

Early Baptist Understanding

The early English Baptists believed in a covenanted church. By this they meant that they held to a gathered church of those who had voluntarily covenanted together under Jesus Christ as Head of the church. In an excellent historical overview, *English Baptist History and Heritage*, Roger Hayden speaks of this, mentioning in particular the church in Gainsborough as an example. One of its members, William Bradford, describes the group significantly in the following way. The church, he says, is a group of Christians seen

> as the Lord's free people, [having] joined themselves (by a covenant of the Lord) into a church estate, in the fellowship of the Gospel, to walk in all his ways, made known, or to be made known unto them, (according to their best endeavors) whatsoever it should cost them, the Lord assisting them.[2]

This is a crucial statement. It indicates the importance of intentionality about membership of the church—"the Lord's free people." We might notice, too, the centrality of both Christ and the gospel in this comment. Of particular significance, though, is the prominence and the centrality of the covenant for membership of the local church ("a covenant of the Lord"), which appears to be evidenced in unity and sharing ("the fellowship of the Gospel"), and its daily authenticity, for it clearly cost them to covenant together in this way. Here is clear expression that the concept of church at this time was of a community of regenerate members.

---

2. Quoted by Hayden, *English Baptist History*, 19.

John Smyth, "the venerable originator of the world-wide Baptist movement," is of a similar persuasion.³ He writes,

> [T]he outward church consists of *penitent persons only*, and of such as believing in Christ bring forth fruits worthy [of] amendment of life. . . . [A]ll penitent and faithful Christians are brethren in the communion of outward life, wheresoever they live, by what name soever they are known.⁴

Noticeable, again, is the emphasis on community based on repentance and Christian faith that brings forth a changed, a godly life ("amendment of life," "the communion of outward life").

Thomas Helwys speaks in a similar vein. The following short passage indicates the boundedness of the community, a boundedness concretely formed by mutual fellowship and baptism, through the word of God and the Holy Spirit.⁵

> [T]he Church of Christ is a company of faithful people, separated from the world by the word and Spirit of God, being knit unto the Lord and one another, by baptism, upon their own confession of the faith and sins.⁶

Indeed, the theological undergirding of this early concept of church was the eternal covenant of God's grace as it became actualized, concrete, and contemporary in the life of believers joined together in church. Interestingly, in his developing theological understanding, John Smyth changed the notion of baptism (as entrance to local church membership) from being a seal of God's grace, which itself is a rather passive concept, to being a more active declaration of entering into a covenant that had already been received.⁷

The church as a covenant community, sharing God's covenant love in Christ, understood itself to be accountable to the God of the covenant, and (as a natural corollary to this accountability) to each other in covenant relationship. According to Hayden, before adopting a General Baptist position, John Smyth's understanding of the church was

---

3. Pearse, *Great Restoration*, 189; see 179–202.

4. Quoted in Wright, *Free Church*, 56; emphasis added.

5. See Brown, *Boundaries*, generally for perceptive comments on "boundedness"; particularly pp. 77, 85, 114.

6. Quoted in Wright, *Free Church*, 56.

7. See Hayden, *English Baptist History*, 23. See also p. 21.

dominated by the covenant idea, defining it as "a visible community of saints," that is, as "two or more joined together by covenant with God and themselves." Consequently, Christians had what Smyth termed "a duty of love" to each other as believers.[8] Indebted to the early separatist Francis Johnson, Smyth reduced the idea of the church to three primary, defining characteristics. Two of the characteristics that defined the church were (1) that members were to be converted people (that is, in Smyth's language, "saints only") and (2) that they shared "communion in all holy things and the power of the Lord Jesus Christ, for the maintaining of that communion." But significantly, for the present study, the third characteristic was that "the true form" of church was "the uniting of [members] together in the covenant."[9]

The important *London Confession* of 1644 appears to hold to the same covenant idea with a similar emphasis on mutuality and support. For example, it describes the church as

> a company of visible Saints called and separated from the world, by the word and Spirit of God, to the visible profession of the faith of the Gospel . . . joyned to the Lord, and each other, by mutuall agreement . . . being fitly compact and knit together, according to the effectuall working of every part, to the edification of itselfe in love.[10]

Similarly, the *Second London Confession* (1689) speaks of the Lord calling out from the world those who join the church as members. It makes the almost casual statement that this is done not only that they might worship together, but also that they may "walk in obedience," and "walk together . . . for their mutual edification." It says that they "willingly consent to walk together according to the appointment of Christ, giving up themselves, to the Lord and one another by the will of God."[11] Again, the emphasis is upon intentionality ("willingly consent to walk"), the ecclesial centrality of Jesus Christ ("the appointment of Christ"), and a mutual sharing in fellowship created by covenant commitment.

---

8. Ibid., 21.

9. Ibid., 20.

10. *London Confession* (1644), 33, 35. Cited from Lumpkin, *Baptist Confessions*, 165, 166, respectively.

11. *Second London Confession* (1689), 5, 14. Cited from Lumpkin, 286.

The later *Orthodox Creed* (1678) continues to hold the covenant idea as central to General Baptist thought.[12] Reflecting on Baptist covenantal thought, Martin suggests the impact of the idea of genuine community "is incalculable."[13] Roger Hayden spells this out as follows.

> The new covenant is the basis for humanity's acceptance before God, since the old covenant has failed. The new covenant in Christ is the foundation for a new relationship between God and humanity, and it is on this that the Church is built. The new covenant is God's "free grace and love to fallen man" and is freely and fully offered to all men on the terms of the Gospel, viz. repentance and faith.[14]

The practical emphases from this early period include a genuine sense of fellowship and community based on mutual, covenanted commitment to one another and to God, together with a commitment to "walk together and watch over each other." This incorporates authentic sharing, care, and edification. It is seen in the shared life of the church—including its discipline, of course.[15]

Contemporary Thought on Church as (Covenant) Community

Roger Hayden suggests that the demise of the theological concept of the church as a covenanted community happened much later with the impact upon the church of evangelicalism, which introduced a greater emphasis on individualism and personal option or choice. He comments that after the rise of evangelicalism "'Church' no longer defined the community of Christ, it simply met an individual's spiritual need."[16] There is some truth in this, of course.

However, despite this assertion, it seems to me that Baptists, generally, have been and continue to be strident in maintaining a covenant idea of church membership and commitment. For instance, amongst others, the Baptist Union of Great Britain seems committed to a cov-

---

12. For the *Orthodox Creed* (1678) see Lumpkin, *Baptist Confessions*, 297–334.
13. See Martin, *Church*, 29.
14. Hayden, *English Baptist History*, 32.
15. See, for example, Bowers, *Bold Experiment*, 173–89. Bowers states that "gathered community" churches "composed of members who have a positive commitment to Christ, demand of them godly lives" (173).
16. Hayden, *English Baptist History*, 64.

enant model of church. Their fairly recent publication *Patterns and Prayers for Christian Worship*, appears to demonstrate this. It is explicit in the section "Reception into Membership," which, is introduced with the statement,

> We enter into covenant with *them* to share with each other in building up the Church to the glory of God, working alongside one another in his service in the world, and encouraging one another in the love of God.[17]

Changing the metaphor, but maintaining the idea, the church is asked whether it welcomes the candidate into the family of God in this local church. Then, the pertinent question to the members present, "Do you promise to love, encourage, strengthen, guide, pray for, and care for" the candidate as they join the fellowship?[18] The covenant concept clearly continues to underline and to shape the horizontal responsibilities that members, committed to one another, have towards each other. Two contemporary Baptist writers continue to suggest a similar mutual commitment and even a covenant understanding of the church. It is to these attempts at contemporary ecclesiology that we now briefly turn.

In his useful and well-used volume, *Radical Believers: The Baptist Way of Being the Church*, Paul Beasley-Murray writes of the church as "a believers' church," giving importance to intentionality following conversion, faith, and baptism.[19] He speaks of a reciprocal commitment between (in the first place) ourselves and God "a life-long commitment to the way of Christ."[20] There follows from this primary commitment (in the second place) a commitment to the people of Christ.

> It means, for instance, that we may no longer look only to our own interests, but also to the interests of others (Phil 2:4). It means that sharing with God's people who are in need and practicing hospitality (Rom 12:13) come to the top of our agenda.[21]

Later he said that "Commitment to Christ, therefore, *inevitably* involves commitment to his people and church membership."[22]

17. Baptist Union of Great Britain, *Patterns*, 104; emphasis original.
18. Ibid., 106.
19. Beasley-Murray, *Radical Believers*, 9.
20. Ibid., 15, 21, respectively.
21. Ibid., 21.
22. Ibid., 50; emphasis added. See also pp. 49, 54.

Beasley-Murray is adamant that we look at church with a covenant focus. This whole matter of church membership, he asserts, is about covenant: "First and foremost church membership is about covenant relationships," indeed, "commitment to one another . . . is the essence of a church covenant."[23] In fellowship groups (which for Beasley-Murray epitomize believers' church) the dynamic of relationships (or, in his term, "meaningful fellowship") means that "love can be displayed, life can be shared, maturity can be developed, gifts can be discovered."[24] Later, in his chapter on "Living the Lordship of Christ," he speaks of an outward, missional movement from covenant relationships to the world: "In our relationship with others we are called to represent Christ to one another *and the world*."[25] We merely note this important idea here, but we will return to it later below.

More recently, the Principal of Spurgeon's College in London, Nigel Wright, agrees with the covenanted nature of church. He speaks of a regenerate church; indeed, he states that "The doctrine of salvation defines the doctrine of the church."[26] And he insists that it should be seen a, what he call, "a gathering church."[27] This rather nuanced phrase is Wright's understandable attempt to move away from the rather static term "gathered church," employed in earlier times but not completely out of vogue today" "gathering church) encourages a dynamic in which the community has an identity defined by its centre, Jesus Christ, and an inclusive circumference rather than an exclusive boundary. It is suggestive of dynamic people who are *actively* light and salt in the world.[28]

---

23. Ibid., 49, 55, respectively. Interestingly, Beasley-Murray writes this in the context of looking at the covenant made by John Smyth and his followers at Gainsborough in 1606.

24. Ibid., 54.

25. Ibid., 60–61; emphasis added. In his choice of words at this point Beasley-Murray seems to be reflecting Luther's understanding of believers being *alter Christus* to each other.

26. Wright, *Free Church*, 51, 55, respectively. Again, his comment comes in a section in which he reflects on the ecclesiology of both John Smyth and Thomas Helwys (55–57). See als, Smith, *All God's People*, 376.

27. Wright, *Free Church*, 49–69.

28. See Jones, *Believing Church*, 38–41. Brown, *Boundaries*, 77–80, in discussing church "canon" (by which he means church life in all its aspects, its particularity) employs the helpful image of a galaxy. Unlike a planet with its static nature, its "brute given-ness," a galaxy functionally exerts its own gravitational pull ("a kind of inner drive") with its ragged edges and its inner swirl.

As Nigel Wright concludes, "The gathering church therefore exists as an *open* community of disciples."[29] In his earlier book, *New Baptists, New Agenda*, Wright says, "The effective church is the open church." He continues,

> This seems to me to be a fundamental aspect of effective congregational life: the capacity to build a committed membership while *at the same time* remaining radically and welcomingly open to those as yet beyond.[30]

Nevertheless, Wright suggests that the members of the church belong to one another (indicating commitment) in "a covenanted relationship." He appears, whether consciously, or unconsciously, to continue the early Baptist position in which the initial, overarching covenant of God is somehow reflected in the membership: "As God has made covenant relationship with us so we are drawn into *explicit and expressed commitment* to each other in the church."[31]

Interestingly, in translating this typically Baptist ecclesiology, Wright argues that the present system of membership is inadequate for the church today. He suggests that we need to think in terms of process, envisaging the church as a series of concentric circles with a "very definite core both of beliefs, values, and committed people." He distinguishes between "community membership" and "covenant membership." Earlier, he had spoken of these as "formal" and "organic" membership, respectively.[32] "Community" or "formal" membership, is open to all; "covenant" or "organic" membership, is open only to those committed together in covenant relationship. The former sees people genuinely cared for in the church's pastoral oversight whilst allowing them to move in the process at their own speed; the latter (based as it is on willing commitment) is intended "to be demanding of people's discipleship."[33] Then, he says, we might envisage a healthy dynamic "that draws people in from the circumference to the centre," from a more formal membership to an organic one.[34] And, as the early General Baptist model indicated, Wright

---

29. Wright, *Free Church*, 51; emphasis added.
30. Wright, *New Baptists*, 75, 76, respectively; emphasis added.
31. Wright, *Free Church*, 58; emphasis added. See also, Wright, *New Baptists*, 79.
32. See Wright, *New Baptists*, 76–79.
33. Wright, *Free Church*, 61.
34. Ibid., 62.

asserts that membership is about close relationships in the overarching context of the love of God.

> We are engaged with each other in such a way that we receive from each other aspects of the manifold grace of God, setting an example to each other. . . . This is the continual activity of the church of Christ, to be a discipling community.[35]

The church meeting and the priesthood of all believers—which this suggests—are corresponding ideas, of course. The booklet, "What Makes a Baptist?" elucidates this as follows:

> In the Baptist model of a believers' church every member has a role to play, whether in teaching, faith-sharing, evangelism, social action, pastoring, guiding, serving, prophetic insight, praying, healing, administration or hospitality.[36]

Mike Nicholls asserts that "every believer has a ministry and true ministry is the work of the whole church." Wright speaks of "the leadership of some and the ministry of all."[37]

This important Reformational emphasis is expressed, by implication at least, in each of the five core values of the Baptist Union of Great Britain. The values suggest that a church is a community that is prophetic, inclusive, sacrificial, missional, and worshipping; and in so doing they address each covenant member of that community, challenging them to live—by the power of the Spirit—as Christ in the local church itself, in the denomination, and in society and the wider world. Each believer is responsible for a prophetic concern, to be inclusive, sacrificial, missional, and each is called upon to worship the Lord.[38] The individual responsibility is to be seen in one's life lived out through the grace of God, but importantly it also comes to expression in the church meeting, which is a significant Baptist ecclesial characteristic. So, though each covenanted church member will be personally challenged, the Baptist

---

35. Similarly, Richter and Francis, *Gone But Not Forgotten*, 144, suggest that one solution might be for churches consciously or unconsciously to recognize different types or levels of membership, encompassing this 'extended family of faith.' People may be invited to sign up as 'seekers,' 'friends of the church,' 'associates,' or 'kindred spirits.'

36. "What Makes a Baptist?" 8.

37. Cited by Hayden, *English Baptist History*, 262.

38. Baptist Union of Great Britain, *5 Core Values*, 2–3. See Grenz, *Created for Community*, 218–27, on this subject.

way is to empower the church corporately to make decisions. Beasley-Murray states with good reason that

> The Baptist model of the church meeting is exciting. *Every* member has a part to play. *Every* member counts. Yet at the same time it is a highly demanding model. It expects much from the membership, and it expects much from the church meeting. . . . [It] involves seeking the mind of Christ in relation to all matters of faith and practice.[39]

We have seen, then, that there is a commitment to a covenant model of church amongst Baptists—a model that has lasted 400 years. The question that confronts us is how this covenant model might work for today's generation. Or, to put it another way, is the covenant model sufficient for a church in post-modern society? That is, is it a model that will be good beyond 400?

Church as (Covenant) Community Today

It is noticeable that there *are* writers who are questioning what it means to belong to a community in post-modern culture. In his helpful book, *The Search to Belong*, Myers asserts that "people crave connection, not contracts," thereby denying any significant relationship between commitment and community. He says, "When we search to belong, we aren't really looking for commitment. We simply want to connect."[40] Likewise, Pete Ward in *Liquid Church* suggests that attempts to develop community in (what he terms) "liquid modernity" are an illusion—though he *does* maintain the central importance of relationships.[41] His conclusion is that the desire that used to create community now creates communication instead.[42] And, this is certainly understandable in an age of Facebook and MySpace. Other writers urge a redefinition of commitment and membership, criticizing the extent to which regular

---

39. Beasley-Murray, *Radical Believers*, 66; emphasis added.
40. Myers, *Search to Belong*, 27, 12, respectively.
41. Ward, *Liquid Church*, 24, 46, respectively. By "liquid modernity" Ward refers to what others speak of as "postmodernity," "late modernity," or "hyper-modernity."
42. Ibid., 88; also, 90. See also Radley, *Place*, 7–9, 16.

attendance at church meetings appears to become equated with faithful church membership.[43]

Notwithstanding, others question the prioritizing of belief above belonging in churches seeking to be relevant to post-modern culture. Brian Harris, for instance, asserts the central importance of community-belonging whilst holding an open, missional ecclesiology.[44] Christopher Walker agrees, stating that missional church is "First and foremost . . . a community."[45] An, perhaps this change in perspective is the key to our translating early Baptist ecclesiology to today's church. I believe, given the biblical images of church and the theological arguments sketched above, that the covenant/commitment model for the church as community has mileage in and for contemporary society, but particularly in its mediatorial and missional role in the changed missional context that confronts us.[46]

In his fascinating essay "The 'Gift' of the Church. *Ecclesia Crucis, Peccatrix Maxima*, and the *Missio Dei*," M. Jinkins says that "The church exists in the history of the world for the sake of *missio Dei*, and for no other reason.[47] Though I would argue that the church has at least two functions—doxological and missional (see, for example, John 4:23–24)—I believe that Jinkins is essentially right. Community today, based upon and reflecting covenant and commitment, is essential, but needs to demonstrate an outward focus and priority. That is, as a membership we don't live for ourselves, we live (primarily) for God, and also for others.

In much of what Nigel Wright says he unashamedly follows the contemporary ecclesiological thought of German theologian Jürgen Moltmann. For example, Wright speaks of Moltmann's excellent work *The Church in the Power of the Spirit* as "the best 'Baptist' book on the church available despite not having been written by a Baptist."[48] In both that book and his later work *The Open Church*, Moltmann calls for the friendship of Jesus to be the key to membership in a missional commu-

---

43. See, for example, Pearse and Matthews, *We Must Stop Meeting Like This*; Thwaites, *Church*.

44. Harris, "'Behave, Believe, Belong.'" See also Moynagh, *Changing World*, 67–70.

45. Walker, *Seeking Relevant Churches*, 30. See particularly pp. 25–38.

46. On the biblical images for the church, see the seminal work Minear, *Images*, particularly 66–220.

47. Jinkins, "'Gift' of the Church," particularly 208.

48. Wright, *New Baptists*, 64. See Moltmann, *Church*.

nity in the present context.⁴⁹ The following statement is worth quoting in full:

> The church will not overcome its present crisis through reform of the administration of the sacraments, or from the reform of its ministries. It will overcome this crisis through the rebirth of practical fellowship.⁵⁰

The Baptist theologian James McClendon also writes concerning the importance of membership in the light of the church's missional calling, but he does so with a realistic, helpful, and biblical concern for the church's pneumatological-eschatological situation, in which the "fellowship of the Holy Spirit implies a common life whose practices suit, not this present age, but the age to come—a community at once redeemed and redemptive."⁵¹ He, too, insists on an intentional church membership, speaking as he does of "a disciple church." He adds, "If membership in the church is intentional, then the church becomes a live circuit for the power of the Holy Spirit."⁵² However, he does not explicitly speak of covenanted church. McClendon's concern is with the time in which we find ourselves, and upon the presence of the Holy Spirit among us, significantly, speaking of this as "the Spirit's koinonic presence."⁵³ The community "lives between the times," but notice that its task is in "adapting, adjusting, transforming, interpreting so that the church can be the church *even as it helps the world to see itself as world*."⁵⁴ Notice, though, that the fellowship of the Spirit implies a common life whose

---

49. See, for example, Moltmann, *Church*, 115–18, 289–99, 314–17; idem, *Open Church*, 9, 29, 50–63, 125. Guder, *Continuing Conversion*, 178–79, writes, "every Christian community should see itself as a community of missionaries. Its responsibility to them is to guide them to identify God's calling, to recognize the gifts and opportunities they have, to provide them the biblical and theological training to incarnate the gospel in their particular fields, and then to commission them to that ministry . . . groups in congregations which sense a common interest in a particular mission should be prepared for that work and mandated to it by the congregation. . . . Such structures of vocation to ministry should become the basic understanding of membership in the mission community." See also, Gibbs, *Church Next*, 31–32.

50. Moltmann, *Church*, 317.

51. McClendon, *Systematic Theology*, 2:366. See, generally, 2:366–71. It is noteworthy that McClendon says that "in each 'local church' (the expression is a redundancy) the wonder of community formation in Christ has occurred" (2:366).

52. Ibid., 2:371.

53. Ibid., 2:367.

54. Ibid., 2:367; emphasis added.

practices suit, not this present age, but the age to come—a community at once redeemed and redemptive.[55] The other aspect of McClendon's ecclesiology is that he centres it on Jesus Christ. He says, for example, that the church is "a company of equals, equally gifted by God's Spirit, equally responsible for the community-building whose accomplishment is the fullness of Christ."[56]

So, clearly, there are theologians (some of whom come from a covenant model of church, some who do not) who generally speak of membership in a similar way. They all emphasize the fellowship aspect, though some are beginning to speak of the crucial missional role in which such members are to be engaged.

Reflections

The Baptist theologian Stanley Grenz says, "No *true* community of faith fails to set its sights outward toward the world in which it is called to live." [57] The emphasis is important here. Grenz means that a community living and working together *as community* will be outward focused. It is that dynamic combination of, and relationship between, community, on the one hand, and mission, on the other, that demonstrates that the covenant idea is both valid and relevant to the church's situation in a postmodern world. So, in his seminal work *Transforming Mission*, David Bosch suggests that "Christian mission gives expression to the dynamic relationship between God and the world."[58] Later, he articulates this again more fully:

> Mission is, quite simply, the participation of Christians in the liberating mission of Jesus. It is the good news of God's love, *incarnated in the witness of a community*, for the sake of the world.[59]

---

55. Ibid., 2:366.

56. Ibid., 2:369. See also, Volf, "Community Formation," 217, who speaks in a similar way: "For in so assembling, Christians attest that Christ is the determining ground of their lives—that in him they have found freedom, orientation, and power." See also, Volf, *After Our Likeness*, 137–45; Barger, *New and Right Spirit*.

57. Grenz, *Created for Community*, 224; emphasis added.

58. Bosch, *Transforming Mission*, 9.

59. Ibid., 519; emphasis added. Notice, too, the comment by Zizioulas, *Being as Communion*, 21: "Christ himself becomes revealed as truth not in a community, but as a community." See also, Dyrness, *Let the Earth Rejoice!*, 190.

We should notice the italicized words that emphasize that it is God's love in Christ that is "incarnated in the witness of a community," and ponder their application today. Certainly, though many Baptists "still feel the double pull of social responsibility issues and mission," contemporary Baptist theologians and writers would underline the central significance of holistic mission in today's society—*including* social action (promoting justice, social welfare, healing, education, and peace in the world). In this divinely given task the church as community, in authentic *koinonia* relationship, seeks to transcend barriers of gender, language, race, class, age, and culture to reach others for Jesus Christ.

In an excellent article that addresses the effects of postmodernism on the church, Australian Peter Corney says that we need first to show that Christianity meets the deepest and most profound needs of people. Because people are less linear in their approach to communication and knowledge than the previous generation, they are more interested in our personal narratives, in our story. He continues,

> Connected with this is the importance that this generation places on relationships. Presenting the Gospel in relational terms, and in the context of relationships, will be helpful. Authentic Christian community will be crucial. People need to see and experience the Gospel lived. When all ideologies are suspect, and when family and community have broken down, Christian communities which are loving, caring, and open will be profoundly attractive.[60]

We might think of the example of the nascent church presented in the Book of Acts in which believers were together in community, and in which they "devoted themselves to the apostles' teaching and to fellowship, to the breaking of bread and to prayer," in which they shared what they had to help those in need, and to which many were added daily (Acts 2:42–47). Notice, too, a similar description of the church in Acts 4:32–35 in which the apostolic preaching of the resurrection of Jesus Christ is somehow inherently linked with the divine grace "powerfully at work in them all" (v. 33). Evidently, the characteristics and the values of such a community people derive from the life of Christ, the empowering of the Holy Spirit, and the Father's continuing love and will be worked

---

60. Corney, "Have You Got the Right address?," 3. The title of the article is derived from a comment by Helmut Thielicke, which Corney quotes: "The Gospel must be constantly forwarded to a new address, because the recipient is repeatedly changing place of residence."

out within the church itself and in the wider circles of the denomination and the world, a world that needs to see the love and grace of God in concrete, relational, *incarnated* terms—at once prophetic, humble, inclusive, sacrificial, and missional, centred on true worship of the living God.[61]

---

61. Wilkinson-Hayes, *Baptist Basics*, 10.

15

Worship and the Unity of Baptists Today[1]

NEVILLE CALLAM

Introduction

People who have participated extensively in corporate worship events in Baptist churches around the world cannot fail to notice the bewildering variety that exists. Would one find anything in common in the worship experience available on a Sunday morning in the Magobini Church in Tanzania, the Chelm Church in Poland, the Hyderabad Church in India, the Moscow Church in Russia, the Cathedral Church in Georgia, the East Queen Street Church in Jamaica, the Vienna or Alfred Street Church in the USA, and the Once Church in Argentina?[2]

Efforts to account for the wide diversity that exists cannot simply resort to the language of cultural differences. In a single cultural context, vast differences may be found in the approaches Baptist churches take in corporate worship. Nor can the diversity be attributed merely to the penchant among Baptists to claim divine leading for what they do when they gather in communities expressing the intent to worship God together. Some people may be content to emphasize that Baptist and

---

1. "The person who can speak for all Baptists has not yet been born, and his parents are already dead!"—an ancient adage cited by David Coffey, president of the Baptist World Alliance.

2. I am reminded of the comment, "Anyone attempting to identify practices which are universal to Baptists is either unusually courageous or simply uninformed!" (BWA, *We Baptists*, 52).

other Christian churches enjoy a God-given freedom to decide how they worship. Others, recognizing the vital importance of corporate worship to Baptist life, may raise questions about the significance and usefulness of the perplexing diversity that exists.

Especially over the last forty or fifty years, there has been a growing realization in the Baptist churches regarding the relationship between worship and unity. While those probing this dimension of worship have tended to keep the ecumenical community in view, might it be useful to ask whether the bewildering diversity in corporate worship among Baptists does in fact serve the unity of the Baptist churches.

Characterizing Worship among Baptists

Walter Shurden contends that Baptists emphasize "church freedom."[3] This refers to freedom of the local churches "under the Lordship of Christ to determine their membership and leadership, to order their worship . . . and to participate in the larger Body of Christ, of whose unity and mission Baptists are proudly a part." The church enjoys the "freedom to worship creatively" and this engenders differences in worship styles that are rooted in congregational church government. Shurden explains that it is this conviction that leads to a rejection of impersonal and mechanical features of worship. Yet, it makes room for various styles of worship—some "surprisingly formal" and others "exceedingly informal."

Reaching beyond Shurden's assertions, Nathan Nettleton claims that the "most notable feature of Baptist worship practice, especially when looked at across the centuries as well as round the globe, is its diversity."[4] He adds the striking claim that "this diversity is actually something which Baptists have a theological commitment to maintaining."[5] Not surprisingly, Nettleton explains that Baptist people "do not usually seek to express or symbolize their unity by agreeing on texts or patterns of worship that will be common to many congregations."[6] Diversity in Baptist worship, he argues, is the "inevitable consequence" of Baptists' affirmation of the autonomy of the local congregation.[7] Of course, this

---

3. Shurden, *Baptist Identity*, 39–41.
4. Nettleton, "Baptist Worship," 81.
5. Ibid.
6. Ibid., 72.
7. Ibid. Cf. BWA, *We Baptists*, 48–61.

view derives from a reading of Baptist origins that grounds the resolution of questions of worship forms in the authority, that is, the competence, of the local congregation to order its own life. According to this view, Baptists believe that when they gather in worshipping communities, they should discern "how God, through the Scriptures, [is] calling them to order their worship."[8] Nettleton claims that because Baptists are open to more light and truth breaking forth from God's word, liturgical nonconformity is likely to be an ongoing feature of their life.

In surveying the development of worship traditions among Baptists, Nettleton credits the changes that appear to a number of sources, including the Evangelical revival in British Protestantism and revivalism in the American frontier movement.[9] Nettleton notes the impact of different sources that have undoubtedly left their marks on corporate worship among Baptists. These include the ecumenical, liturgical renewal, charismatic, and church growth movements. The diverse pattern that results, Nettleton suggests, is a sign of the Baptist openness to change.

In the midst of his vigorous portrayal of the remarkable diversity that he regards as normative for Baptist worship, Nettleton claims that "there is a widespread dissonance between what Baptists think they do and what they actually do in their worship."[10] While he relates this to the attitude of many Baptists to the use of liturgical texts, might Nettleton's claim not extend beyond this to the very issue of the structure and content of worship among Baptists?[11] If we allow that Baptists do not regard diversity in worship forms as necessarily a hindrance to unity, can we accurately claim that for Baptists the quest for common worship patterns and texts may prove in itself to be an obstacle to unity? If the claim is credible that "Baptists do not *begin* with the assumption that greater homogeneity in worship is a desirable objective," can it not also be said that in worship practice, once we get behind the actual elements that make up a corporate worship service among Baptists, we may actually discern an *ordo* or pattern in services of Holy Communion held in many Baptist churches around the world?[12]

---

8. Best and Grdzelidze, *Worship Today*, 73.
9. Cf. White, *Brief History*, ch 5.
10. Nettleton, "Baptist Worship," 79.
11. Ibid., 79–80.
12. Ibid., 80; emphasis added.

My contribution in this essay must not be taken to represent an attempt to nudge Baptist churches toward a boring uniformity in worship content and style. Is it not commonly agreed that, from the beginning, considerable diversity has always marked the worship of God's people gathered in the church?[13] What we see emerging among many Baptists—and we consider this commendable—is a liturgical *ordo*, a pattern, or shape of worship that is able to embrace diverse elements mediated in ways that are actually culturally conditioned. Should Baptist churches detect in their corporate worship life the *ordo* we claim to mark our Lord's Supper services, the lessons arising from this should be noted. For example, whether or not a particular confessional tradition emphasizes textuality or orality, formality or spontaneity, this does not eliminate the possibility of the existence of a liturgical *ordo* in that tradition. Nor does this deny the reality that this *ordo* may be deemed a source for the fundamental unity of which corporate worship among Baptists may be said to give expression.

Reflections on Baptist Worship in Berlin

In October 1998, 500 Baptists from 193 Baptist World Alliance member bodies serving in 58 countries gathered in Berlin to consider the subject of Christian worship among Baptists. Those assembled desired to accomplish many aims. They wanted to identify biblical and theological emphases informing the role of worship in the life of the church and of the individual. They desired to investigate the "rich variety of worship forms practiced in ... Baptist churches and to explore how various models impact on the Baptist worship experience." They set out to "celebrate and appreciate different cultural approaches to worship in the Baptist world today" and to "celebrate in worship our common life as Baptists both through well established liturgy and through creative, innovative and complementary forms of worship."[14] The conference examined a "variety of worship emphases, never to elevate one over another and always with a spirit of inquiry and wonder ... in love and with grace."[15]

Six papers presented at the conference dealt with "How worship takes place in different regions"—namely, Eastern Europe, African

13. White, *Brief History*, 13–39; Martin, *Worship in the Early Church*.
14. Cupit, *Baptists in Worship*, 235.
15. Ibid., 7.

American, Western Europe, Euro American, Latin America, and the Caribbean.[16] Significantly, at no time during the conference was consideration given to whether the "rich diversity" that marks the worship life of Baptist churches does indeed serve the unity of the Baptist family. Nor did the conference address the subject of the inculturation of worship and whether there are legitimate limits to it.

BWA General Secretary Denton Lotz was the only presenter to address the relation of worship and unity, but in all too few words.[17] Lotz described the Baptists gathered at the conference as "a diverse group, speaking many languages, representing many cultures, and worshipping in different ways."[18] Noting that "worship is the great activity that unites [Baptists] worldwide," Lotz declared,

> For it is in worship that we come not as Americans or Germans, not as Russians or Africans, not as Brazilians or Australians, not as Koreans or Indians, but we come as men and women who have been . . . crucified with Christ and transformed into a believers' church. It is that unity we experience in worship that is the visible sign of God's hand upon us. When that is lacking then we become just a voluntary association with perhaps some common goals, but no spirit and no life! Worship of the Lord Jesus Christ is the center of our unity.[19]

Rather than developing these interesting insights, which seemed not to have been a part of the focus of the conference, Lotz explained how mission, fellowship, encouragement, Christian formation, and social justice issues are related to the heart of worship as whole-life engagement in response to the revelation of God's love. It is all too easy to celebrate the variety that marks Baptist worship without considering whether and if this diversity is as laudatory as some Baptists are inclined to assume.

Worship and Baptist Identity

In 2004, the Faith and Order Commission of the World Council of Churches produced a text offering a "survey of the understanding and practice of worship . . . in a wide variety of Christian Churches, com-

---

16. Ibid., 91–136.
17. Ibid., 226–34.
18. Ibid., 229.
19. Ibid.

munities and contexts."[20] Three Baptist contributions appear in the text. Burchel Taylor contributes "The Jamaica Baptist Worship Tradition," Nathan Nettleton provides an interpretation of "Baptist Worship in Ecumenical Perspective," and Paul Sheppy contributes an overview and analysis on "Worship and Ecumenism."[21]

Nettleton claims that Baptists "have tended to rally round the cause of common mission, rather than common prayer."[22] He grounds this in Baptist beginnings in nonconformity with its insistence on freedom from external human authority in the determination of its liturgical practice. Liturgical nonconformity, he says, has freed the local church congregations to respond to developments in worship in ways they discerned the Spirit was leading them. Nettleton credits this for Baptist liturgical practice not developing a unique pattern. The result is that, while today there are dominant patterns in Baptist worship, there is no single pattern that is common to all. This does not prevent Nettleton from identifying what he describes as "family resemblances."

Nettleton identifies the following features as characteristic of Baptist worship: the importance ascribed to personal sincerity and individual experience, the centrality of preaching, the prominence of singing, extempore prayers, and ambivalence towards written liturgical texts.[23] Concerning worship and unity among Baptists, Nettleton presents his conclusion:

> [T]he emphasis, in ecumenical dialogue, on the quest for common liturgical texts as a pathway to greater unity . . . is essentially foreign to the Baptist mindset. While it is recognized that things such as a common hymnal have sometimes fostered a greater sense of familial bond between Baptist congregations, Baptists have never seen differences in worship language, style or structure as an obstacle to unity, even among themselves. Conversely, however, the quest for common patterns and texts in worship may well prove, in itself, to be an obstacle to unity for Baptists. The belief that God's call to each congregation is particular, and the consequent insistence on protecting each congregation's right to discern and obey the details of that call without external human interference, mean that Baptists do not begin with the

---

20. Best and Heller, *Worship Today*, ix.
21. Ibid., 199–202, 72–83, 311–22, respectively.
22. Ibid., 72
23. Ibid., 78.

assumption that greater homogeneity in worship is a desirable objective. Rather, they would tend to suspect that the quest for common worship might come at the expense of the Spirit's mission of incarnating the body of Christ in each community in ways which are truly indigenous to it.[24]

There is no doubt that Baptists prize what is often referred to as "the autonomy of the local church." Yet, is it not also a fact of Baptist history that "associating" has also been a value that is highly regarded? Not surprisingly, over the years many churches that are connected historically have not only used the same hymn books, but also the same worship manuals.[25] Furthermore, in recent years discussion on local church autonomy has become rather more nuanced than it has tended to be. Care is being taken to ensure that this autonomy is seen to rest on the church's capacity to discern how the Holy Spirit is leading and is not intended to affirm self-centred independence and self-sufficiency.

The treatment of autonomy in a publication in 1999 by the Study and Research Division of the Baptist World Alliance is highly instructive.[26] While it affirms the local church's "freedom and responsibility to conduct its own life and mission [including] questions of worship," it states clearly that in some cases the "emphasis on the spiritual competency of the local church may have led to an exaggerated sense of autonomy and independence." It continues:

> For some, the autonomy of the local church is absolute so that the role of any convention or union is minimal and only advisory. . . . Other Baptists insist on the necessity of churches associating together; for them any definition of the church that does not include this interdependence is inadequate. According to the latter view, the local church needs to belong to a larger association of churches which can more fully reflect the nature of the church as it seeks to find the mind of Christ.[27]

The Symposium on Baptist Identity and Ecclesiology held in Elstal, Germany (March 2007) made the following affirmations.[28] First, the

---

24. Ibid., 79–80.

25. See, for example, Payne and Winward, *Orders and Prayers*; Baptist Union of Great Britain, *Patterns and Prayers*; Ellis and Blyth, *Gathering for Worship*.

26. BWA, *We Baptists*.

27. Ibid., 25.

28. See BWA, "Statement."

local church is wholly church but not the whole church. Second, the theological and practical necessity of relating to sister churches for discernment and action illustrates this through the notion of covenant expressed by the early English Baptist phrase, "to walk together in ways known and to be made known."

A major paper presented by Nigel Wright at the Elstal Symposium reveals that many Baptists are trying to keep autonomy and interdependence in a proper balance.[29] If there was once secure confidence in the particularity of divine disclosure to people in one context, this does not preclude the possibility of common structures that people from autonomous communities may share. Wright argues that

> Baptist Christians . . . believe . . . that they exist *under the rule of Christ* and that this rule brings them into freedom. Because Christ rules and imparts his mind and his will through the scriptures and through the Spirit to those communities which gather around him and meet in his name, we are able to say that those communities are empowered to discern and do his will (1 Cor 2:6–16).

On this basis, he affirms the "competence of the church of Jesus Christ, its freedom and ability to discern and do the will of God for its own life."[30] Wright emphatically asserts that

> the autonomy of the local church does not mean that our congregations can be a law unto themselves or cut themselves off from each other. We are accountable to each other. The autonomy of the local church should not be interpreted as congregational individualism or isolation. . . . [T]he the autonomy, freedom and authority of the church as a whole, and of the distinct churches within it, is only ever an autonomy under the authority of Christ. . . . It is not the rule of the people, or of the majority, that is at stake within the church but of the Lord himself and our efforts are devoted to finding out what the Lord wants.

Further, he emphasizes that

> the fundamental competence of the local congregation . . . is not the same as omni-competence. If a local congregation is able to interpret and administer the scriptures, this does not mean that it has no need of anybody else. This would be contrary to God's

---

29. Ibid., 499. See also Wright, *Free Church*, 115–37, 183–203.
30. Ibid., 499.

chosen way of shaping the church. God deliberately causes us to need each other within the Body of Christ (1 Cor 12:12–21).

On this basis, he explains that "there are some matters we are unable to resolve or decide in our individual churches and where we need to refer to the wider body of Christ. A strength of the Baptist way is to recognize that all of us together are wiser than any of us on our own."[31] Finally, Wright offers a clearly worded conclusion:

> The freedom and autonomy of the local church is one of the characteristic Baptist principles. However, stressing this aspect of our freedom in Christ at the expense of our belonging to each other in the wider Body is not in our interests or in that of our mission. More importantly, to interpret this as the kind of independence which says we do not need each other is to misunderstand our heritage. We do need each other. We benefit from giving and receiving. We embody Christ's way when within our congregations and between them, across the world, we honour and serve each other. The autonomy of the local church needs to be celebrated, but always in the context of being part of a world-wide family and movement called together to serve the abiding purposes of God.[32]

Such a nuanced understanding of local church autonomy is hospitable to the emergence of structures, procedures, and resources that are held in common, but are adapted to the specific circumstances in which a local Baptist church carries out ministry.

Worship Conference in Czech Republic

In 2007 the International Baptist Theological Seminary (IBTS) convened a conference to address "how convictional intentional communities worship."[33] One of the presenters at the conference, a leading Baptist worship scholar, Christopher Ellis, argues for the inadmissibility of people conferring "authoritative status on any stage of the developing story of Baptist worship." Ellis points out that "change and continuity" are features of the churches' response to "changing social and cultural

---

31. Ibid., 9–10.
32. Ibid., 12.
33. Jones and Parushev, *Currents in Baptistic Theology*, 5.

contexts."[34] On the subject of an *ordo* of worship among Baptists, Ellis asks the question,

> [I]s there a genetic code which makes worship among Baptists recognizably Baptist? I believe there is but I do not see it as a list of ingredients so much as a set of values which find varying forms of expression in different settings. There is, if you like, a family likeness rather than a genetic cloning.[35]

Ellis identifies this *ordo* as "a cluster of values which express Baptist ecclesiology in particular ways [such as] attention to scripture, devotion and openness to the Spirit, the church as community, [and] eschatology or concern for the Kingdom."[36] From his research, Ellis argues for the priority among Baptists of concern for sincerity on worship over the juxtaposition of elements of the corporate worship event. He grants, however, that the ordering of the parts of a worship event does have significance and conveys meaning. Ellis is concerned especially to make the case that "there is not a single structure which is to be regarded as correct or right . . . [even though] some will be better, or more helpful, than others."[37] Addressing the same conference, Nathan Nettleton asserted that while "every worshipping community will utilize some consistent elements" there is "no real right or wrong" way to order the "basic movements" characterizing the narrative structure in a worship service.[38]

---

34. Ellis, "Understanding Worship" 33. For Ellis' perspectives on worship, see his *Gathering*.

35. Ellis, "Understanding Worship," 36.

36. Ibid., 27. In another essay, Ellis identifies the following as the five core values of Baptist worship: the importance of Scripture and attention to its perceived commands; devotional concern for personal faith and piety; a concern for the religious affections and an openness to the Holy Spirit; committed participation in a community in which fellowship and relationships are highly valued; and an encounter with God that looks to the horizon of God's kingdom. See Ellis, "Who Are the Baptists?" 81–83. In an earlier work, *Corporate Worship*, I argued for discernible "movements" in Baptist worship that could be identified in the Jamaican context. See Taylor, "Jamaican Baptist Worship."

37. Ellis, "Understanding Worship," 37.

38. Jones and Parushev, *Currents in Baptistic Theology*, 88.

Ecumenical Consensus and the *Ordo* of Communion Service among Baptists

A certain ecumenical consensus has emerged around the *ordo* of Christian worship, which is described in the Ditchingham Letter and Report as "the undergirding structure which is to be perceived in the ordering and scheduling of the most primary elements of Christian worship."[39] This *ordo* may be understood rather as a description of what actually happens when people gather for worship than as a stipulated requirement for authentic corporate worship. What is this ecumenical consensus around the basic outlines of this *ordo*?

This *ordo*, which is always marked by pairing and by mutually reinterpretive juxtapositions, roots in word and sacrament held together. It is Scripture readings and preaching together, yielding intercessions; and with these it is *Eucharistia* and eating and drinking together, yielding a collection for the poor and mission in the world. It is a formation in faith and baptizing in water together, leading to participation in the life of the community. It is ministers and people enacting these things, together. It is prayers through the days of the week and the Sunday assembly seen together; it is observances through the year and the annual common celebration of the *Pascha* together.[40]

One feature of the Baptist understanding of worship is that total-life discipleship, and not merely the worship event, is its true context. The worship event is linked with the routine of daily life. This is why the *ordo* links public worship and the lived experience of the worshippers. Baptist worship on "Communion Sunday" reflects this underlying *ordo*. Put differently, the celebration with thanksgiving of Christ's death and resurrection is linked with the call to mission engagement, and baptism in water is linked to formation in faith and growth in Christian discipleship as a lifelong commitment. Worship is seen to be at the heart of both Christian life in community and life in the world, and is understood to be the calling of all believers, including the congregations and their leaders.[41]

When the entire worship event on Communion Sunday is seen as a single event, the worship includes a number of elements which interact

---

39. Best and Heller, *So We Believe*, 6. See, also, Lathrop, *Holy Things*, pt 1.
40. Ibid., 6.
41. Ibid.

with each other in subtle ways, which may not at first appear evident. Through the medium of speech or song, there is an invocation of the Spirit on the gathered community together with all that is in their midst. So it is an invocation also on the elements of bread and wine set before the congregation gathered for the Lord's Supper. Whatever the medium utilized, there is the confession of sin and with increasing frequency an assurance of forgiveness grounded in Scripture. It is easy to consider these elements to be absent when we look only at the words spoken in worship and refrain from analysis of the content of the lyrics marking the many hymns and songs that are sung from the multiple sources used in Baptist worship.

In his paper "Tracing Baptist Theological Footprints over the Past Four Hundred Years," delivered at the Seventh Baptist International Conference on Theological Education, Ian Randall referred to the tradition of reading Scripture in the congregation led by John Smyth. One or two chapters of the Bible preceded prayer and an exposition of the text, as the congregation together discovered the power of the Bible.[42] Still today, Scripture is read and the readings usually form the basis of preaching, which often involves making clear what the text may be saying to those reading it together.[43] Similarly, whether the prayer of intercession precedes or follows the sermon, the central point of the sermon does influence the prayer, whether prepared or impromptu.[44]

During the Lord's Supper, eating and drinking accompany a recollection of the major events of the life of Christ and participants are reminded of the meaning of this corporate act.[45] In many places, the tendency to orally link the Lord's Supper and the financial offerings has

---

42. This paper will appear in the journal *Perspectives in Religious Studies*.

43. While in some places less and less time is spent reading the Scriptures, this is not the case among many Baptists who continue to insist that the church family should not allow shorter worship services to compromise the time needed for Bible readings.

44. In some places there is a diminution of concern for the world and even for fellow Christians residing outside the community gathered for worship. Petitions for those gathered seem to cancel concern for those outside the walls of the gathering. The trend toward an elimination of intercessions in some cases seems to reflect an extreme self-centredness that is not in keeping with Baptist understandings of what sincere corporate worship would require.

45. In some places, the celebration of the Lord's Supper is under threat from the continuing reduction of time for corporate worship. The short time devoted to Holy Communion is denuding the Communion of its full meaning and is undermining its important place in the corporate worship event.

receded. This seems to result from the holistic approach to ministry that emphasizes the connection between worship and the missional calling of the community. Baptist communities tend to appreciate the ethical implications of their missional calling as a predicate of baptism. This includes an unshakeable commitment to the poor. As Burchel Taylor has indicated,

> True worship is . . . always potentially subversive [especially] in an idolatrous environment. . . . This makes worship a dangerous exercise . . . because of the prophetic challenge it constitutes. . . . It, however, puts into proper perspective the true formative centre of all life.[46]

Perhaps nowhere is the need more urgent for serious analysis of our corporate worship traditions as Baptists than in the way we celebrate the Holy Communion. In churches where the Communion service is not a long service of the Word, with only five to ten minutes devoted to the Lord's Supper—a tradition that still exists in some Baptist churches—the bewildering diversity that is said to characterize our worship services may be more apparent than real in the light of the *ordo* that one may discern.

Baptist worship during Communion Sunday reflects *epiclesis* and *anamnesis*, confession and thanksgiving, reading, preaching, intercession reflecting the believers opening their hearts to the world, and the dismissal for missional engagement.[47] In other words, the *ordo* of the Communion service focuses on the invocation of the Spirit and the rehearsal of major moments in Jesus' life. It reflects the community's penitent acknowledgement of its sinfulness and the thanksgiving that believers raise for the grace of forgiveness. It also includes the link between Word and sacrament/ordinance.[48] The preached Word and the Lord's Supper are always held together.

Does the suggestion of an existing *ordo* of Communion services among Baptists suggest that we are trying to force emerging Baptist traditions into dominant models reflected in the "ways of thinking about the theory and practice of worship" in what Paul Sheppy calls the "old

---

46. Taylor, *Saying No*, 71.
47. See Wainwright, "Eucharistic Dynamic."
48. See Callam, "Introduction"; Fiddes, *Tracks and Traces*, 157–92.

church"?[49] Put another way, are we trying to "regularize [the new church] by means of the hierarchical authority of the old [church]?"[50] I think not, though we face that danger when we analyze several areas of ecclesial life! Yet, awareness of the extent to which there is a common liturgical shape that characterizes the churches may provide encouragement for all who believe in the catholicity of the church.[51] We are not saying that the shape we broadly share must always remain as it is. We are merely claiming that the *shape* as currently conceived may be deemed a shared reality. At any rate, whatever shape the liturgy takes, it must be mediated through Christian inculturation. This saves the liturgy from a boring sameness, even if it has roughly a common structure.

Conclusion

The hope for an emerging common *ordo* becoming even more widely manifested in Baptist corporate worship events may lie in church leaders being encouraged to consider the question. Although more Baptist communities may need to raise the question about the frequency of their Communion services, to the extent that the churches share a common structure in these services I believe that this holds the promise of a more clearly visible witness to Baptist unity. Seen in this perspective, the amazing diversity in our worship services will not then disappear. However, the diversity will be more apparent than real. Furthermore, the diversity manifested will be but an example of how unity of intent and purpose may be concealed within apparent diversity. The order of elements in Communion services may differ, but the *ordo* or undergirding structure of worship may be largely similar. The growing witness to this *ordo* of Communion service in Baptist churches could serve to strengthen the bonds of unity that we celebrate as Baptists.

---

49. See Sheppy, "Worship and Ecumenism," esp. 314–15, 322.

50. Ibid., 314.

51. It is interesting that in his excellent book *Towards Baptist Catholicity*, Harmon's discussion on worship among Baptists (151–77) reflects the serious limitations of over-reliance on the epithet *lex orandi lex credendi*, which, by itself, tends to elicit an over-emphasis on the didactic as compared to the doxological focus of worship. A careful reading of Harmon's essay will show the danger of not also affirming with equal vigor the *lex credendi lex orandi* side of the maxim.

16

The Emerging Portrait: A Response

BRIAN HARRIS & NIGEL WRIGHT

Introduction

The conference "Beyond 400" took place at Vose Seminary in Perth, Western Australia, over two full days. This concluding chapter captures the reflections of Brian Harris and keynote speaker Nigel Wright, both principals of Baptist colleges and both responsible for the training and encouragement of future pastors, as they pondered over some of the key issues that arose from the conference papers and seminar discussions. It is hoped that this conclusion will foster and encourage further thought, research, and discussion that will bring glory to Jesus Christ, the Head of the church, and that it will help us to move beyond 400 into the exciting and challenging future God has for his people.

Brian Harris: Some Words for the Journey

The task of trying to summarize themes that have emerged from a rich mosaic of papers is daunting. The risk of leaving out significant refrains is great and of necessity, the task is reductionist. Indeed, if you are left wondering why I did not mention something that stood out so clearly for you, perhaps this exercise will not be in vain, as it will simply highlight the rich feast we have enjoyed—there has been so much good fare and not all of it can be tasted. In trying to do justice to the task, I have operated from the belief that words can be friends. Sometimes a word can capture the essence of what it is we are grappling with. Some words have jumped out at me as I've read and listened to the papers presented. They are words that I believe need to be our companions as we grapple with what it means to be Baptist in our journey beyond 400.

Complexity—with Accompanying Respect

The first word I'd choose is "complexity." It is not one that Baptists have often embraced. As Nigel Wright demonstrates in his paper "Baptist Christians: Repentant and Unrepentant," we have usually been very sure we are right. Indeed, schism and division has never been far away, for we have been a little too sure that our understanding of the faith is correct and that other versions are therefore, at best, seriously flawed. While the many splits that we have had within our ranks—Nigel Wright's quote from Geldbach, "When in doubt, let's split," summarizes it well—should have led to a ready acknowledgment that not all questions are easily answered, in practice we have usually been uncomfortable with complexity and have sought the security of definite and non-negotiable answers. At a time of increasing complexity, a new attitude is needed.

This became increasingly clear in Scott Higgins's paper, "Baptists in Mission to and with the Poor: What Do We Need to Learn?" Higgins demonstrated that in spite of good intentions, from the perspective of development our missional efforts have sometimes been destructive. Clearly this is a suggestion we need to take with the utmost seriousness. Too often the history of the church has been one of unwittingly doing harm in the name of God. Provocatively, Higgins raises the possibility that, well intentioned though Rick Warren's PEACE plan is, in the end the harvest could be unintended and damaging. At least, we need to recognize that the issues are complex, and that a reductionist approach where the simplest answer is quickly embraced might have little to commend it.

If complexity is a word we are willing to adopt in our Beyond 400 journey, it presupposes that we create a climate where conversation is embraced and nurtured. Baptist history should give us cause for hope in this regard. After all, isn't congregational government about participation, empowerment, and often robust debate? And doesn't upholding the priesthood of all believers require that we listen respectfully to one another? We have always realized that the voice of Jesus could be coming to us through the hesitant, stumbling contribution of a barely articulate saint.

Yet it seems that this is an aspect from our past that is currently in jeopardy. Janice Newham demonstrates in her fascinating paper, "Leadership Style and Church Culture," that church growth and cultural changes have challenged traditional Baptist models of leadership and congregational participation. New models that stress the importance of strong leadership tend not to champion either participation or respect for alternate viewpoints. Finding the intellectual robustness to cope with complexity will require a fresh embracing of the best aspects of congregational government and the priesthood of all believers. It is true that both these emphases are in jeopardy because they have lapsed into a sorry caricature of what they should be. Congregational government has sometimes been a cover for congregational pettiness. Small-mindedness and tinkering with trivia will not serve us well in an increasingly complex landscape. Strong leadership is indeed needed, but it needs to be deeply respectful and participatory leadership—leadership that brings the best out of others by calling them to their highest goals and aspirations, rather than impotently watching as church meetings endlessly "tut-tut" over issues such as the unfortunate color choice for the church toilets!

As we embrace complexity, perhaps another word will be a minor refrain—"respect." We need to have respect for those who follow Jesus in a slightly different way, but also respect for the mission of God beyond the self-imposed boundaries of the church. If we buy into the concept of the *missio Dei*, we will not look for the fingerprints of God only within our local church gatherings. It is perhaps for this reason that Graham Hill's paper on emerging-missional ecclesiology suggests that the first indicator of an effective missional church is that it is incarnational rather than attractional in its ecclesiology. Incarnation has a habit of fostering respect for those amongst whom we are incarnated. Rather than hiding behind caricatures of what constitutes the worldliness we should abandon, as we listen to the stories of those in our community we will discover that God writes straight lines with crooked sticks, and is often to be found in unexpected places.

After his experience as a patient in a psychiatric institution in the 1930s, Anton Boisen, founder of the clinical pastoral education movement, pleaded that theology students not only study books but also "living human documents." The phrase is memorable. It should be adopted not only by pastoral counselors, but by all who seek to follow the one who was incarnated in Bethlehem so many years ago. Respect implies no "one size fits all" packaging of the gospel, as if people who have been made in the image of God can tidily be packaged into a narrow range of denominational labels and experiences. Rather, as the Spirit of God moves we should expect to find an embrace of some of the best aspects of human culture, a veering away from those which miss the mark, and a freshness that characterizes a community that is simultaneously deeply in awe of all of God's creation whilst always alert to the tarnishing impact of the fall. As an eschatologically oriented community we will move through our time and setting with eyes open to signs of the coming kingdom which are provisionally embedded in the present moment, while always remembering that our overall cry is "*Maranatha*—come Lord Jesus." A respectful incarnational ecclesiology will help us to navigate through a complex landscape with the grace and hopefulness befitting those who follow the risen Christ.

Freedom—with a Chastened Humility

A second key word that comes to me is "freedom." In many ways this is a predictable Baptist word. As Nigel Wright demonstrated, we have traditionally stood for at least four freedoms: freedom from state interference, freedom from priestly succession, freedom from liturgical forms, and freedom of conscience and inquiry. As he rightly suggests, these are aspects of our heritage we must uphold, truths about which we must be unrepentant.

May I highlight one small aspect of freedom that seems to me to be of special importance in our current climate? Freedom of conscience and inquiry raises an integrity issue. We often speak of integrity as though it is largely a matter of sexual and financial integrity, occasionally also alluding to issues of power and control, but we regularly overlook the area of intellectual integrity. The freedom to ask new questions, or to ask old questions in fresh ways, seems to me to be a requirement if we are to enter into a Beyond 400 world.

Wright suggests that part of our freedom will be the freedom to be both repentant and unrepentant for aspects of our past. Perhaps we could speak of having a chastened attitude to our history. I like the word "chastened" as it does not suggest that everything is wrong, just that everything is not as good as we might have thought. It's about humility, or to use another image, it is going forward with a limp, but, as with Jacob, a limp that comes as a result of a genuine God encounter. So if "freedom" is a key word, "chastened" needs to be the minor word to accompany it.

Martin Sutherland laments that too often the song most closely associated with Baptist theology is "The Sound of Silence." This is not because we have nothing to say—and Sutherland's paper of that title highlights several notable Baptist theologians—but because we have failed to create a climate where theological enquiry is valued. Indeed, at our worse moments we have stifled debate and excluded dissenters from our ranks, as some of the recent history of the Southern Baptists demonstrates all too clearly. Such debacles reflect an unfortunate amnesia. At our core we are not people who are afraid of difficult questions. Indeed, we were the ones who asked why the Reformers had not gone far enough in their attempt to reclaim a convincing version of New Testament Christianity. We wondered why believers' baptism was not a part of a newly reformed church when it was so evidently a part of the New Testament church. Even though, as Richard Moore demonstrates in his scholarly paper "Baptist Witness to New Testament Baptism beyond 2009," Baptists do not consider baptism essential to salvation; they willingly paid the significant price associated with adopting an alternate viewpoint on baptism in their quest to ensure that *sola Scriptura*, or perhaps more accurately *suprema Scriptura*, was more than a rallying cry, but the actual heartbeat of the movement.

Wright's closing statement in his paper is therefore very significant: "The openness to change that is part of the further-light principle is written into our DNA. It is our tradition that we can change our tradition. This is the way of open-ended pilgrimage which sets us free to embark upon and explore our futures."[1] This "open-ended pilgrimage" is best served when we are free to ask questions without fear of censure or ridicule. And if we are able to ask our questions with humility, and with the heart of a pilgrim people, ready and able to change because we are not so tied to the status quo that change is intolerable, our freedom to enquire might lead to further light for many others. This freedom will serve us well in our Beyond 400 journey, especially if we continue to

---

1. See page 32.

allow our insights to be informed by the broad and generous parameters given in Scripture, which has always been our founding and shaping text. Indeed, the freedom to listen to the biblical text in new ways will be part of our future. Baptist theologian Stanley Grenz advocates the communal pneumatological discernment of the meaning of Scripture—a hermeneutical approach that, while sometimes difficult to put into practice, has characterized Baptist communities. The freedom to simultaneously and communally listen to the Spirit and the Scriptures is a freedom we should enthusiastically adopt as we journey beyond 400.

Becoming—with a Commitment to Moving Beyond

Whether it is the analogy of Pilgrim on his journey to the Celestial City, referred to in Edwina Murphy's paper, "Cyprian and *The Pilgrim's Progress*," or Martin Sutherland's stress in his paper "The Sound of Silence? Baptist Thought in Obama's World" that underlying traditional Baptist distinctive is the dynamics of *becoming* church, both scholars stress the idea that we are not a community that has arrived. We are on the way. We are becoming in the course of the journey. As Sutherland emphasizes, "For all our frustrating ways, we are still a people committed to the encounter with Christ in the gathering."[2]

Nigel Wright also stresses the importance of becoming when he writes,

> We return at this point to the traditional four marks of the church, and suggest that in place of seeing them as qualities that churches can claim to possess (who after all can credibly claim to be "one, holy, catholic, and apostolic"?) we understand them as a missionary agenda as we move towards their eschatological realization. In this sense then, the church is to be understood as a proclaiming, reconciling, sanctifying, and unifying community. These activities are the work of Jesus Christ in the world and of the church as Christ's instrument.[3]

We are indeed a community on a journey.

If "becoming" is to be our third word, as with "complexity," it should perhaps have an accompanying word. Perhaps that could be "be-

---

2. See page 59.

3. See pages 27–28. Wright acknowledges his indebtedness to Grenz, *Renewing the Center*, 319–21.

yond"—not just "Beyond 400" as in the theme of this conference, but beyond whatever marker we have in place at any particular time or in any particular setting. Michael O'Neil's paper on moving beyond a Baptist identity crisis helpfully explores the theological constructs of some key Baptist theologians. One such theologian is Stanley Grenz, who is helpful in this regard when he suggests that all theological construction should be eschatologically oriented.[4] Such an orientation allows us to evaluate the present in the light of our ultimate destination, and to adjust accordingly. This gives us the freedom to affirm many aspects of our time and place, whilst also striving to more clearly reflect that which we are called to become. Life in a not-yet-arrived world is never dull or predictable. It transforms debate over worship styles or on systems of church governance. Wherever we are, we are still becoming, and called to move beyond previous markers of progress. Martin Sutherland is correct when he suggests that

> the beating heart of Baptist theology is ecclesiology. Not, it must be stressed, a general attention to the nature of the church, but a particular, "baptistic" understanding of the dynamics of the community of Christ. McClendon identifies a core sense of immediacy—the sense that the church now *is* the primitive church, being created anew in every moment, and that each generation stands with the apostles at the brink of the new day. It is a vision "neither developmental nor successionist, but mystical and immediate . . . better understood by the artist and poet than by the metaphysician and dogmatist."[5]

This intuitive sense of what it means to both be true to the primitive church whilst needing to be church in the immediate, whilst journeying towards the future, will need to be claimed afresh as we move beyond 400.

So could these be our words for a Beyond 400 era? *Complexity* accompanied by the *respect* that flows when we move beyond trite answers; *freedom* with a *chastened humility*, for we have not always been true to our vision; *becoming* and always willing to move *beyond*. Some may ask what these words have to do with Baptist distinctives. Other than freedom, they are hardly words that have been our obvious companions. True, but perhaps as we move beyond 400 we can again affirm our key

---

4. Grenz, *Social God*.
5. See page 55. He quotes here McClendon, *Ethics*, 33.

distinctives—regenerate church membership, symbolized by our commitment to baptism, the autonomy of the local church, congregational government, religious liberty, separation of church and state, and so on. But in affirming them, perhaps we could adopt an ethos that embraces each distinctive while readily acknowledging the complexity of most issues, and the respect that should therefore flow from us; the importance of being free to ask and to explore, and the chastened awareness that we are often not good at this; and the delight that though we are characterized by key distinctives we are a people who are still becoming, as we hesitantly but surely move beyond 400.

Nigel Wright: Summary Reflections

It has been a great pleasure to take part in this project, and once more I express my gratitude for the opportunity to give and receive over the days of the conference. I am delighted that the event has been such a success and, given that it is the first of its kind in Western Australia, I do believe that this should be a great encouragement to do similar things in the future. It is clear that the appetite for careful and sustained thought is amongst us and that it should be nourished on occasions such as this. May even greater things be in store for the future.

For me this is the most difficult session of those for which I have had responsibility. With my other sessions, I had a prepared text and simply needed to read it in a way that suggested I understood what I was talking about. My assignment now, however, is more immediate and demanding since it requires me to think on my feet. What I have to do is distill some of the things I think I have been hearing in the sessions and seminars we have held. Inevitably this is filtered through my own biases and interests. I have, of course, read most of the papers, but a conference like this involves more than the papers. It includes the asides, the conversations, the questions that are raised from the floor, and the responses that they evoke. I have sought to look for tendencies and directions in the dialogues as a whole, and to do this, of course, always under the heading of "Beyond 400"—with the concern for the future of churches of a Baptist (or baptist) persuasion. Rather than interact extensively and in detail with specific papers, therefore, and risk neglecting others, I have chosen a variety of broad headings under which I can cluster some thoughts.

Theology

Perhaps not surprisingly, I begin with theology. The fact that we are here together at a theological conference is itself a statement as to the importance we attach to theological discussion. As an outsider I reflect back to you that there is no shortage of theological acumen and insight in this room, and that devotion to serious yet "street-level" theological reflection is increasing in this part of the globe. I confess I am not fully persuaded about the comment—which I think goes back to James William McLendon Jr.—that Baptists have historically been weak or disinterested in theology. It is certainly the case that in their early confessions of faith Baptists tended to lean heavily upon other traditions, particularly Presbyterian. However, systematic theologians enough have emerged from the Baptist movement. I might name here the eighteenth-century divine John Gill, or the nineteenth century's A. H. Strong, or E. Y. Mullins in the early twentieth; and there appears to me to be an abundance of twentieth-century Baptist systematic theologians, among whom I would number Carl Henry, Millard Erickson, James Leo Garrett, P. K. Jewett, Wayne Grudem, Stanley Grenz, Paul Fiddes, and Roger Olson. From my perspective, Baptist dogmatic theologians have been relatively and increasingly abundant in their output.

The fact is that systematic theology of this kind is a product of the post-Enlightenment intellectual environment, with its particular concern for both epistemology and intellectual belief. This does not deprive it of its value. Despite the names listed, therefore, I am more sympathetic to the notion that few Baptist theologians have developed a distinctively Baptist way of approaching theology, a Baptist methodology, and that this is an enterprise that should occupy some of us. In particular, I confess myself very taken with my fellow speaker Martin Sutherland's conviction that such a theology would proceed, as does our ecclesiology, from the reality of the risen Christ in the midst of the gathered community, with a concern to explicate this presence and to construct a theological account of reality on the basis of it. I can see that this is a different approach from that which has characterized theology since the Enlightenment, with its constant attempt to justify belief in the light of critical, historical reason. This would be a theology that does not need to justify itself or its starting point, although as it develops it would certainly need to give attention to its own coherence and credibility as well as its consonance with the identity of Christ. Yet, would it in fact be so different from the way in which theology has actually been conducted in history of the Christian church?

Far from setting Baptist theology on the margins of the theological enterprise, set apart from the Great Tradition, does it not rather return it to where the church began, since the creeds are precisely an attempt to do this—to spell out the logic of the belief that God is present in Christ and that Christ continues to be present in the church as the primary sacrament of the divine presence? My immediate response to these important and challenging insights, which I personally would like to take forward more extensively at some point, is to affirm, as I argued in my first paper, the need to hold together in a fruitful rather than a conflicting way the catholic and the radically Protestant, and that this continuing conversation constitutes a way forward for Baptists.

Mission

A second cluster of reflections concerns the nature and breadth of Christian mission. I have welcomed the opportunity to share here in a number of papers that put before us a "thick" theology of mission, in particular the concern for the poor, rather than the "thin" one that has sometimes characterized evangelical movements. Evangelical Christians have been constructively shifting their theological ground in this area: being one-time laggards always afraid of slipping into a social gospel, in recent years they have placed themselves among the more adventurous thinkers and practitioners, simultaneously developing the agencies that will extend their endeavors. Yet the challenge I have heard at this conference has to do with the depth and quality of our analysis.

In a day when even some African economists raise the question of whether Western aid solves or simply compounds the problem of poverty, Christian aid agencies need to be sure of their ground and of their analysis. Are we sure that our personal initiatives, motivated by compassion, or our small-scale church activities to help the poor, are not playing into the hands of larger economic and global forces that simply postpone the day when problems will be addressed and justice done? I do not have the answer to this question, and am unlikely to think myself towards it. However, the question itself should shake us, lest we find ourselves seeking to do good and succeeding in doing something less than that. What we need to help us is a stable and coherent analysis in accordance with which we can act, and as yet it is not clear to me that we have one. There is scope here for more work, and perhaps someone feels the challenge to commit to it.

While on the theme of mission, I will take opportunity to air a concern. I confess myself to be a conversionist. In other words, I believe that the whole of the work of God in Christ is about the conversion of human beings and their world to the God who is the ground of their being and who therefore is the source of their true humanity. In Christ we see God bringing about that conversion, with Christ himself being the representative Converted One, the "Last Adam" (1 Cor 15:45), the first-fruits, and the agent of a new humanity. During my ministry I have argued for a "thick" understanding of mission and a broad perspective of God's work of transforming heaven and earth. But I do believe I have lived to see a day when we are in danger of muting the notes of sin, repentance, new birth, conversion, and personal salvation. It is as though in affirming a broad view of salvation we are in danger of losing the focus upon the need for individuals to be reconciled to God. I am not suggesting that in any way we should renege upon the gains of moving to a fuller theology of mission. But I am saying that we must do this without losing the enduring evangelical claim that individuals need to be converted to God. After all, if we are to share in the mission of God we need *people* who will does this, and people will not be motivated to do this until and unless they have experienced the saving work of God in their own lives. In these respects I am unashamedly a pietist (a much misunderstood term) who believes that doctrine needs to be experienced.

Congregations

This brings me to the theme of the congregation, which has been represented here by a variety of studies extending from the study of a particular congregation—the kind of study that I am persuaded will be an increasing and exciting one in future years—to reflections upon emerging church and leadership styles. In fact, what we have heard here tends to echo what we are aware of in the broader world of church. We are in constant debate with each other about competing and contrasting ways of being church. Is big really beautiful? Are we accommodating to celebrity culture in the development of leader- rather than community-orientated churches? Are we compromising on Baptist distinctives when we shift the governmental centre of gravity towards a leadership team, or CEO-like figure, rather than the congregation? Are we, in fact, treating churches as corporations, with growth as the marker of success, at the cost of ecclesial integrity? Should churches opt for a "beneath the radar" existence, a "mongrel church" rather than a "super church" model? Does it not take a certain kind of courage to settle for modesty rather than celebrity? Are postmodern, "emerging" churches the way forward, or will it become clear in time that "fresh expressions" of church are going to be no more effective in reaching people than those with traditional or simply "contemporary" styles?

This is a ferment of ideas, but it does reflect the current church scene and the multiple critiques of completing claims, which are legion. It can be taken either as a sign of profound confusion or of evangelical creativity, or perhaps both. What is clear to me is that we are in a mixed economy, that widely varying forms of church exist and have their place within this economy, that the motivations behind these differing forms also vary, that there is little to be gained by pitting these against each other in any aggressive way, but that there is an entirely valid and necessary debate about what constitutes the "ecclesial minimum" or authentic church. Put briefly, there are certain elements that need to exist before any group can properly be designated "church." I have my own ideas about what these elements are, and these would include confession of Christ, gathering in his name to pray and worship, baptism, and Communion. Some would contest the latter elements, but we might all agree that if everything is church then nothing is church, and some process of elimination is required to distinguish between church and non-church, and perhaps between what may be simply a mission activity and what may be an ordered church community. This then becomes an invitation to discuss the question of "order," which some would dismiss as being boring and others, like me, find deeply interesting as well as deeply Baptist.

In addition to our discussion about congregations, questions have also arisen about denominational or interchurch relations and the claim they have on us. Our own tradition is deeply divided as to the status given to these relationships. Opinions range across a spectrum that at one end sees denominational affiliation as a matter of pragmatic convenience, and at the other sees it as one of ecclesial and covenantal significance. To take the former view leads to the conclusion that there are no great issues of conscience involved in leaving a denomination. This would simply be an acknowledgment that the alliance is no longer appropriate or useful and that although disengagement is unfortunate and time consuming it is not theologically significant. In so far as this subject has been discussed at this conference this is the tendency that has been represented. A more ecclesial or covenantal understanding is based on the notion that Christ is present not only in the local congregation but in the wider communion of churches, especially when that communion gathers in a representative way in an association or assembly, and that disaffiliation or secession is not just unfortunate but also at some level a breach in the body of Christ, a withdrawal of covenant commitment. I have come personally to tend more in this direction and believe that the ecclesial nature of our interchurch relations requires more consideration than it has been given historically. This is not to say that there may not be issues of conscience that lead us to no longer walk together, but it does increase the sense of tragedy and failure when this happens.

Sacraments

Some final words are in order about the theology of sacraments. Once more we need to say that this is another of those contested areas in Baptist life and will continue to be so beyond 400. Truth to tell, according to my own observation it is only more recently that an assumed consensus has been increasingly questioned and much of that questioning seems to emanate from the British Isles, which is, taken at surface reading, out of step on this issue with the global Baptist movement (although with increasing support from "catholic Baptists" in the United States).

Baptists have understandably reacted against the idea that the ordinances or sacraments of the church are effective *ex opera operato*, which they understand (rightly or wrongly) to mean even without the presence of faith in the recipient. They have understood this to be deeply contrary to the Reformation teaching about the need for faith in the reception of any spiritual grace if sacraments were not to be turned into quasi-magical acts. They have also observed that even the Reformers were not entirely consistent on this point—with Calvin, as an example, teaching that infant baptism planted a "seed of faith" within the infant. Baptists, then, have usually been placed by themselves and others in the Zwinglian camp, which reduces sacraments to "bare memorials" devoid of gracious divine activity in themselves but witnessing to the primary divine acts in which that grace was certainly active—the cross and resurrection. Again, whether this was really Zwingli's view would be worth a debate or two. As a consequence many Baptists have preferred to speak of "ordinances" rather than "sacraments," placing the emphasis on obedience to what Christ has ordained—the witnesses of baptism and of the Lord's Supper. Those who choose to refer to "sacraments" are usually wishing to increase the sense of God's activity through the means of grace that have been given.

The word "sacrament" evokes various reactions and, because it is construed in various ways, it may be more helpful to drop it from this discussion, at least provisionally. At a more basic level, what some British Baptists have become increasingly uneasy with is the sense that in baptism and the Lord's Supper "nothing happens." If fact, for the sake of distancing the Baptist way from more Catholic ways of being church, this is a point that has often been stressed in preaching. Lest people gather the wrong idea, they are told that in baptism, for instance, "nothing is going to happen." The act is "just a witness." Against this claim, more sacramental Baptists have wanted to say that *where there is sincere faith in the recipient* something *is* going to happen by the action of God's Spirit in both baptism and Communion. *What* will happen is that those who receive in faith will participate more fully in the saving action of God through the cross and resurrection which is applied to them by the Spirit of God in the present. Put like this, and laying the language of "sacrament" temporarily to the side, it is hard to see that any Baptist would want to disagree. So perhaps we are more sacramental than we think we are. Above all, beyond 400 we surely want to promote a life of common worship that is eventful, where we believe that God comes to us by the Spirit and transforms us, singly and together, for good.

Conclusion

I cannot pretend for a moment that I have brought together all the important themes of this conference. I am delighted for the publication of the papers presented, as it will enable those of us who have attended, and many others who have not, to benefit from the careful and creative thinking that so many have contributed and explore it at greater leisure. Such a conference as this will never touch bottom or exhaust the themes we have identified. But it may well stimulate and inspire us to continue the glorious activity of "faith seeking understanding." May it help us to shape the future that lies open before us in ways that will be beneficial to us all.

APPENDIX A
Explicit Baptismal Vocabulary in the New Testament

Greek word		GOSPELS & ACTS					7 LETTERS							Comments
		MT	MK	LK	JN	AC	Rom	1 Cor	Gal	Eph	Col	Heb	1 Pet	
βαπτιζω (76x)	verb	7	12	10	13	21	2	10	1					
βαπτισμα (19x)	noun	2	4	4		6	1			1			1	
βαπτισμος (4x)	noun		1								1	2		
βαπτιστης (12x)	noun	7	2	3										Of John the Baptist; confined to the Synoptic Gospels
		16	19	17	13	27	3	10	1	1	1	2	1	TOTAL = 111

Matt 3 [1.6.7.11.11.13.14.16] 11 [11.12] 14 [2.8] 16 [14] 17 [13] 21 [25] 28 [19]

Mark 1 [4.4.5.8.8.9] 6 [14.24.25] 7 [4.4] 8 [28] 10 [38.38.38.39.39.39] 11 [30]
[+16 [16] = Longer Ending]

Luke 3 [3.7.12.16.16.21.21] 7 [20.29.29.30.33] 9 [19] 11 [38] 12 [50.50] 20 [4]

John 1 [25.26.28.31.33.33] 3 [22.23.23.26] 4 [1.2] 10 [40]

Acts 1 [5.5.22] 2 [38.41] 8 [12.13.16.36.38] 9 [18] 10 [37.47.48] 11 [16.16] 13 [24] 16 [15.33] 18 [8.25] 19 [3.3.4.4.5] 22 [16]

Rom 6 [3.3.4]

1 Cor 1 [13.14.15.16.16.17] 10 [2] 12 [13] 15 [29.29]

Gal 3 [27]

Eph 4 [5]

Col 2 [12]

Heb 6 [2] 9 [10]

1 Pet 3 [21]

APPENDIX B
The Nine Instances of Christian Baptism Reported in Acts

No.	Ref.	Baptizee/s	Baptizer	1 Word	2 Response F = Faith	3 Holy Spirit	4 Evidence
1	2.38, 41	Day of Pentecost	Peter & apostles	2.14–36	2.37		
2	8.12, 13, 16	Samaritans, *including* Simon Magus	Philip	8.12 8.14	F 8.12 F 8.13		
3	8.36, 38	Ethiopian eunuch	Philip	8.35	8.36		
4	9.18 + 22.16	Saul [Paul]	Ananias	9.3–6		9.17	
5	10.47–48 +11.16	Cornelius & company	Peter	10.34–43	F 11.17	10.44 11.17	10.46
6	16.15	Lydia & household	Paul	16.13	16.15 (?) pistos		
7	16.33	Philippian jailor & household	Paul	16.31–32	F 16.31		
8	18.8	Crispus, leader of synagogue & household + many Corinthians	Paul	18.5, 8	F 18.8a F 18.8b		
9	19.3, 4, 5	Ephesian Christians who formerly knew only John's baptism	Paul	9.1–4	19.2	19.6	

5 Conditions	6 Name	7 Baptism	8 Effects/ Outcomes	9 Hands laid on	10 Holy Spirit	11 Evidence	12 Household
2.38	JC 2.38	2.41	2.38				
		8.12		[later] Peter & John (8.17)	8.14–15		
		8.13			8.17		
[22.16]		8.38–39	8.39 [22.16]				
9.17–18		9.18	9.17, 19				
	JC 10.48	10. 47–48;	10.46 speaking in tongues, praising God				H
16.14		16.15	16.15				H
		16.33	16.34				H
		18.8					H
	LJ 19.5	19.5		19.6	19.6	19.6	

Bibliography

Aland, B., et al. *Novum Testamentum Graece.* 27th ed. Stuttgart: Deutsche Bibelstiftung, 1993.
Aland, K. *Did the Early Church Baptize Infants?* Translated by G. R. Beasley-Murray. 1963. Reprint, Eugene, OR: Wipf & Stock, 2004.
Aland, K., and B. Aland. *Novum Testamentum Graece et Latine.* Stuttgart: Deutsche Bibelgesellschaft, 1984.
Augustine. *A Treatise on the Merits and Forgiveness of Sins, and on the Baptism of Infants.* In *Augustine: Anti-Pelagian Writings,* edited by P. Schaff, 11–78. $NPNF^1$ vol. 5.
Austin, M. "The Figural Logic of the Sequel and the Unity of *The Pilgrim's Progress*." *Studies in Philology* 102 (2005) 484–509.
Ayedze, K. A. "Tertullian, Cyprian and Augustine on Patience: A Comparative and Critical Study of Three Treatises on a Stoic-Christian Virtue in Early North Africa." PhD diss., Princeton University, 2000.
Baileys, Alan J. "Evangelical and Ecumenical Understanding of Mission." *IRM* (October 1996) 485–504.
Baker, M. D. *Religious No More: Building Communities of Grace and Freedom.* Downers Grove, IL: InterVarsity, 1999.
Banks, R. "Denominational Structures: Their Legitimacy, Vocation and Capacity for Reform." In *In the Fullness of Time,* edited by D. Peterson and J. Pryor, 277–300. Homebush West: Lancer, 1992.
———. *The Tyranny of Time.* Homebush West, Australia: Lancer, 1983.
Baptist Union of Great Britain. *5 Core Values.* Didcot: BUGB, 1996.
———. *Patterns and Prayers for Christian Worship: A Guidebook for Worship Leaders.* Oxford: Oxford University Press, 1991.
———. *What Are Baptists?* Didcot: BUGB, n.d.
Baptist World Alliance. *We Baptists.* Franklin, TN: Providence House, 1999.
———. "Statement from the Baptist World Alliance Symposium on Baptist Identity and Ecclesiology (Are Baptist Churches Autonomous?)." Symposium held 21–24 March 2007, Elstal, Germany. Online: http://www.bwanet.sitewrench.com/statementfromelstal.
Bardy, G. *The Christian Latin Literature of the First Six Centuries.* Translated by Mary Reginald. London: Sands, 1930.
Barger, R. *A New and Right Spirit: Creating an Authentic Church in a Consumer Culture.* Herndon: Alban Institute, 2005.

Barrett, L. Y., editor. *Treasure in Clay Jars: Patterns in Missional Faithfulness*. Grand Rapids: Eerdmans, 2004.
Bartchy, S. S. "Community of Goods in Acts: Idealization or Social Reality?" In *The Future of Early Christianity: Essays in Honor of Helmut Koester*, edited by B. Pearson, 309–18. Minneapolis: Fortress, 1991.
———. "Table Fellowship." In *Dictionary of Jesus and the Gospels*, edited by J. B. Green et al., 796–800. Downers Grove, IL: InterVarsity, 1992.
———. "Table Fellowship with Jesus and the 'Lord's Meal' at Corinth." In *Increase in Learning: Essays in Honor of James G. Van Buren*, edited by R. J. Owens Jr. and B. E. Hamm, 45–61. Manhattan, KS: Manhattan Christian College, 1979.
Barth, K. *Church Dogmatics IV/4*. Edinburgh: T. & T. Clark, 1964.
———. *The Teaching of the Church Regarding Baptism*. London: SCM, 1948.
Barth, M. *Rediscovering the Lord's Supper: Communion with Israel, with Christ, and among the Guests*. Atlanta: John Knox, 1988.
Bartley, J. *Faith and Politics after Christendom: The Church as a Movement for Anarchy*. Carlisle, UK: Paternoster, 2006.
Bauman, Z. *The Art of Life*. Cambridge, UK: Polity, 2008.
———. *Community: Seeking Safety in an Insecure World*. Cambridge, UK: Polity, 2001.
———. *Consuming Life*. Cambridge, UK: Polity, 2007.
———. *The Individualized Society*. Cambridge, UK: Polity, 2001.
———. *Liquid Fear*. Cambridge, UK: Polity, 2006.
———. *Liquid Life*. Cambridge, UK: Polity, 2005.
———. *Liquid Love: On the Frailty of Human Bonds*. Cambridge, UK: Polity, 2003.
———. *Liquid Modernity*. Cambridge, UK: Polity, 2000.
———. *Liquid Times: Living in an Age of Uncertainty*. Cambridge, UK: Polity, 2006.
Beasley-Murray, P. *Radical Believers. The Baptist Way of Being the Church*. Didcot: BUGB, 1992.
Bebbington, D. *The Dominance of Evangelicalism. The Age of Spurgeon and Moody*. Downers Grove, IL: InterVarsity, 2005.
Berkhof, L. *Systematic Theology*. Edinburgh: Banner of Truth, 1959.
Berkouwer, G. C. *The Church*. Grand Rapids: Eerdmans, 1976.
Best, T., and T. Grdzelidze. *BEM at 25: Critical Insights into a Continuing Legacy*. Faith and Order Paper 205. Geneva: WCC, 2007.
Best, T., and D. Heller. *So We Believe, So We Pray: Towards Koinonia in Worship*. Faith and Order Paper 171. Geneva: WCC, 1995.
———. *Worship Today: Understanding, Practice, Ecumenical Implications*. Faith and Order Paper 194. Geneva: WCC, 2004.
Bloesch, D. *The Church: Sacraments, Worship, Ministry, Mission*. Downers Grove, IL: InterVarsity, 2002.
Blue, B. B. "Love Feast." In *Dictionary of Paul and His Letters*, edited by G. F. Hawthorne et al., 578–79. Downers Grove, IL: InterVarsity, 1993.
Bobertz, C. A. "Cyprian of Carthage as Patron: A Social Historical Study of the Role of Bishop in the Ancient Christian Community of North Africa." PhD diss., Yale University, 1988.
Boff, L. *Ecclesiogenesis: The Base Communities Reinvent the Church*. Glasgow: Collins, 1982.
Bosch, D. J. *Transforming Mission: Paradigm Shifts in the Theology of Mission*. American Society of Missiology Series 16. Maryknoll, NY: Orbis, 1991.

Bowers, F. *A Bold Experiment: The Story of Bloomsbury Chapel and Bloomsbury Central Baptist Church, 1848–1999*. London: Bloomsbury Central Baptist Church, 1999.
Brown, D. *Boundaries of Our Habitations: Tradition Theological Construction*. New York: SUNY Press, 1994.
Brown, J. *John Bunyan: His Life, Times, and Work*. London: Hulbert, 1928.
Brown, M. "Virtual Sacraments?" Brownblog, June 22, 2009. Online: http://brownblog.info/?p=886.
Buckley, J. J. "Christian Community, Baptism and Lord's Supper." In *The Cambridge Companion to Karl Barth*, edited J. Webster, 195–211. Cambridge: Cambridge University Press, 2000.
Bullock, A., and O. Stallybrass. *Fontana Dictionary of Modern Thought*. London: Fontana, 1977.
Bunyan, J. *Grace Abounding to the Chief of Sinners*. London: Religious Tract Society, 1907.
———. *The Pilgrim's Progress*. Westwood, NJ: Barbour, 1990.
Burns, J. P. *Cyprian the Bishop*. London: Routledge, 2002.
Buschart, W. D. *Exploring Protestant Traditions: An Invitation to Theological Hospitality*. Downers Grove, IL: InterVarsity, 2006.
Callam, N. *Corporate Worship in a Christian Context*. Jamaica Baptist Union, 2006.
———. "Introduction to the study document on *One Baptism* text." In *Faith and Order at the Crossroads: Kuala Lumpur: The Plenary Commission Meeting*, edited by T. Best, 130–35. Faith and Order Paper 196. Geneva: WCC, 2005.
Capper, B. "The Palestinian Cultural Context of Earliest Christian Community of Goods." In *The Book of Acts in Its Palestinian Setting*, edited by R. Bauckham, 323–56. Book of Acts in Its First Century Setting 4. Grand Rapids: Eerdmans, 1995.
Carey-Holt, S. *God Next Door: Spirituality & Mission in the Neighbourhood*. Brunswick East: Acorn, 2007.
Castagna, L. "Vecchiaia e morte del mondo in Lucrezio, Seneca e San Cipriano." *Aevum Antiquum* 13 (2000) 239–63.
Catechism of the Catholic Church. London: Chapman, 1994.
Chan, S. *Spiritual Theology: A Systematic Study of the Christian Life*. Downers Grove, IL: InterVarsity, 1998.
Chen, Shaohua, and Martin Ravallion. "The Developing World Is Poorer Than We Thought, But No Less Successful in the Fight Against Poverty." World Bank Policy Research Working Paper 4703. Washington, DC: World Bank Development Research Group, August 2008. Online: http://papers.ssrn.com/sol3/papers.cfm?abstract_id=1259575.
Chester, T. *The Busy Christian's Guide to Busyness*. Leicester, UK: InterVarsity, 2006.
———. "The Rhythms of a Missional Church." Author's blog, January 29, 2009. Online: http://timchester.wordpress.com/2009/01/28/the-rythyms-of-a-missional-church/.
Chester, T., and S. Timmis. *Total Church: A Radical Reshaping around Gospel and Community*. Nottingham, UK: InterVarsity, 2007.
Chilton, B. D. *Jesus' Prayer and Jesus' Eucharist: His Personal Practice of Spirituality*. Valley Forge, PA: Trinity, 1997.
Chrysostom, J. *The Homilies of St. John Chrysostom, Archbishop of Constantinople, on the First Epistle of St. Paul the Apostle to the Corinthians*. 2 vols. Oxford: Parker, 1839.
Clark, M. *A Short History of Australia*. Ringwood, Victoria: Penguin, 1995.
———. "Two Mid-Third Century Bishops: Cyprian of Carthage and Dionysius of Alexandria. Congruences and Divergences." In *Ancient History in a Modern University*, edited by T. W. Hillard et al., 2:317–28. Grand Rapids: Eerdmans, 1998.

Clarke, G. W., translator. *The Letters of St. Cyprian of Carthage*. 4 vols. Ancient Christian Writers 43–44, 46–47. New York: Newman, 1984–89.
Coffey, D. "Foreword." In *Radical Believers: The Baptist Way of Being the Church*, by P. Beasley-Murray, 4. Didcot: BUGB, 1992.
Cole, N. *Organic Church: Growing Faith Where Life Happens*. San Francisco: Josey-Bass, 2005.
———. *Organic Leadership: Leading Naturally Right Where You Are*. Grand Rapids: Baker, 2009.
Colwell, J. E. *Promise and Presence: An Exploration of Sacramental Theology*. Carlisle, UK: Paternoster, 2005.
Conyers, A. J. "The Changing Face of Baptist Theology." *RevExp* 95.1 (1998) 21–38.
Corney, P. "Have You Got the Right Address? Post-Modernism and the Gospel." *GRID* (1995) 1–3.
Costello, Tim. *Another Way to Love: Christian Social Reform and Global Poverty*. Brunswick East, Victoria: Acorn, 2009.
Cross, T. L. "The Rich Feast of Theology: Can Pentecostals Bring the Main Course or Only the Relish?" *JPT* 16 (2000) 27–47.
Croucher, R. "Charismatic Renewal: Myths and Realities." Reproduced on the John Mark Ministries blog, April 7, 2004. Online: http://jmm.aaa.net.au/articles/12475.htm.
Cupit, L. A. *Baptists in Worship*. McLean, VA: Baptist World Alliance, 1999.
Cyprian. *De lapsis* (*The Lapsed*) / *De catholicae ecclesiae unitate* (*The Unity of the Catholic Church*). Translated by M. Bévenot. Ancient Christian Writers 25. New York: Newman, 1957.
———. *Ad Donatum* (*To Donatus*). Translated by R. J. Deferrari. In Deferrari, *FC*.
———. *De habitu virginum* (*The Dress of Virgins*). Translated by A. E. Keenan. In Deferrari, *FC*.
———. *De dominica oratione* (*The Lord's Prayer*). Translated by R. J. Deferrari. In Deferrari, *FC*.
———. *Ad Demetrianum* (*To Demetrian*). Translated by R. J. Deferrari. In Deferrari, *FC*.
———. *De mortalitate* (*Mortality*). Translated by M. H. Mahoney. In Deferrari, *FC*.
———. *De opera et eleemosynis* (*Works and Almsgiving*). Translated by R. J. Deferrari. In Deferrari, *FC*.
———. *De bono patientiae* (*The Good of Patience*). Translated by G. E. Conway. In Deferrari, *FC*.
———. *De zelo et livore* (*Jealousy and Envy*). Translated by R. J. Deferrari. In Deferrari, *FC*.
———. *Ad Fortunatum* (*Exhortation to Martyrdom, to Fortunatus*). Translated by R. J. Deferrari. In Deferrari, *FC*.
Daley, B. E. *The Hope of the Early Church: A Handbook of Patristic Eschatology*. Cambridge: Cambridge University Press, 1991.
Daniélou, J. *The Origins of Latin Christianity*. Translated by D. Smith and J. A. Baker. A History of Early Christian Doctrine before the Council of Nicaea 3. London: Darton, Longman & Todd, 1977.
Davison, G. "Suburban Character." *People and Place* 7.4 (1995) 26–31.
Deferrari, R. J., editor. *The Fathers of the Church: A New Translation*. Vol. 36. New York: Fathers of the Church, 1958.
DeVries, Dawn. "The Incarnation and the Sacramental Word: Calvin's and Schlieremacher's Sermons on Luke 2." In *Towards the Future of Reformed Theology: Tasks, Topics,*

Traditions, edited by D. Willis and M. Welker, 386–405. Grand Rapids: Eerdmans, 1999.

Dockery, D. S. "Millard J. Erickson." In *Baptist Theologians*, edited by T. George and D. S. Dockery, 640–59. Nashville: Broadman, 1990.

Doogue, G. "Billy Graham's Pretty Faith Was Not Enough." *The Australian*, 28 February 2009.

Drane, J. W. *The Mcdonaldization of the Church: Consumer Culture and the Church's Future*. Macon, GA: Smyth & Helwys, 2001.

Dugger, Celia W. "Ending Famine, Simply by Ignoring the Experts." *New York Times*, December 2, 2007, sec. World/Africa. Online: http://www.nytimes.com/2007/12/02/world/africa/02malawi.html.

Dunn, G. D. "Infected Sheep and Diseased Cattle, or the Pure and Holy Flock: Cyprian's Pastoral Care of Virgins." *JECS* 11 (2003) 1–20.

Dyrness, W. A. *Let the Earth Rejoice!: A Biblical Theology of Holistic Mission*. Pasadena, CA: Fuller Seminary Press, 1991.

Edward, Peter. "The Ethical Poverty Line: A Moral Quantification of Absolute Poverty." *Third World Quarterly* 27 (2006) 377.

Eller, V. *Could the Church Have It All Wrong?* House Church Central, 1997. Online: http://www.hccentral.com/eller9/index.html#toc.

———. *In Place of Sacraments: A Study of Baptism and the Lord's Supper*. Grand Rapids: Eerdmans, 1972.

Ellis, C. J. "Understanding Worship: Trends and Criteria." In *Currents in Baptistic Theology of Worship Today*, edited by K. G. Jones and P. R. Parushev, 25–39. Prague: International Baptist Theological Seminary, 2007.

———. "Who Are the Baptists?" In *Currents in Baptistic Theology of Worship Today*, edited by K. G. Jones and P. R. Parushev, 25–39. Prague: International Baptist Theological Seminary, 2007.

Ellis, C. J., and M. Blyth. *Gathering for Worship: Patterns and Prayers for the Community of Disciples*. Norwich, UK: Canterbury, 2005.

Elwood, C. *The Body Broken: The Calvinist Doctrine of the Eucharist and the Symbolization of Power in Sixteenth-Century France*. Oxford Studies in Historical Theology. New York: Oxford University Press, 1999.

Erasmus von Rotterdam. *Novum Instrumentum, Basel 1516*. Basel: Frommann-Holzboog, 1986.

Erickson, M. J. *Christian Theology*. 3 vols. Grand Rapids: Baker, 1983–85.

Erickson, M. J., et al. *Reclaiming the Center: Confronting Evangelical Accommodation in Postmodern Times*. Wheaton, IL: Crossway, 2004.

Evans, C. A. "Jesus' Action in the Temple: Cleansing or Portent of Destruction?" *CBQ* 51 (1989) 237–70.

———. "Jesus and the Continuing Exile of Israel." In *Jesus & the Restoration of Israel: A Critical Assessment of N. T. Wright's "Jesus and the Victory of God,"* edited by C. C. Newman, 77–100. Downers Grove, IL: InterVarsity, 1999.

Eusebius. *Historia ecclesiastica (The Church History of Eusebius)*. Translated by A. C. McGiffert. In *NPNF*[2] vol. 1, edited by P. Schaff and H. Wace. Peabody, MA: Hendrickson, 1994.

Fahey, M. A. *Cyprian and the Bible: A Study in Third-Century Exegesis*. Tübingen: Mohr, 1971.

Fee, G. D. "History as Context for Interpretation." In *The Act of Bible Reading: A Multidisciplinary Approach to Biblical Interpretation*, edited by E. Dyck, 10–32. Downers Grove, IL: InterVarsity, 1996.

Ferguson, E. B. *Baptism in the Early Church: History, Theology, and Liturgy in the First Five Centuries*. Grand Rapids: Eerdmans, 2009.

———. "The Lord's Supper in Church History: The Early Church through the Medieval Period." In *The Lord's Supper: Believers Church Perspectives*, edited by D. R. Stoffer, 21–45. Scottdale, PA: Herald, 1997.

Fiddes, P. *Participating in God: A Pastoral Doctrine of the Trinity*. London: Darton, Longman & Todd, 2000.

———. *Tracks and Traces: Baptist Identity in Church and Theology*. Studies in Baptist History and Thought 13. Milton Keynes, UK: Paternoster, 2003.

Freeman, C. W., et al. *Baptist Roots: A Reader in the Theology of a Christian People*. Valley Forge: Judson, 1999.

Frost, M., and A. Hirsch. *The Shaping of Things to Come: Innovation and Mission for the 21st-Century Church*. Peabody, MA: Hendrickson, 2003.

Furlong, M. *Puritan's Progress*. New York: Coward, McCann & Geoghegan, 1975.

Gehring, R. W. *House Church and Mission: The Importance of Household Structures in Early Christianity*. Peabody, MA: Hendrickson, 2004.

Geldbach, E. "The Petrine Ministry and the Unity of the Church: A Baptist Perspective." In *Petrine Ministry and the Unity of the Church: "Toward a Patient and Fraternal Dialogue": A Symposium . . .* , edited by J. F. Puglisi. Collegeville, MN: Liturgical, 1999.

George, C. F. *How to Break Growth Barriers. Capturing Overlooked Opportunities for Church Growth*. Grand Rapids: Baker, 1993.

———. *Prepare Your Church for the Future*. Grand Rapids: Baker, 1992.

George, T. "The Future of Southern Baptist Theology." In *Baptist, Why and Why Not, Revisited*, edited by T. George et al., 23–39. Nashville: Broadman & Holman, 1997.

———. "The Reformation Roots of the Baptist Tradition." *RevExp* 86.1 (1989) 9–22.

———. "The Renewal of Baptist Theology." In *Baptist Theologians*, edited by T. George and D. S. Dockery, 13–25. Nashville: Broadman, 1990.

———. "The Sacramentality of the Church." In *Baptist Sacramentalism*, edited by A. R. Cross and P. E. Thompson, 21–35. Studies in Baptist History and Thought 5. Milton Keynes: Paternoster, 2003.

———. *Theology of the Reformers*. Leicester: InterVarsity/Apollos, 1988.

Gibbs, E. *Church Next: Quantum Changes in How We Do Ministry*. Downers Grove, IL: InterVarsity, 2000.

Gibbs, E., and R. K. Bolger. *Emerging Churches: Creating Christian Community in Postmodern Cultures*. Grand Rapids: Baker, 2005.

Giles, K. *What on Earth Is the Church? A Biblical and Theological Enquiry*. Downer's Grove, IL: InterVarsity, 1995.

Greaves, R. L. *Glimpses of Glory: John Bunyan and English Dissent*. Stanford: Stanford University Press, 2002.

Grenz, S. J. *The Baptist Congregation: A Guide to Baptist Belief and Practice*. Vancouver, BC: Regent College Publishing, 1998.

———. "Conversing in Christian Style: Toward a Baptist Theological Method for the Postmodern Context." *BHH* 35.1 (2000) 82–103.

———. *Created for Community: Connecting Christian Belief with Christian Living*. Grand Rapids: Baker, 1998.
———. *Renewing the Center: Evangelical Theology in a Post-Theological Era*. Grand Rapids: Baker Academic, 2000.
———. *Revisioning Evangelical Theology: A Fresh Agenda for the 21st Century*. Downers Grove, IL: InterVarsity, 1993.
———. "Salvation and God's Program in Establishing Community." *RevExp* 91 (1994) 505–20.
———. *The Social God and the Relational Self*. Louisville: Westminster John Knox, 2007.
———. *Theology for the Community of God*. Grand Rapids: Eerdmans, 1994.
Grieb, A. K. *The Story of Romans: A Narrative Defense of God's Righteousness*. Louisville: Westminster John Knox, 2002.
Grudem, W. *Systematic Theology: An Introduction to Biblical Doctrine*. Downers Grove, IL: InterVarsity, 1994.
Guder, D. L. *The Continuing Conversion of the Church*. Grand Rapids: Eerdmans, 2000.
———. *Missional Church: A Vision for the Sending of the Church in North America*. Grand Rapids: Eerdmans, 1998.
Guinness, O. *Dining with the Devil: The Megachurch Movement Flirts with Modernity*. Grand Rapids: Baker, 1993.
Hall, D. J. *The End of Christendom and the Future of Christianity*. New York: Trinity, 2002.
Hamman, A-G. "Le rythme de la prière chrétienne ancienne." In *Études Patristiques: Méthodologie-Liturgie-Histoire-Théologie*, 159–81. Paris: Beauchesne, 1991.
Hansen, G. W. *Galatians*. IPV New Testament Commentary 9. Downers Grove, IL: InterVarsity, 1994.
Harmon, S. *Towards Baptist Catholicity: Essays on Tradition and the Baptist Vision*. Studies in Baptist History and Thought 27. Milton Keynes, UK: Paternoster, 2006.
Harris, B. S. "From 'Behave, Believe, Belong' to 'Belong, Believe, Behave'—A Missional Journey for the 21st Century." In *Text and Task: Scripture and Mission*, edited by M. Parsons, 204–17. Carlisle, UK: Paternoster, 2005.
Hart, L. D. *Truth Aflame: Theology for the Church in Renewal*. Rev. ed. Grand Rapids: Zondervan, 2005.
Hayden, R. *English Baptist History and Heritage*. Didcot: BUGB, 2005.
Haymes, B., et al. *On Being the Church: Revisioning Baptist Identity*. Studies in Baptist History and Thought 21. Carlisle, UK: Paternoster, 2008.
———. *A Question of Identity*. Leeds, UK: Yorkshire Baptist Association, 1986.
Hays, R. B. "The Conversion of the Imagination: Scripture and Eschatology in 1 Corinthians." *NTS* 45 (1999) 391–412.
———. *Echoes of Scripture in the Letters of Paul*. New Haven: Yale University Press, 1989.
———. *The Faith of Jesus Christ: The Narrative Substructure of Galatians 3:1—4:11*. Grand Rapids: Eerdmans, 2002.
———. *First Corinthians*. Interpretation. Louisville: John Knox, 1999.
Hill, C. "John Bunyan and his Publics." *History Today* 38.10 (1988) 13–19.
———. *A Turbulent, Seditious, and Factious People: John Bunyan and His Church, 1628–1688*. Oxford: Oxford University Press, 1988.
Hill, C. E. *Regnum Caelorum: Patterns of Future Hope in Early Christianity*. Oxford: Clarendon, 1992.

Hill, G. J. G. "An Examination of Emerging-Missional Ecclesiological Conceptions: Missional Ecclesiology and the Ecclesiologies of Miroslav Volf, Joseph Ratzinger and John Zizioulas." PhD diss., Flinders University of South Australia, 2009.

Hirsch, A. "Adaptive Challenges and the Church." Forgotten Ways blog, February 14, 2009. Online: http://www.theforgottenways.org/blog/2009/02/14/adaptive-challenges-and-the-church/.

———. *The Forgotten Ways: Reactivating the Missional Church*. Grand Rapids: Brazos, 2006.

Hitchens, C. *God Is Not Great: The Case against Religion*. London: Atlantic, 2007.

Holmes, S. R. *Listening to the Past: The Place of Tradition in Theology*. Carlisle, UK: Paternoster, 2002.

Hunsberger, G. R., and C. Van Gelder, editors. *The Church between Gospel and Culture: The Emerging Mission in North America*. Grand Rapids: Eerdmans, 1996.

Hunsinger, G. "Baptized into Christ's Death: Karl Barth and the Future of Roman Catholic Theology." In *Disruptive Grace: Studies in the Theology of Karl Barth*, 253–78. Grand Rapids: Eerdmans, 2000.

Jamieson, A. *A Churchless Faith: Faith Journeys beyond the Churches*. London: SPCK, 2002.

Jenkins, P. *The Next Christendom: The Coming of Global Christianity*. Oxford: Oxford University Press, 2002.

Jeremias, J. *The Eucharistic Words of Jesus*. Translated by N. Perrin. London: SCM, 1966.

———. *Infant Baptism in the First Four Centuries*. Translated by David Cairns. London: SCM, 1960.

Jerome. *Lives of Illustrious Men (De viris illustribus)*. Translated by E. C. Richardson. In $NPNF^2$ vol. 3, edited by P. Schaff and H. Wace. Peabody, MA: Hendrickson, 1994.

Jewett, R. "Are There Allusions to the Love Feast in Romans 13:8–10?" In *Common Life in the Early Church: Essays Honoring Graydon F. Snyder*, edited by J. V. Hills et al., 265–78. Harrisburg, PA: Trinity, 1998.

Jinkins, M. "The 'Gift' of the Church. Ecclesia Crucis, Peccatrix Maxima, and the Missio Dei." In *Evangelical Ecclesiology: Reality or Illusion?*, edited by J. G. Stackhouse Jr., 179–209. Grand Rapids: Baker, 2003.

Johnson, G. K. *Prisoner of Conscience: John Bunyan on Self, Community and Christian Faith*. Studies in Evangelical History and Thought. Milton Keynes, UK: Paternoster, 2003.

Joynt, Michael Scott. Foreword to *The Abolition of Slavery and Public Christianity: Reflections on the Dangers of Privatising Faith, Mindful of Contemporary Challenges Facing Britain Today*, by Daniel Boucher. London: CARE, 2009.

Jones, K. *A Believing Church: Learning from Some Contemporary Anabaptist and Baptist Perspectives*. Didcot: BUGB, 1998.

Jones, K., and P. Parushev, editors. *Currents in Baptist Theology of Worship Today*. Praha, Czech Republic: International Baptist Theological Seminary, 2007.

Kärkkäinen, V.-M. *An Introduction to Ecclesiology: Ecumenical, Historical and Global Perspectives*. Downers Grove, IL: InterVarsity, 2002.

Kelly, G. *Retrofuture: Rediscovering Our Roots, Recharting Our Routes*. Downers Grove, IL: InterVarsity, 1999.

Kelly, R. "Twitter Study Reveals Interesting Results about Usage—40% is 'Pointless Babble.'" Pear Analytics blog, August 12, 2009. Online: http://www.pearanalytics

.com/blog/2009/twitter-study-reveals-interesting-results-40-percent-pointless-babble/.
Kimball, D. *The Emerging Church: Vintage Christianity for New Generations.* Grand Rapids: Zondervan, 2003.
Kingsley, J. G., Jr. "John Bunyan and the Baptists." *BHH* 13.4 (1978) 3–7.
Knott, J. R., Jr. "Bunyan and the Holy Community." *Studies in Philology* 80.2 (1983) 200–225.
Koenig, J. *The Feast of the World's Redemption: Eucharistic Origins and Christian Mission.* Harrisburg, PA: Trinity, 2000.
Kreider, E. *Given for You: A Fresh Look at Communion.* Leicester, UK: InterVarsity, 1998.
Ladd, G. E. *A Theology of the New Testament.* Grand Rapids: Eerdmans, 1993.
Lane, A. N. S. *Justification by Faith in Catholic-Protestant Dialogue: An Evangelical Assessment.* London: T. & T. Clark, 2002.
Lathrop, G. *Holy Things: A Liturgical Theology.* Minneapolis: Fortress, 1998.
Leibovitz, L. "Communication Breakdown." *Forward*, March 18, 2009. Online: http://www.forward.com/articles/104050/.
Leonard, T. "US cities may have to be bulldozed in order to survive." *Telegraph*, June 12, 2009. Online: http://www.telegraph.co.uk/finance/financetopics/financialcrisis/5516536/US-cities-may-have-to-be-bulldozed-in-order-to-survive.html.
Lindemann, A. "The Beginnings of the Christian Life in Jerusalem according to the Summaries in the Acts of the Apostles." In *Common Life in the Early Church: Essays Honoring Graydon F. Snyder*, edited by J. V. Hills et al., 202–18. Harrisburg, PA: Trinity, 1998.
Longenecker, B. W. *The Triumph of Abraham's God: The Transformation of Identity in Galatians.* Nashville: Abingdon, 1998.
Lumpkin, W. L. *Baptist Confessions of Faith.* Valley Forge, PA: Judson, 1969.
Maddox, M. *God under Howard: The Rise of the Religious Right in Australian Politics.* St. Leonards, NSW: Allen & Unwin, 2005.
Malphurs, A. *A New Kind of Church: Understanding Models of Ministry for the 21st Century.* Grand Rapids: Baker, 2007.
Manley, K. R. *From Wooloomooloo to "Eternity": A History of Australian Baptists*, vol. 2: *A National Church in a Global Community (1914–2005).* Studies in Baptist History and Thought 16. Milton Keynes, UK: Paternoster, 2006.
Markham, I. S. *Plurality and Christian Ethics.* Cambridge: Cambridge University Press, 1994.
Marshall, I. H. "Lord's Supper." In *Dictionary of Paul and His Letters*, edited by G. F. Hawthorne et al., 569–75. Downers Grove, IL: InterVarsity, 1993.
Martin, G. W. *The Church. A Baptist View.* London: Baptist Publications, n.d.
Martin M. "Baptistification Takes Over." *Christianity Today*, 2 September 1983, 32–36.
Martin, R. P. *Worship in the Early Church.* Grand Rapids: Eerdmans, 1992.
McBeth, H. L. *The Baptist Heritage.* Nashville: Broadman, 1987.
———. *A Sourcebook for Baptist Heritage.* Nashville: Broadman, 1990.
McClendon, J. W., Jr. *Ethics.* Vol. 1 of *Systematic Theology.* Nashville: Abingdon, 1986.
———. *Doctrine.* Vol. 2 of *Systematic Theology.* Nashville: Abingdon, 1994.
McClung, F. *The Father Heart of God.* Eastbourne, UK: Kingsway, 1985.
McGavran, D. A. *Understanding Church Growth.* Grand Rapids: Eerdmans, 1970.
McGrath, A. E. *Christianity's Dangerous Idea: The Protestant Revolution—a History from the Sixteenth Century to the Twenty-first.* London: SPCK, 2007.

---. *Reformation Thought: An Introduction*. Oxford: Blackwell, 1993.
McKnight, Scott. *A New Vision for Israël: The Teachings of Jesus in National Context*. Grand Rapids: Eerdmans, 1999.
McLaren, B. D. *The Church on the Other Side: Doing Ministry in the Postmodern Matrix*. Grand Rapids: Zondervan, 2000.
McManus, E. R. *An Unstoppable Force: Daring to Become the Church God Had in Mind*. Loveland, CO: Group, 2001.
Middleton, J. Richard. "The Liberating Image? Interpreting the Imago Dei in Context." *Christian Scholars Review* 24.1 (1994) 8–25.
Migliore, D. *Faith Seeking Understanding: An Introduction to Christian Theology*. Grand Rapids: Eerdmans, 1991.
---. "Reforming the Theology and Practice of Baptism: The Challenge of Karl Barth." In *Toward the Future of Reformed Theology: Tasks, Topics, Traditions*, edited by D. Willis and M. Welker, 494–511. Grand Rapids: Eerdmans, 1999.
Milne, B. *Know the Truth: A Handbook of Christian Belief*. Leicester, UK: InterVarsity, 1998.
Minear, P. S. *Images of the Church in the New Testament*. London: Lutterworth, 1961.
Mohler, R. A. "A Call for Baptist Evangelicals and Evangelical Baptists: Community of Faith and a Common Quest for Identity." In *Southern Baptists and American Evangelicals: The Conversation Continues*, edited by D. S. Dockery, 224–39. Nashville: Broadman & Holman, 1993.
Molager, J. *Cyprien de Carthage: A Donat et La Vertu de Patience*. Paris: Cerf, 1982.
Molnar, P. D. *Karl Barth and the Theology of the Lord's Supper: A Systematic Investigation*. New York: Lang, 1996.
Moltmann, J. *The Church in the Power of the Spirit: A Contribution to Messianic Ecclesiology*. Translated by Margaret Kohl. London: SCM, 1977.
---. *The Open Church: An Invitation to a Messianic Lifestyle*. London: SCM, 1978.
Moo, D. J. *The Epistle to the Romans*. NICNT. Grand Rapids: Eerdmans, 1996.
Moore, R. K. "Forming Our Theology of Infancy/Childhood: Shall We Be Informed by Augustine of Hippo or Jesus of Nazareth?" Unpublished paper, Baptist Pastors' Conference, Katanning (4 May 1993).
---. "Justification by Faith—or Justification by Baptism? Recent Lutheran-Roman Catholic Dialogue." Unpublished paper, ANZATS/ANZSTS Conference, Adelaide, 9 July 2002.
Moynagh, M. *Changing World, Changing Church: New Forms of Church, Out-of-the-Pew Thinking, Initiatives That Work*. Oxford: Monarch, 2001.
---. *Emergingchurch.Intro*. Oxford: Monarch, 2004.
Murray, S. "Anabaptists." In *The Dictionary of Historical Theology*, edited by T. A. Hart, 13–16. Carlisle, UK: Paternoster; Grand Rapids: Eerdmans, 2000.
---. *Church after Christendom*. Milton Keynes, UK: Paternoster, 2005.
---. *Post-Christendom: Church and Mission in a Strange New World*. Carlisle, UK: Paternoster, 2004.
Myers, J. R. *The Search to Belong. Rethinking Intimacy, Community, and Small Groups*. Grand Rapids: Zondervan, 2003.
Naphy, W. G. *The Protestant Revolution: From Martin Luther to Martin Luther King Jr.* London: BBC, 2007.

Nettleton, N. "Baptist Worship in Ecumenical Perspective." In *Worship Today: Understanding, Practice, Ecumenical Implications*, Faith and Order Paper 194, edited by T. Best and D. Heller. Geneva: WCC, 2004.

Newman, H. *Certain Difficulties Felt by Anglicans in Catholic Teaching*. London: Longmans, Green, 1900.

Nickerson, S., and L. Ball. *For His Glory: 100 Years of the Queensland Baptist College of Ministries*. Brisbane: QBCM, 2004.

Niebuhr, H. R. *Christ and Culture*. New York: Harper & Row, 1975.

———. *Nova vulgata Bibliorum sacrorum editio*. Vatican City: Vatican Library Press, 1979.

Norman, R. S. *The Baptist Way: Distinctives of a Baptist Church*. Nashville: Broadman & Holman, 2005.

Obama, Barack Hussein. *The Audacity of Hope: Thoughts on Reclaiming the American Dream*. Melbourne: Text Publishing, 2006.

———. Inaugural address as 44th President of the United States, 20 January 2009, Washington, DC. *Congressional Record* 155.11, S667-70. Online: http://www.gpoaccess.gov/crecord/09crpgs.html.

O'Grady, J. F. *Pillars of Paul's Gospel: Galatians and Romans*. New York: Paulist, 1992.

O'Neil, M. D. "Ethics and Epistemology: Ecclesial Existence in a Postmodern Era." *JRE* 34 (2006) 21–40.

Orwell, G. "Politics and the English Language." In *Inside the Whale, and Other Essays*, 143–57. London: Penguin, 1958.

Payne, E. A. *Free Churchmen, Unrepentant and Repentant, and Other Papers*. London: Kingsgate, 1965.

Payne, E. A., and S. F. Winward. *Orders and Prayers for Church Worship: A Manual for Ministers*. London: Kingsgate, 1960.

Pearse, M. *The Great Restoration: The Religious Radicals of the 16th and 17th Centuries*. Carlisle, UK: Paternoster, 1998.

Pearse, M., and C. Matthews. *We Must Stop Meeting Like This*. London: Kingsway, 1999.

Pontius. *Vita Cypriana (The Life and Passion of Cyprian, Bishop and Martyr)*. Translated by Ernest Wallis. *ANF* vol. 5.

Porter, S. E., and A. R. Cross, editors. *Baptism, the New Testament and the Church: Historical and Contemporary Studies in Honour of R. E. O. White*. JSNTSup 171. Sheffield: Sheffield Academic, 1999.

———. *Dimensions of Baptism: Biblical and Theological Studies*. JSNTSup 234. London: Sheffield Academic, 2002.

Pugh, J. *Fantasyland Faith: The Redemptive Role of Ethical Leaders within Neurotic Church Systems*. Saarbrücken: VDM, 2007.

Radley, S. *Place: Church and Mission*. Cambridge, UK: Grove, 1997.

Rainer, T. S., and E. Geiger. *Simple Church: Returning to God's Process for Making Disciples*. Nashville: B & H, 2006.

Randall, I. M. *Communities of Conviction: Baptist Beginnings in Europe*. Schwarzenfeld: Neufeld, 2009.

Reumann, J. *The Supper of the Lord: The New Testament, Ecumenical Dialogues, and Faith and Order on Eucharist*. Philadelphia: Fortress, 1985.

Richter, P., and L. Francis. *Gone but Not Forgotten*. London: Darton, Longman & Todd, 1998.

Riddell, M., M. Pierson, and C. Kirkpatrick. *The Prodigal Project: Journey into the Emerging Church*. London: SPCK, 2001.

Ringe, S. H. *Jesus, Liberation, and the Biblical Jubilee: Images for Ethics and Christology.* Overtures to Biblical Theology 19. Philadelphia: Fortress, 1985.
Robinson, S. *Mosques and Miracles: Revealing Islam and God's Grace.* Mt. Gravatt, Queensland: City Harvest, 2003.
———. *Praying the Price.* Kent, UK: Sovereign World, 1994.
Roxburgh, A. J. "Reframing Denominations from a Missional Perspective." In *The Missional Church and Denominations: Helping Congregations Develop a Missional Identity*, edited by C. V. Gelder, 75–103. Grand Rapids: Eerdmans, 2008.
———. *The Missionary Congregation, Leadership, and Liminality.* New York: Trinity, 1997.
Sachs, Jeffrey D. *Common Wealth: Economics for a Crowded Planet.* New York: Penguin, 2008.
Sage, M. M. *Cyprian.* Patristic Monographs 1. Cambridge, MA: Philadelphia Patristic Foundation, 1975.
Sanders, E. P. *Jesus and Judaism.* London: SCM, 1985.
Sanders, J. O. *Spiritual Leadership.* London: Marshall, Morgan & Scott, 1967.
Schein, E. H. *Organisational Culture and Leadership.* 2nd ed. San Francisco: Jossey-Bass, 1992.
Schneider, W. E. *The Reengineering Alternative: A Plan for Making Your Current Culture Work.* Burr Ridge, IL: Irvin Professional, 1994.
Schreiner, T. R., and S. D. Wright. *Believer's Baptism: Sign of the New Covenant in Christ.* Nashville: B & H, 2006.
Scourfield, J. H. D. "The *De mortalitate* of Cyprian: Consolation and Context." *Vigiliae Christianae* 50 (1996) 12–41.
Sen, Amartya. *Development as Freedom.* New York: Knopf, 1999.
Senn, F. C. "The Reform of the Mass: Evangelical, but Still Catholic." In *The Catholicity of the Reformation*, edited by C. E. Braaten and R. W. Jenson, 35–52. Grand Rapids: Eerdmans, 1996.
Sharrock, R. *John Bunyan.* London: Hutchinson's University Library, 1954.
Shelley, B. L. *Church History in Plain Language.* Nashville: Nelson, 1995.
Shenk, W. R. *Write the Vision: The Church Renewed.* Valley Forge, PA: Trinity, 1995.
Sheppy, P. "Worship and Ecumenism." In *So We Believe, So We Pray: Towards Koinonia in Worship*, Faith and Order Paper 171, edited by T. Best and D. Heller, 311–22. Geneva: WCC, 1995.
Shurden, W. B. *The Baptist Identity: Four Fragile Freedoms.* Macon, GA: Smyth & Helwys, 1993.
Simson. W. *Houses That Change the World: The Return of the House Churches.* Emmelsbull: C & P, 1999.
Smalley, S. S. "Banquet." In *New Bible Dictionary*, edited by I. H. Marshall and D. R. W. Wood, et al., 120. Leicester, UK: InterVarsity, 1996.
Smith, D. L. *All God's People: A Theology of the Church.* Wheaton, IL: Bridgepoint, 1996.
Smith, L. T. *Decolonizing Methodologies: Research and Indigenous People.* Dunedin, NZ: University of Otago Press, 1999.
Smith, P. "Voices That Must Be Heard." *The Tablet* (25 July 2009) 4.
Smyth, John. "Propositions and Conclusions concerning the True Christian Religion, Containing a Confession of Faith of Certain English People, Living at Amsterdam." In *Baptist Confessions of Faith*, edited by W. L. Lumpkin, 140. Valley Forge, PA: Judson, 1969.
Spencer, N., and J. Chaplin, editors. *God and Government.* London: Theos/SPCK, 2009.

Stranahan, B. P. "Bunyan and the Epistle to the Hebrews: His Source for the Idea of Pilgrimage in *The Pilgrim's Progress*." *Studies in Philology* 79 (1982) 279–96.
Stein, R. H. "Baptism in Luke-Acts." In *Believer's Baptism: Sign of the New Covenant in Christ*, edited by T. R. Schreiner et al., 35–66. Nashville: B & H, 2006.
———. "Last Supper." In *Dictionary of Jesus and the Gospels*, edited by J. B. Green et al., 444–50. Downers Grove, IL: InterVarsity, 1992.
Studer, B. "Hoffnung." In *Reallexikon für Antike und Christentum*, edited by E. Dassmann, 1161–244. Stuttgart: Hiersemann, 1991.
Sutherland, M. "Gathering, Sacrament and Baptist Theological Method." *PJBR* 3.2 (2007) 41–57.
Sweet, L., ed. *The Church in Emerging Culture: Five Perspectives*. Grand Rapids: Zondervan, 2003.
Taylor, B. *Saying No to Babylon: A Reading of the Book of Daniel*. Kingston, Jamaica: Express Litho, 2006.
———. "The Jamaican Baptist Worship Tradition." In *Worship Today: Understanding, Practice Ecumenical Implications*, Faith and Order Paper 194, edited by T. Best and D. Heller, 199–202. Geneva: WCC, 2004.
Thiselton, A. C. *The First Epistle to the Corinthians: A Commentary on the Greek Text*. Carlisle, UK: Paternoster; Grand Rapids: Eerdmans, 1999.
Thwaites, J. *The Church beyond the Congregation*. Carlisle, UK: Paternoster, 1999.
Tinker, M. "Language, Symbols, and Sacraments." *Churchman* 112.2 (1998) 131–49.
Tomlinson, P. *How a Man Handles Conflict at Work*. Minneapolis: Bethany House, 1996.
Troeltsch, E. *The Social Teaching of the Christian Churches*. London: Allen & Unwin, 1932.
Van Til, Kent A. *Less Than Two Dollars a Day: A Christian View of World Poverty and the Free Market*. Grand Rapids: Eerdmans, 2007.
Vanhoozer, K. J. "The Voice and the Actor: A Dramatic Proposal about the Ministry and Minstrelsy of Theology." In *Evangelical Futures: A Conversation on Theological Method*, edited by J. G. Stackhouse Jr., 61–106. Grand Rapids: Baker, 2000.
Volf, M. *After Our Likeness: The Church as the Image of the Trinity*. Grand Rapids: Eerdmans, 1998.
———. "Community Formation as an Image of the Triune God: A Congregational Model of Church Order and Life." In *Community Formation in the Early Church and the Church Today*, edited by R. N. Longenecker, 213–37. Peabody, MA: Hendrickson, 2002.
Wagner, C. P. *Churchquake! How the New Apostolic Reformation Is Shaking Up the Church as We Know It*. Ventura, CA: Regal, 1999.
Wainwright, G. W. "Church and Sacrament(s)." In *The Possibilities of Theology: Studies in the Theology of Eberhard Jüngel in His Sixtieth Year*, edited by J. Webster. Edinburgh: T. & T. Clark, 1994.
———. *Eucharist and Eschatology*. London: Epworth, 2003.
———. "Lord's Supper, Love Feast." In *DLNTD*, 688–89.
———. "The Eucharistic Dynamic of BEM." In *BEM at 25: Critical Insights into a Continuing Legacy*, Faith and Order Paper, 205, edited by T. Best and T. Grdzelidze, 60–62. Geneva: WCC, 2007.
Wakefield, G. S. *Bunyan the Christian*. London: HarperCollins, 1992.
Walker, C. *Seeking Relevant Churches for the 21st Century*. Melbourne: JBCE, 1997.

Wallace, Jim, "Tony Jones talks to Jim Wallace of the Australian Christian Lobby." ABC, *Lateline*, September 8, 2007. Transcript online: http://www.abc.net.au/lateline/content/2007/s2001198.htm.

Walsh, P. "The Joys of Letting Go." *Oprah Radio*, November 30, 2007. Online: http://www.oprah.com/oprahradio/The-Joys-of-Letting-Go.

Ward, P. *Liquid Church*. Peabody, MA: Hendrickson, 2002.

Warren, Rick. "Myths of the Modern Megachurch." Keynote speech for the Pew Forum biannual Faith Angle conference, Key West, May 2005. Transcript online: http://pewforum.org/Christian/Evangelical-Protestant-Churches/Myths-of-the-Modern-Megachurch.aspx.

Webber, R. E. *The Younger Evangelicals: Facing the Challenges of the New World*. Grand Rapids: Baker, 2003.

Weber, M. *Economy and Society: An Outline of Interpretive Sociology*. Berkeley: University of California Press, 1978.

Weber, R. *Biblia Sacra: Iuxta Vulgatam versionem*. Stuttgart: Wu[place umlaut over u]rttembergische Bibelanstalt, 1975.

Webster, J. *Barth's Ethics of Reconciliation*. Cambridge: Cambridge University Press, 1992.

Whale, J. S. *The Protestant Tradition: An Essay in Interpretation*. Cambridge: Cambridge University Press, 1955.

"What Makes a Baptist?" Didcot: Baptist Union of Great Britain, n.d.

White, B. R. *The English Separatist Tradition*. Oxford: Oxford University Press, 1971.

White, J. *A Brief History of Christian Worship*. Nashville: Abingdon, 1993.

White, J. *The Church and the Parachurch: An Uneasy Marriage*. Portland, OR: Multnomah, 1983.

Wiebe, B. *Messianic Ethics: Jesus' Proclamation of the Kingdom of God and the Church in Response*. Scottdale, PA: Herald, 1992.

Wilkinson-Hayes, A. *Lifestyle*. Baptist Basics 10. Didcot: Baptist Union of Great Britain, 2009.

Williams, R. *Mission-Shaped Church: Church Planting and Fresh Expressions of Church in a Changing Context*. London: Church House, 2004.

Williams, Roger. *Complete Writing*. 7 vols. New York: Russell & Russell, 1963.

Williams, Rowan. "Secularism, Faith and Freedom." Lecture delivered to the Pontifical Academy of Social Science in Rome, 23 November 2006.

Williams, S. K. "The 'Righteousness of God' in Romans." *JBL* 99 (1980) 241–90.

Winter, B. "The Problem with 'Church' for the Early Church." In *In the Fullness of Time*, edited by D. Peterson and J. Pryor, 203–217. Homebush West: Lancer, 1992.

Wolin, S. *The Presence of the Past: Essays on the State and the Constitution*. Baltimore: Johns Hopkins University Press, 1989.

World Council of Churches. *Baptism, Eucharist and Ministry*. Faith and Order Paper 111. Geneva: WCC, 1982.

Wright, Christopher J. H. *Living as the People of God: The Relevance of Old Testament Ethics*. Downers Grove, IL: InterVarsity, 1983.

———. *Old Testament Ethics for the People of God*. Downers Grove, IL: InterVarsity, 2004.

Wright, D. F. "Infant Dedication in the Early Church." In *Baptism, the New Testament and the Church: Historical and Contemporary Studies in Honour of R. E. O. White*, edited by S. E. Porter and A. R. Cross, 352–78. JSNTSup 171. Sheffield: Sheffield Academic, 1999.

Wright, Nigel G. *Disavowing Constantine: Mission, Church and the Social Order in the Theologies of John Howard Yoder and Jürgen Moltmann.* Carlisle, UK: Paternoster, 2000.

———. *Free Church, Free State: The Positive Baptist Vision.* Milton Keynes, UK: Paternoster, 2005.

———. "Government as an Ambiguous Power." In *God and Government*, edited by N. Spencer and J. Chaplin. London: Theos/SPCK, 2009.

———. "National Churches." In *A Dictionary of Baptist Life and Thought*, edited by J. H. Y. Briggs, 345–46. Studies in Baptist History and Thought 33. Carlisle, UK: Paternoster, 2009.

———. *New Baptists, New Agenda.* Carlisle, UK: Paternoster, 2002.

———. *Participating without Possessing: The Public and the Private in Christian Discipleship.* Horley, UK: Industrial Christian Fellowship, 2003.

———. "Post-Denominationalism and the Renewal of a Denominational Witness." Unpublished paper presented at the Burleigh Conference, Adelaide, 2001.

———. Review of *Toward Baptist Catholicity* by Stephen Harmon. *Ecclesiology* 5 (2009) 383–85.

Wright, N. T. *Jesus and the Victory of God.* Christian Origins and the Question of God 2. Minneapolis: Fortress, 1996.

———. "Jesus, Israel and the Cross." In *SBL Seminar Papers: 1985*, edited by K. H. Richards, 75–95. Atlanta, GA: Scholars, 1985.

———. "Romans and the Theology of Paul." In *Pauline Theology*, vol. 3: *Romans*, edited by D. M. Hay and E. E. Johnson, 30–67. SBLSymS 4. Minneapolis: Fortress, 1995.

———. *Scripture and the Authority of God.* London: SPCK, 2005.

———. "The Letter to the Romans." In *The New Interpreter's Bible*, edited by L. Keck, 10:393–770. Nashville: Abingdon, 2002.

———. *The Meal Jesus Gave Us: Understanding Holy Communion.* Louisville: Westminster John Knox, 2003.

Wynne-Jones, Jonathan. "Facebook and MySpace can lead children to commit suicide, warns Archbishop Nichols." *Telegraph*, August 1, 2009. Online: http://www.telegraph.co.uk/news/newstopics/religion/5956719/Facebook-and-MySpace-can-lead-children-to-commit-suicide-warns-Archbishop-Nichols.html.

Yoder, J. H. *Body Politics: Five Practices of the Christian Community before the Watching World.* Nashville: Discipleship Resources, 1992.

———. "Sacrament as Social Process: Christ the Transformer of Culture." In *The Royal Priesthood: Essays Ecclesiological and Ecumenical*, 359–73. Grand Rapids: Eerdmans, 1994.

———. *The Christian Witness to the State.* Institute of Menonite Studies Series 3. Newton, KS: Faith and Life, 1964.

———. *The Politics of Jesus: Vicit Agnus Noster.* 2nd ed. Grand Rapids: Eerdmans, 1994.

Zizioulas, J. D. *Being as Communion: Studies in Personhood and the Church.* Crestwood, NY: St. Vladimir's Seminary Press, 1985.

www.ingramcontent.com/pod-product-compliance
Lightning Source LLC
Chambersburg PA
CBHW071242230426
43668CB00011B/1552